ARTIFICIAL INTELLIGENCE:
Towards Practical Application

G D I

Technology Assessment and Management 1

ARTIFICIAL INTELLIGENCE: Towards Practical Application

Proceedings of the joint Technology Assessment Conference of
the Gottlieb Duttweiler Institute and
the European Coordinating Committee for Artificial Intelligence
Rüschlikon, Zürich, Switzerland, 12-13 April 1984

edited by

Thomas BERNOLD
Project Manager
Gottlieb Duttweiler Institute

and

Günter ALBERS
European Coordinating Committee
for Artificial Intelligence (ECCAI)
Organiser Industrial Liaison Session

1985

NORTH-HOLLAND – AMSTERDAM · NEW YORK · OXFORD

ISBN: 0 444 87719 3

Published by:

ELSEVIER SCIENCE PUBLISHERS B.V.
P.O. Box 1991
1000 BZ Amsterdam
The Netherlands

Sole distributors for the U.S.A. and Canada:

ELSEVIER SCIENCE PUBLISHING COMPANY, INC.
52 Vanderbilt Avenue
New York, N.Y. 10017
U.S.A.

PRINTED IN THE NETHERLANDS

INTRODUCTION

After the famous Fifth Generation conference in Tokyo 1981 Artificial Intelligence(AI) has received extended public attention. The impact of the wave of publicity on the development of this field of Advanced Information Technology has yet to be assessed. The expectations and also anxieties about the potential of AI, however, were high, encouraged further by the early interest of venture capital. Aggressive marketing by the American companies and the announcement of sizable capital investment by the Japanese have speeded up the development pace. Despite the recent European efforts such as ESPRIT, ALVEY and other national programs there is the growing fear that Europe may run again the risk of falling behind in this field of technology.

Despite the great publicity of intentions and the inummerable reports, articles and features, there remained a lack of genuine and reliable information about the realistic objectives and actual development of research. The non-specialist observer and the newcomer to the present situation in the field of Artificial Intelligence appears still rather confused. As there is nowadays no generally accepted theory and there is constant change due to the strong innovative drive, even within the AI community it is difficult to assess the state of the art and the recent developments in research and application. What, actually, is new? What has AI to offer, with its subareas Expert Systems and Knowledge Engineering, 3rd Generation Robotics, and Natural Language Systems? What advantages are there over conventional information technology? How could its implementation affect the structure of organisations? How long is the time horizon, how much should one invest and what sort of investment risk is involved? What are the implications for the further development of AI?

This selection of papers presented in collaboration between the Gottlieb Duttweiler Institute and ECCAI (European Coordinating Committee for Artificial Intelligence) at the international conference on Technology Assessment and Technology Transfer at the Gottlieb Duttweiler Institute in Ruschlikon/Zurich: Artificial Intelligence - Information Processing on the Threshold of Practical Application? is intended to provide a first European view of the current state of applications and the emerging developments in this area of Advanced Information Processing. The four viewpoints Technology, Practical Application, Economic Impact and Research and Training, have been chosen to illustrate the various interdependencies of the different groups presently involved in Artificial Intelligence. The proceedings concentrate on Expert Systems, Flexible Manufacturing/Robotics and Intelligent Interfaces, being the subareas of the fastest growing commercial relevance in AI. The contributions have been chosen from universities as well as from commercial areas, and there is a particular emphasis on the question of organizational impact which, as we feel, has not yet received its proper amount of attention. Only peripheral editing has been applied in order to import genuinely the current situation and the views of the different players in the domain of AI.

The expected emerging commercial success of Artificial Intelligence, particularly in the field of Expert Systems, where the applied knowledge of experts of a specific field is transferred to computing systems, is closely linked to a change of paradigm in parts of the research community. The initial intention of developing universal mechanisms and theories of intelligence for problem solving has been postponed, at least temporarily, in favour of systems that function in narrowly defined domains with very restricted task specific knowledge. The coining of the word "Knowledge Engineer" illustrates nicely the shift to the doable, constructable and also economically exploitable.

An indication of the commercial success of AI, and especially of Expert Systems, will be their rate of diffusion throughout business, industry and administration. It is easy to confuse potential and expectation with reality. At present the majority of applications are still in an experimental stage and it takes people with a long genesis of knowledge on the technology to design and operate them. Neither hard- nor software are yet simple and flexible enough, apart from being expensive, to have reached a level of user-friendliness to attract a wider interest by medium and small business and industries. Some consultants even fear that all the mistakes that have been made during the introduction of conventional data processing, such as ignoring the user's needs and preferences, might be repeated which would imply that a breakthrough similar to the PC's, as making AI a tool for everyone, might be still a considerable way off. Thus there is evidence that the development and the use of Expert Systems will stay inside universities and R & D units of large companies for some time. Nevertheless, it is important to note that many spinnofs of AI research enter the world of conventional data processing quietly, in disguise such as, e.g., programming environments.

The impact and potential of AI, even if only partially realized, is real and growing, but success always means a sound knowledge of the area it is applied to. For the organisational area AI might be of help to overcome the present difficulties. Nevertheless, the history of the development of Managerial Decision Support Systems implies that the basic processes have to be understood and capabilities and conceptions have to be evaluated. How well do the present day models represent this reality? How much are those models computationally executable ? How much is really known about the different classes of decisions and decision making?

Besides the technical and conceptual problems there is the danger that automated systems could serve as an excuse for not taking up the responsibility of decision making. It is a well known fact that many consultants are used exactly this way already today.

This observation stresses once again the human dimension. Any exploration of the potential as well as the limitation of AI has to include a deep analysis of this dimension.

The actual application of the new technologies as e.g. of Expert Systems in Industry will indicate which direction future development will take. The realization of its potential could help to augment skills and to enlarge responsibility and control of the operator and workers. However, it would imply a shift from a generation-old paradigm of Taylorisation in the industrial progress. Mechanisation, automation and robotisation went usually parallel to the partial deskilling of the workforce.

The short history of AI shows that the acceptance of this new technology varies according to regional differences in cultural background, tradition and structure. This trend is most likely to continue. There are areas in Europe where a growing reluctance against too fast a change, and the actual rate of innovation in general can be felt. "From high to good tech" is a slogan which indicates the current mood of small and medium firms. This includes even a revival of the so called applied or meso-technologies. The force is strong enough to have attracted scientific interest to conduct an empirical survey to assess its relevance.

These considerations are meant to sketch the contours of the socio-cultural environment AI, as any other technology, is part of. They go beyond the scope of these proceedings, but we believe that they need to be mentioned particularly in the context of a science in which an essential part is derived from the studies of human cognition and behaviour.

Finally we would like to stress research and training as a particularly sensitive topic. Typical for the present situation are the diverging interests between universities and industrial research groups. An obvious reason are differences in the definition of objectives and in the timespan for their realization. Basic research is an investment in long term development but has no quick financial return. The conflict arises mainly over the shortage of trained scientific personnel. There is the justified fear that universities will loose a whole generation of researchers to industry and might not fulfil their function to do long term oriented research and education. The European Community suffers in addition from the strong competition of a well funded and organized American research establishment which attracts many of the young graduates.

The new programs of the administrations such as ESPRIT and ALVEY have recognized the needs of both universities and industries as well as the present deficiency of European know-how. There is an intention to bridge the gap but only the next few years will prove the soundness of their plans which are mostly application and industry oriented, and not so much to basic research, as overseas. Nevertheless, it is obvious that a number of compromises will have to be made. Education and training as the universities stress should however be beyond compromises. So far the industrial research centers have sent their personnel to American universities. European centers should stop this braindrain weakening the future perspective of AI on this side of the Atlantic.

Thomas Bernold, Günter Albers

ACKNOWLEDGEMENTS

We want to express our special thanks to Dr. J.-M. Cadiou for the excellent presidency which has been a major contribution to the success of the AI-conference.

We further want to thank the GDI-collaborators as well as M. Hertel and C. Schleith of ECCAI for the beneficial assistance during the organisation and realization of the conference.

We feel obliged to Mrs. A.-M. Brennwald and Mrs. D. Kunz-Wechler for the special attention they paid to the production of the proceedings.

Thomas Bernold / Günter Albers

TABLE OF CONTENTS

Introduction by the editors
T. Bernold, G. Albers v

Manufacturing and Artificial Intelligence
K.G. Kempf 1

TECHNOLOGY

Knowledge Processing Expert Systems
P. Raulefs 21

Cooperative Access Systems
W. Wahlster 33

The next Generation of Robots: Increased flexibility through the use of sensors
C.W. Burckhardt 47

Visions Systems - State-of-the-Art and Prospects
B. Neumann 51

Expert Systems and Knowledge Engineering
Robotics and Intelligent Interfaces
Summary of Discussions 63

APPLICATION

Artificial Intelligence in a Large-Scale Enterprise - the Experience of Digital Equipment Corporation
B. Rees 67

Expert Systems in Services Sectors: Use of Expert Systems in 6 Sample Cases
D. Sagalowicz 77

Office-Automation: A field for Applied Artificial Intelligence
H. Thompson 81

Requirements on Expert Systems as seen by an Insurance Company
Ch. Jenny 87

Current Work on Expert Systems and Natural Language Processing at Siemens
G. Eibl 97

Computer Assisted Synthesis Planning - a project of the Chemical Industry
W. Sieber 107

A Case Study of the Dipmeter Adviser Development
R. Langley 111

FF: A Nixdorf Expert System for Fault-Finding and Repair Planning - an Outline Description
S. Savory 119

A Prototype Expert System in P.W.R. Power Plant Conducting
J.-F. Héry 129

Knowledge Engineering in CAE - First Industrial Experiences
H. Marchand 135

Advanced Information Processing in Robotics
J.-C. Latombe 143

The Lisp Machine Architecture
D. Schwartz 161

ECONOMIC IMPACTS

Market Trends in Artificial Intelligence in the United States and Japan
K. Wiig 169

Speculations on the Future of Knowledge Engineering in Europe I, II
A.G. Baker / A.W. Pearson 181

The Influence of Artificial Intelligence on Organizational Structure and Rationalization
H.W. Hüsch / E. Staudt 189

Evaluation of Artificial Intelligence with regard to size of Capital Investment and risk
J. Biedermann 201

Possibilities and Limitations of Artificial Intelligence
Panel Discussion 205

INFRASTRUCTURE, RESEARCH AND TRAINING

Problems of the Infrastructure: The Bottlenecks in Research and Training
St. Cerri 209

Research Policy of Administrations - Great Britain (ALVEY)
B. Oakley 213

Cooperation between University, Government and Industry
Excerpts of the Panel Discussion 217

Artificial Intelligence and "Natural Man"
M. Boden 221

APPENDIX

List of Speakers 231

Idea Exchange 233

ARTIFICIAL INTELLIGENCE: Towards Practical Application
T. Bernold and G. Albers (editors)
Elsevier Science Publishers B.V. (North-Holland)

Manufacturing and Artificial Intelligence

Dr. K. G. Kempf
Mgr. - Robotics Technology
McDonnell Douglas Automation Company
St. Louis, Missouri

INTRODUCTION

The question which has stimulated the following discussion is whether the techniques of Artificial Intelligence compete with or complement the techniques of conventional data processing. While I certainly can not answer for all application areas, I believe that the answer for the area in which my own efforts are focused is particularly clear. In manufacturing, AI techniques and conventional data processing techniques are complementary. The two techniques address different classes of problems, both of which are vital in manufacturing today and especially in the future. The following discussion is an attempt to provide a perspective on that class of important problems in manufacturing with which conventional data processing can not cope (or, less pessimistically, has not yet succeeded) but which AI techniques can treat (or, less optimistically, show promise in handling). It is assumed throughout this discussion that the reader is already cognizant of the fact that any modern or future manufacturing facility would collapse without a high level of support from conventional data processing. The focus here is to point out that in the not too distant future, the techniques of Artificial Intelligence will occupy a similar but complementary position.

A significant portion of the human experience is concerned with devising courses of action aimed at changing existing situations into preferred ones. We conceive of an idea, plan how to realize it, then execute the plan. When we perform these steps in the manufacturing arena, we participate in the principal real-wealth producing activity of today. Roughly two-thirds of the real-wealth of a typical industrialized country stems from manufacturing - from people having product ideas, planning how to build the product, then producing the product according to plan. Increases in the general economic well-being and standard of living of people in industrialized countries derive directly from decreasing the cost and increasing the productivity of the manufacruing process.

The first fundamental improvement in our treatment of the commercial manufacturing process in which we have been participating for a few thousand years occurred about two centuries ago. The first industrial revolution was precipitated by the invention and application of the steam engine, a tool used to greatly multiply human physical effort. The second fundamental improvement in commercial manufacturing is beginning to occur today. I say beginning because, while some would argue that the second industrial revolution started some years ago, I believe that we have hardly scratched the surface. Clearly the tool fo the second industrial revolution is the computer, a tool used to magnify the effects of human intellectual effort. While there are other new and useful tools, the computer is an integrating tool for the whole system of manufacturing. With this integrating role, the computer will evolve from being useful in manufacturing today to being essential in the factory of the future.

A SIMPLE MODEL OF MANUFACTURING

Manufacturing comes in many shapes and sizes. Rather than attempt any universal description, attention will be focused on one particular area of manufacturing. The first focusing step splits manufacturing into two major categories, discrete and continuous. Continuous manufacturing of the sort found, for example, in a chemical factory will not be further discussed. The second focusing step selects one of the many sub-categories of discrete manufacturing to serve as a center of discussion. The area of choice is the manufacture of mechanical products - those products made primarily of three dimensional rigid parts. A bicycle is a good example, as is an automobile, as is an airplane. So are a refrigerator and a washing machine. So is a kitchen sink.

This selection does not mean that other manufacturing processes - the discrete manufacturing of electrical/electronic goods or the continuous manufacture of chemical goods as examples - cannot be viewed as sets of computational problems. It simply means that discrete mechanical manufacturing has been selected as a rich source of examples most of which will be within the experience of the intended audience.

To discuss discrete mechanical manufacturing and associated engineering functions as computational problems, a simple (but not overly simplified) model is proposed. This model consists of three stages of ativity including the Part Design Stage, the Tool/Process Design Stage, and the Process Execution Stage.

1.The Part Design Stage of Manufacturing

The first step in part design is a conceptual one dealing with both synthesis and analysis (left side of Figure 1). Here the basic ideas of the product from the design standpoint are generated and teste . There are many constraints on this step. From the product planning function comes the request for a product with a particular set of functions, a performance level for each, and a packaged selling price in the marketplace. From the management function come design and development budgets which should not be exceeded while responding to product planning. Input can also come from researchers investigating the latest advances in relevant technology and from vendors marketing the latest components and subsystems. The goal of the concept synthesis phase is to consider these various constraints, and those constraints imposed by the laws of nature and the rules of engineering, and to create a solution - that is, a conceptual product design. The goal of the concept analysis phase is to subject each trail idea or set of ideas to some rough (possibly hand) calculations to compare feasibility.

The second step in part design is a detailing one, again involving both synthesis and analysis (right side of Figure 1). Once one, or possibly a few, concepts are selected as promising, detail part design begins. Here the part design concept is placed under the engineering microscope for detailed consideration.

All of the same constraints input to the concept synthesis phase are passed along to the detail synthesis phase in expanded form. For example. the list of desired features and functions originally input from product planning for concept synthesis is now broken down, specified, documented, and examined at the level of a user's manual and repairman's guide. Detail analysis deals with extended calculations simulating various expected operating conditions of the product in contrast to the "ballpark" analysis of the conceptual step. The detailing step may include the construction of a prototype and feedback of test data. The detailing step should include analysis for manufacturability of the product as the part design stage continues. The detailing step can sometimes include a search for an existing part which meets requirements, either from the in-house data base or from vendors. The goal of the Part Design Stage is to produce a detailed product specification, usually through detail drafting, to pass on to the Tool/Process Design Stage. Note, however, that a concept can "fail" in the detail step. This is to indicate that the concept considered in detail may be shown not to satisfay one or more of the imposed constraints and so detailing stops and the conceptual step restarts.

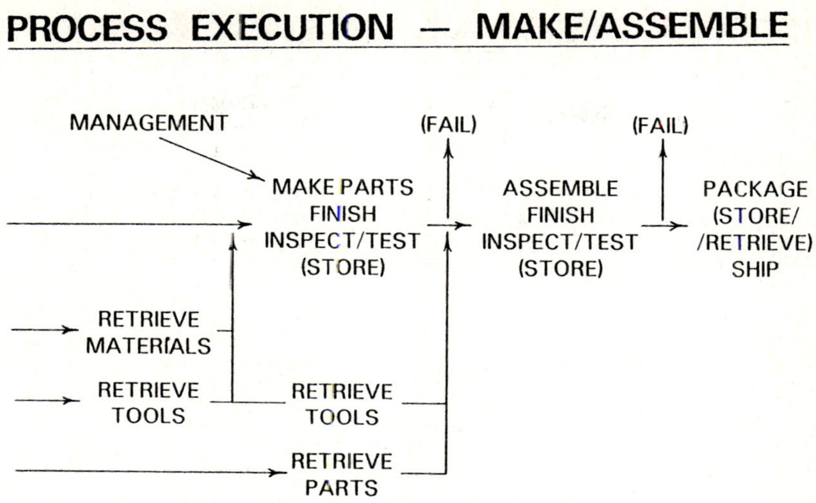

Figure 1

2. The Tool/Process Design Stage of Manufacturing

The Process Design Stage exhibits a high degree of similarity to the Part Design Stage - except that the focus of attention is on designing processes by which to manufacture parts rather than designing the parts themselves. The first step in process design is a conceptual one where the basic ideas of the product from the production standpoint are generated and tested (left side of Figure 2).

A number of the constraints input to this step come from the Part Design Stage in the form of the detailed product specification. Other important constraints come from the production facilities actually available on the factory floor and the inventory of materials, tools and parts. Once again, the management function provides constraints in the form of time/money budgets which should not be exceeded in the Process Design Stage. The goal of the conceptual synthesis phase is to consider these constraints, and those imposed by the rules of engineering and the laws of nature, and to create a solution - a conceptual process design. The goal of the concept analysis phase is to test these concepts for feasibility.

The second step in process design is a detailing one where the process design concept is again placed under the engineering microscope for detailed consideration. The constraints from the conceptual step are passed along in expanded form to the detail step. For example, the constraints of existing factory facilities are broken down to consider the details of the existing and planned workloads, and the availability schedules of materials, tooling, and parts required to commence activity on the factory floor. Detail analysis concerns fine simulation and validation of the processes designed as opposed to the coarse analysis done in the conceptual step.

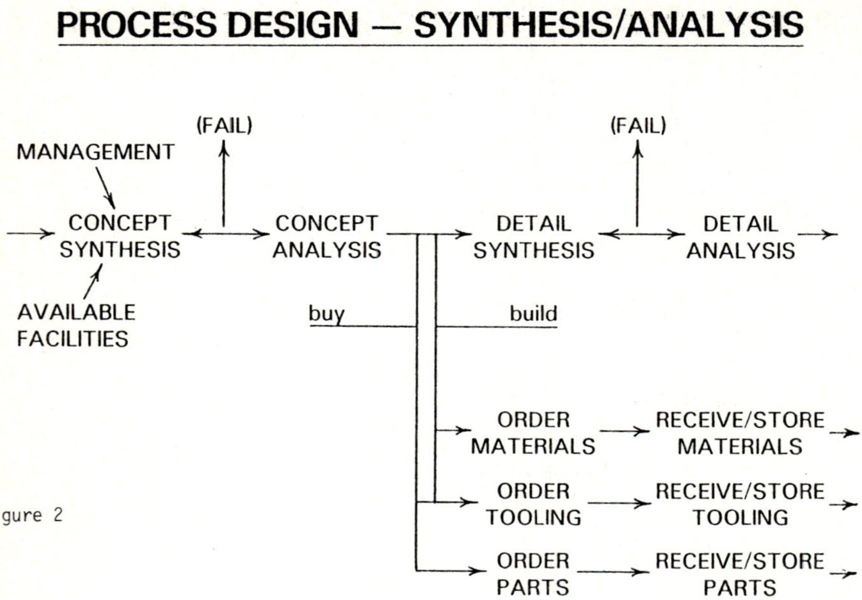

Figure 2

During the Process Design Stage a number of build/buy decisions are made. If it is possible to buy a part (or a tool), and its cost in time/money is reasonable in the context of the design of the process, then part (or tool) orders must be placed and deliveries entered as constraints. If, on the other hand, parts (or tools) are more effectively made in-house, orders for materials (or tools) must be placed and the resulting constraints considered. Special emphasis on tools must be added here. A separate but complete manufacturing scenario for tools could be described in parallel to this one for products. It has been estimated, for example, that in the automotive industry roughly 20 % of the design efforts goes into the car, and 80 % goes into the tooling to make the car. This description of a model of product manufacturing will continue in spite of this fact on the basis that tool-making can still be considered as discrete mechanical manufacturing with the tool as the product. This points out that discrete mechanical manufacturing is multilayered with many similar activities proceeing in parallel for complementary reasons.

Note that a possible outcome for either of these process design steps can be failure. One or more of the imposed constraints may be shown not to be satisfiable and so the previous step restarted, usually at considerable expense in terms of both time and money. If successful, the result of the Tool/Process Design Stage is a detailed production specification to pass on to the Process Execution Stage.

3. The Process Execution Stage of Manufacturing

After the product has been designed in detail and the manufacturing process planned in detail, the next obvious stage is the execution of the process to make the product.

The first step in process execution is one in which raw materials and tooling are brought together with other manufacturing equipment - NC machine tools, for example - to produce parts (left side of Figure 3). This might also entail finishing the parts (deburring, polishing, plating, painting, etc.), inspecting and/or testing, and placing the parts in storage until required. The second step in Process Execution includes bringing together parts and tooling along with other manufacturing equipment - biological robots (humans) for example - to assemble products (right side of Figure 3). Again, finishing, inspecting, testing, and storing may be required. In this model of manufacturing, the packaging function is included as a kind of generalized assembly - assembling the product with its shipping and merchandising container (far right side of Figure 3).

PARTS DESIGN — SYNTHESIS/ANALYSIS

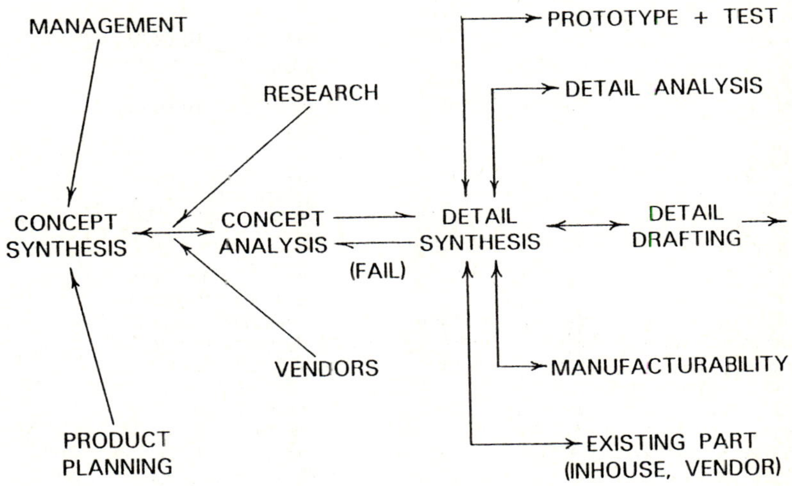

Figure 3

As might be expected, the Process Execution Stage is also constrained. The constraints encapsulated in both the detailed product specification and the detailed process specification are used as inputs to process execution. From the management function come production time and cost budgets. The laws of nature come to the forefront in this stage since the activities are taking place on the factory floor whereas both of the previous stages have taken place mainly in the design and production offices. Two categories of natural laws will be discussed later and so are introduced here. The first are Newton's Laws, the cornerstones of engineering theory and practice, and the natural laws referred to in previous stages as the constraints of nature. The second laws are those of Murphy expressing the stark reality of the shop floor. These latter laws have not been considered as constraints in earlier stages, but certainly are in process execution. This is because on the shop floor, Murphy generally takes precendence over Newton.

Note yet again that, while the goal of this stage is the product ready for the market place, failure is a possible outcome. In some cases this may simply mean that another try at the execution of the production plan is in order. In more drastic cases, the plan may be faulty and Process Design Stage must be reactivated. In the most traumatic cases, faults in the design may only become apparent at this point in manufacturing and the Part Design Stage restarted.

MANUFACTURING AS A SET OF COMPUTATIONAL PROBLEMS

So much for the simple model of discrete mechanical manufacturing. The point is that there are a number of interesting computational problems in the three manufacturing stages just described. Many of these problems, at least the ones which are the focus of this document, stem from the combinatorial complexity inherent in manufacturing. There are at least two different sources of this complexity - one is most obvious in the Part Design Stage, the other is most obvious in the Process Execution Stage. In the Process Design Stage, both sources are present to a lesser degree.

1. Combinatorial Complexity in Part Design

The source of the combinatorial complexity in the Part Design Stage lies in the basic nature of engineering synthesis and analysis (Figure 4). In science, as distinct from engineering, one studies natural systems in which the inputs can usually be controlled (or at least measured), the outputs can usually be observed, and the goal is the discovery of the natural laws governing the system.

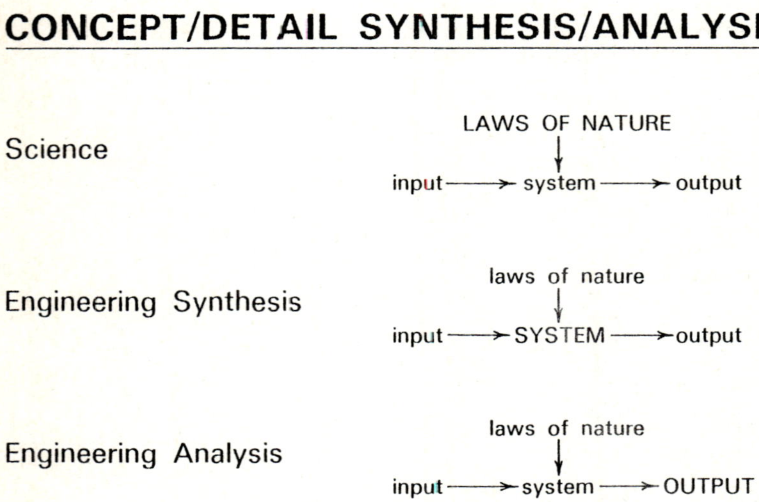

Figure 4

The goal of engineering synthesis is quite different. Given the natural laws, a partial specification of the input and output requirements, and the experiental rules of "good engineering synthesis" as constraints, the practitioner is required to create an artificial (i.e. manufacturable) system which conforms to and satisfies all of these constraints. The goal of engineering analysis is different still. Given the natural laws, a partial specification of the inputs, and the rules of "good engineering analysis" as constraints, and given an artificial system (or model thereof) as an object of study, the practitioner is required to create an analysis which models the expected outputs from the system while conforming to the constraints. In the manufacturing context, it is this constraint-directed synthesis/analysis which is the source of combinatorial complexity.

Mechanical parts synthesis is the use of scientific principles, technical information, and imagination in the definition of a mechanical structure to perform pre-specified functions with a high degree of economy and efficiency. Part synthesis is the activity of adding detail to a description until full detail is reached relative to some context. In the concept synthesis context, full detail is a complete set of ideas that fit together and appear feasible. In the detail synthesis context, full detail is a complete set of drawings of the parts as a structural definition. Difficulties are generated by the fact that these synthesis tasks are often ill-defined and always under-constrained. The tasks are ill-defined in that there does not exist a clear goal and so problem definition and problem solution go on concurrently rather than serially. The tasks are under-constraint in that, even with a clear goal, there are never enough restrictions given to limit to one the number of systems which could serve as solutions to the synthesis problem. In brief, the designer is faced with a practically infinite number of ways to hit a moving target - and is expected to select one which exhibits a high degree of economy and efficieny. Synthesis becomes a long series of difficult decisions, some of which must be restracted as the goal becomes clearer. The designer is faced with combinatorial complexity at two levels - first in making each individual decision (later called tactical decisions), then in choosing the next decision to consider (later called strategic decisions).

Mechanical parts analysis is the use of scientific principles, technical information, and imagination in the critical examination of designs and design ideas in the context of their behaviour under various operating conditions. Again combinatorial complexity is present to make the engineering task more difficult. The analyst must choose from the potentially infinite number of combinations and permutations of physical inputs that any non-trivial product might experience in its service life, those that can be investigated in the finite amount of time available. In addition, the analyst must be familiar with the vast array of laws of nature and rules of analysis and select from the ones sutiable for the problems at hand. Finally, the analyst must decide among all of the ways in which the object to be analyzed could be modelled, and also decide the level of detail to include. Once again, the designer is faced with tactical and strategic combinatorial complexity.

The result of these difficulties is added expense in the creation of real-wealth. The ever increasing complexity of products means an ever increasing time expended in decision making. The problem solver is presumed to have a larger and larger range of background information relevant to the context of the problem. Faced with rising complexity, the designer lapses into trying to modify his "standard solutions" when faced with new problems rather than accepting the risk of being innovative. Given the combinatorial complexity inherent in design, the engineer knows that the optimal solution cannot be found (in fact, probably wouldn't be recognized if it was generated) and so must somehow be able to generate (through synthesis) and recognize (through analysis) a "satisfactory" solution. In the face of combinatorial complexity, judgemental errors are easily possible and if undetected until the Process Design Stage or the Process Execution Stage lead to low quality or ineffectual products and/or costly overruns or failures.

2. Combinatorial Complexity in Process Execution

The source of combinatorial compexity in the Process Execution Stage lies in the basic nature of the factory environment specifically and the overall commercial manufacturing environment in general. The goal of the manufacturing engineer is to execute process plans in as cost and time efficient a manner as possible. Budgetary constraints have been specified by management. The natural laws of space and time provide constraints which cannot be ignored in the factory. A very large number of constraints are input in terms of the product specification emanating from the Part Design Stage and the process specification emanating from the Process Design Stage. The combinatorial complexity experienced on the shop floor is generally not due to ill-defined goals or under-constrained tasks. It has been the objective of the earlier stages to clarify the goals and to enumerate and satisfy the constraints. Since the earlier stages are never perfect, ill-defined goals and under-constrained tasks are sometimes encountered on the factory floor, but are not the crux of the argument here.

The problem is that the manufacturing environment contains a inescapable element of randomness. Stated briefly, for an involved multistep process in the factory requiring communication and synchronization, there are only a few ways for the process to succeed and an essentially infinite number of ways in which the process might fail. Process specifications are often found to be fragile in the domain of Murphy's Laws. The best maintained production machinery sometimes fails. The highest quality tools sometimes break, The most reliable employee sometimes gets sick. The specially reserved stock for a particular process sometimes gets misplaced in the warehouse or accidentally used for another job. The most reliable of suppliers sometimes delivers late. Snow storms and flash floods and tornados do occur. Any process specification is founded on a number of assumptions about the conditions in the execution environment. For the process plan to execute smoothly, all of the assumptions must hold true. The more involved the process or set of processes, the greater the number of assumptions. But of course, each assumption carries with it some chance of being fals once tested in the real world. It does not require example calculations to see that, for the execution of a process plan of any reasonable size, the probability of at least one of the assumptions being false at any particular time can be very high, and the possibility of a number of assumptions failing simultaneously can be non-negligible.

For the process engineer on the factory, combinatorial complexity comes from trying to manage the contingencies inherent in process execution. There are tactical decisions to be made concerning the possibilities of repairing a process once it has gone wrong. There are strategic decisions required having to do with selecting which fault in a multiple failure situation to attend to first, or which potential error condition to prepare for if things are running well. Decisions must sometimes be made to start over, or to contact the personnel in the Process Design Stage, or to contact the personnel in the Part Design Stage.

The result of the difficulties associated with this second class of combinatorial complexity is again added expense in the creation of real-wealth. The ever increasing complexity of processes means an ever increasing possible execution time. The fault repairer is required to have an ever growing range of background information relevant to operating on the factory floor. Judgemental errors can be made which simply compound the execution problems. Again the result is costly overruns and failures.

3. Combinatorial Complexity in Process Design

In the Process Design Stage of manufacturing, both types of combinatorial complexity play a role since this stage forms the link between the Part Design Stage and the Process Execution Stage. The process designer certainly faces combinatorial complexity in the sense of ill-defined, under-constrained task - process design does include creative design tasks. The process designer also faces the combinatorial complexity of real world randomness - process design must take into account as much as possible and practical the uncertain nature of events in the real world. In this sense, the Process Design Stage faces the most difficult challenge in overcoming the hazards of combinatorial complexity.

As stated at the beginning of this section, the simple model of manufacturing presented points to a number of interesting computational problems in manufacturing. Many of of the problems are numeric in nature, requiring what might be considered "normal" computational techniques, but a significant subset of the problems involves combinatorial complexity. Although these latter problems are strongly implicated in adding expense to manufacturing functions, not enough effort has been focused on computation solutions for them.

A SIMPLE MODEL OF ARTIFICIAL INTELLIGENCE

From the beginning of computing as a discipline, a number of classes of problems have been fairly well understood. The major, almost exclusive, application of computers today is in solving the numerically difficult or computationally tedious problems which fall into these classes. Computers have had a tremendous impact on our lives through the automated solution of problems in these classes, at least partly because humans are not very efficient in the face of numerical difficulty or computational tedium. Imagine an airline reservation system or financial institution or engineering company without its number crunching computer. Solving equations, calculating payrolls, and generally keeping track of numbers is the obvious work of the computer - a role from which it derives its popular name. In the context of this paper, the problems in these classes exhibit three common features. The first characteristic is that these problems do not involve combinatorial complexity in their solution. They may be numerically difficult and require mathematical creativity, and they may be computationally tedious and require programming skills, but they are seldom inherently ill-defined or under-constrained. Secondly, there is usually a well-known, relatively standard solution process for these problems. In some cases, payroll calculations for example, the processes were commonly used by humans before computers and have simply evolved as they have been transferred onto the machine. The third characteristic is that these problems generally include the requirement for a particular or optimal answer. In the mind of every recipient of a paycheck, there is the single correct answer - close is not good enough. For most seekers after the solutions to an equation, there is "the" right answer - again close will just not do. Problems exhibiting these three characteristics, and the programs resulting from solution attempts, are the mainstream of computer science.

For roughly the last twenty-five years, another quite different class of problems has been under study. Problems in this class, and programs which implement solution ideas, are among the worst understood in computer science. This sad fact is not true because the problems in this class are not important. It is rather because the problems are so difficult and because there are so few computer scientists doing significant work in the area. In the context of this discussion, there are three common traits exhibited by problems in this class. The first trait is that these problems do exhibit combinatorial complexity. These problems are often inherently ill-defined and always inherently under-constrained. Secondly, there is seldom any known or standard solution process for these problems. There may be a store of "rules of Thumb", "educated guesses", and "standards of good practice" in approaching a problem, but seldom is there a guaranteed solution process. The third trait is that for these problems there is hardly ever an optimal or unique answer. A solution technique which provides a reasonably good answer reasonably often is about as much as can be expected. As a toy example (but difficult) of this class of problem consider the game chess. Given the playing pieces, the board, the rules, chess presents a fairly well-defined goal, but is grossly under-constrained in terms of achieving that goal. While there is no well- known guaranteed solution process to the chess problem, there certainly is a storehouse of advice on "good play". Much of this is on display in the chess section of any well-stocked library. And fianlly, optimal moves are not required. A player need only select incremental solutions to the chess problem which are better than those used by his opponent. It is interesting to note that problems which fall into this class, while being manageable by humans, are not well understood and their solutions have not yet been impacted by the computer.

Both of these categories of problems - those first described as being basically numeric in nature, and those just described as being somewhat different - are found in the manufacturing problem set. In this paper, our focus of attention is on the latter class of problems which are frequently solved efficiently by human beings, and which are the type of problems which are with higher frequency increasing the cost of manufacturing. It is commercially important in terms of the cost of producing real-wealth in an ever more technically advanced marketplace to understand these problems and how humans solve them so that the power of the computer can be brought to bear in automating their solution.

ARTIFICIAL INTELLIGENCE AS A SET OF COMPUTATIONAL TECHNIQUES

It was during the study of these kinds of human problem solving abilities (in a broader context than that of manufacturing) that it was realized that the detailed steps of almost all intelligent human activity were (are) unknown. This realization marked the beinning of Artificial Intelligence (AI) as a separate branch of Computer Science. For the purposes of this discussion, Artificial Intelligence can be thought of as the experimental branch of computer science which relates one complex natural phenomenon - human cognitive ability - with an artificial mechanical analogy - computer programs.

This endeavor can be viewed as both science and engineering. Some AI practitioners study naturally intelligent systems in terms of input and output attempting to deduce the natural laws of intelligence. Building the results into programs for comparison with natural (human) intelligence has sometimes led to a better understanding of human cognition. This can be viewed as the science of AI. Other AI workers are not principally concerned with modelling human behavior. The object is rather to use what is known or suspected to be a "natural law of intelligence", along with a specification of a desirable input/output relationship, to synthesize a computer program. The result of this work has sometimes been a high performance program functioning as a powerful tool for its users. This is AI as engineering.

It is also valid to try to define or understand AI in terms of the particular problems which are the objects of study. From this point of view, AI is the computational study of a number of problems related to human cognitive ability. AI is the study of communication between naturally intelligent entities - it is the computational study of our use of language, both spoken and written. AI is the study of human perception of our physical environment - it is the study of vision and touch as computational processes. AI is the study of human reasoning and human problem solving - in both the average man as "common sense" and in the not-so-average man as "expertise". AI is the study of human learning - from examples, from errors, and from experience. And AI is the study of human manipulation of our physical environment - it is the computational study of dealing with space and time. In the context of this paper, AI can be viewed as the overlap of all of these cognitive abilities in the computational study of the robot as a model of the human. This is especially true in the process Execution Stage of manufacturing.

The third and final perspective on AI offered here - and probably the most useful from the point of view of manufacturing - is AI as a three stage problem solving technique. The first step in this approach is to answer the question: "What knowledge is available to overcome the combinatorial explosion?". Given a combinatorially complex problem for which a less optimal procedure exists, what sources of knowledge can be tapped and what knowledge will be available from these sources? The second step is to seek an answer to the question "how can this knowledge be represented in the computer ?" Having obtained knowledge of the problem in terms of facts, figures, experiential rules-of-thumb, problem solving heuristics, and so on, in what structure should knowledge be stored for maximal accessibility and minimal memory occupancy - i.e., efficiently. Easy accessibility is stressed because the solution of very difficult problems requires very large knowledge bases leading to issues of finding the appropriate piece of knowledge at the appropriate time to push the problem solving process ahead. Compactness is stressed because of the requirement to fit a very large knowledge base into a finite computer (which even our largest machines are). The third step is to try to anser the question "how can this knowledge be utilized in the computer?" Once all available knowledge has been acquired and represented, it must be used to reason over the problem. The question becomes one of applying the knowledge to guide the search for a solution through the maze of combinatorial complexity.

ARTIFICIAL INTELLIGENCE APPLICATIONS IN MANUFACTURING

I trust that the connection that I have been trying to make between manufacturing problems and AI techniques is now obvious. Realization of more efficient production of real-wealth through the manufacturing process requires better solutions to increasingly difficult problems involving combinatorial complexity. The techniques being developed by AI workers offer one of the few realistic chances to manage these problems. While AI techniques are under development in a number of different application areas - and many of these techniques will be important in manufacturing - only a few AI workers have directly attacked manufacturing problems. Included here are two sets of references for the interested reader. Firstly, although this paper has concentrated on discrete mechanical manufacturing, significant references exist in chemical, civil, and electrical/electronics areas. Secondly, brief summaries are given of a number of systems which are of direct impact on the topics highlighted in this document.

At least three systems are described in the literature which should be of interest to the chemical engineer. HEATEX (22, 38) is a program which assists in designing chemical processing plan systems that include heat exchangers. CONPHYDE (38) aids in selecting the appropriate analytic programs to evaluate chemical processing plant designs. WASTE (14)is aimed at the domain of chemical wastewater treatment systems, especially at diagnosing faults such as clogged pipes and valves and broken pumps.

At least six systems of potential interest to civil engineers are described in the literature. One system (25) deals with the problem of laying out rooms in a dwelling while another system (13) handles the problem of selecting and checking structural components on the basis of their conformance to design specifications and building codes. MOVER (38) dignoses faults and recommends repairs for an airport transportation system. Two systems (35, 42) aid in the diagnosis and treatment of nuclear reactor accidents. The sixth program aims at helping decision makers to operate flood control dams and to plan civil defense in flood-prone areas (7).

The number of papers in the AI literature concerning electrical and/or electronic systems is far too high to be treated here, but a few examples can be given. Systems exist at the integrated circuit level which provide intelligent assistance on the layout problem (27, 40). At the component level, work has been done on representation (34), on design (23, 26), on redesign (33), on design verification (3), and on component level debugging (8, 24). At the system level, there are systems which aid in design (30, 31, 32) and systems which aid in debugging (5, 19, 39). There is also a system which assists in maintaining telephone cables (41, 43).

In the context of discrete mechanical manufacturing - the focus of this document - here are two levels of interesting literature. On one hand there are a few papers (11, 12, 18, 37) and two books (1, 2) which treat the topic in a theoretical way or on a survey level. On the other hand there are a few papers which describe particular working system. A selection of the latter are briefly described here.

1. AI in Part Design

One of the earliest applications of AI to manufacturing was the TROPIC system of Latombe (28.). Following on this lead, McDonnel Douglas is currently beginning an investigation of the part design stage of manufacturing. The specific topic under study at this time is the metal joining problem - what knowledge does an expert part designer call into play when deciding whether to join two pieces of metal by welding, gluing, riveting, etc. - and can this knowledge be captured in such a way as to be of assistance to all designers. Initial results are encouraging. Three other systems concerned with part design have been described in the literature ....

A Design by Refinement System: At Ohio State University, Chandrasekaran and Brown have developed an intelligent design tool based on the idea of design refinement (6). The system contains a hierarchy of conceptual design specialists each containing a set of design plans relevant for its level in the hierarchy. The high level specialists maintain a global view of the design while the low level specialists are concerned with specific parts. Each specialist takes as input design parameters and constraints. Success yields a workable design from the lowest level. Failure at any level in the hierarchy leads to another design cycle with further design parameters and tighter constraints. A two level trial system has been implemented to design small tables. At the top of the hierarchy is the "small table design expert" and at the second level there are the "circular top specialist" and the "cylindrical support specialist". This system is capable of responding to an overall requirement description by producing a design including materials and dimensions. The concept is being pursued with Accuray Corporation, a manufacturer of industrial control systems, to produce a system able to design simple pneumatic actuators. The design refinement idea permits automatic systems if all of the design specialists are programs, or interactive systems if some of the specialists are human designers.

A Design by Redesign System: At General Electric Corporate Research and Development Laboratories, Dixon and Simmons have developed an intelligent design tool based on the idea of redesign (10). The system takes as input an available initial design, then iterates through evaluation and redesign steps until an acceptable design is produced. At the heart of the system are the evalutation criteria and scales established in consultation with human experts. Although the domain and status of this system are not clear, it appears to have been applied to simple mechanical systems like V-belts and shafts.

SACON (Structural Analysis CONsultant): The last AI application in the part design stage of manufacturing to be discussed here is an excellent example of the potentially powerful interaction between numeric computation and symbolic computation. SACON is a system developed and partially implemented at Stanford University (4) to advise engineers in the use of a general-purpose structural analysis program called MARC. The MARC program employs finite-element analysis techniques to simulate the mechanical behavior of parts, but offers such a wide choice of analysis methods, material properties and geometries that one year of experience with the program is typically required to learn how to use all of the options proficiently. The objective of the SACON program is to assist the user in selecting from the options an analysis strategy for a particular problem which will provide the correct simulation at the desired accuracy while incurring a minimal computational expense. Although SACON has only been used as an experimental tool, it points the way to artificially intelligent programs which serve an interfacing role between complex numerical programs and humans who whish to use those programs efficiently without investing large blocks of time in proficiency training.

2. AI in Process Design

In the process design stage of manufacturing, McDonnel Douglas is developing intelligent tools to assist process desigrers. The specific topic is again metal joining, an example being an expert welding assistant. This program provides advice on most facets of welding from a point just after the designer has decided to weld up to a point just before an arc is struck on the workpiece. This involves selecting a welding process (MIG, TIG, etc.), deciding a joint and weld type, detailing joint preparation, commenting on jigging and tacking, etc. Three other systems dealing with process design have been described in the literature.....

ISIS: In the process design stage of manufacturing, ISIS embodies a constraint-directed reasoning approach to job-shop scheduling and has been developed and implemented by Fox and coworkers at Carnegie-Mellon University (14, 15, 17). This job-shop scheduling problem consists of selecting a sequence of operations and assigning particular resources and start/end times for each operation. This is an NP-hard problem and is one at which human schedulers are not especially proficient. The symptoms of this lack of proficiency are typically high work in progress, low machine utilization, and general tardiness of order completion. To solve the scheduling problem, ISIS reasons over a variety of constraints including profit constraints (e.g. due date), physical constraints (e.g. machine capabilities), causal constraints(e.g. resource availability), and preference constraints (from the shop floor personnel). Directed by these constraints, the system performs a hierarchical search in the space of alternate schedules, operating in either an automatic or interactive model. ISIS is currently undergoing preliminary testing in a Westinghouse steam turbine blade production facility.

GARI: This program developed and implemented at the University of Grenoble by Latombe and coworkers (9), performs a knowledge-based automatic planning function over machining sequences for the manufacture of mechanical parts. Given a drawing of the desired part, GARI produced a plan specifying the machining cuts to be made, their order, the machine tools to be used, and the surfaces to be employed for clamping and locating during each cut. In producing this plan, GARI takes into account both technological and economic considerations (although compromises are often necessary). The initial version of GARI has been used in an industrial setting, and there have recently been indications that further work on the system will soon commence.

KBS (Knowledge-Based Simulation): In another project at Carnegie-Mellon University, Fox and coworkers are developing a knowledge-based system capable of interactively modelling and simulating factory organizations (14). The system includes a number of features which are aimed at producing simulations that are easier to build and that produce more understandable results than currently available simulators. For example, KBS represents the system at multiple levels of abstraction thus allowing the user to specify the level of simulation and the detail of the results. Furtermore, KBS allows the system to be selectively instrumented to restrict data analysis to areas of interest. To date, KBS has been applied (experimentally) to a number of assembly scenarios found in the factories of Digital Equipment Corporation, the sponsors of the research.

3. AI in Process Execution

McDonnel Douglas also has an active AI research in the process execution stage of manufacturing. A specific example is a real time system with expertise in machine loading and unloading by robot. Conventional robot cells often fail to operate efficiently due to their lack of intelligence. Convential scheduling approaches also fail due to their lack of robustness in the face of time tolerances and unexpected events. Our approach has been to put intelligence on top of a robot controller in the actual cell environment. This yields a loading/unloading cell with the capability of deciding for itself the best "next move" to assure efficiency. Other systems dealing with process execution have been described in the literature ....

PDS (Process Diagnosis System): Fox and coworkers at Carnegie-Mellon University have developed and artificially intelligent system for the online realtime diagnosis of malfunctions in machine processes (14, 16). The operation of the system is based on information acquired from tens to hundreds of sensors attached to the machine(s). While this is the only way to obtain large amounts of timely information, it introduces further problems since no sensor is error-free and sensor performance degrades over time. Therefore, PDS also reasons about the sources of its information in addition to performing diagnosis based on the information. The system is just going into production use at Westinghouse Electric Corporation who have sponsored the research.

Other Shop Floor Diagnosis Systems: Other researchers have also been exploring the use of Artificial Intelligence techniques to maintain the integrity of the process execution phase of manufacturing. Gini and coworkers at the Politecnico di Milano have proposed CAMA (Computer Assisted MAintenance) as a knowledge-based consultation system for automatic maintenance and repair (21.). Further efforts by the same workers has been aimed at automatic error recovery in robot programs while operating in the manufacturing environment (20.). Related work in robotics is also being pursued at the University College of Wales (29.).

4. Related Systems

Two other classes of systems should be mentioned for completeness. There are systems which are focused on product maintenance problems too. One example is the DELTA (Diesel-Electric Locomotive Troubleshooting Aid) or CATS (Computer Aided Troubleshooting System) program currently in use at the General Electric Company. The other class contains programs which aid at the level of manufacturing management. Examples include the Callisto (large project management) (14.), ROME (long range financial planning) (14.), and INET (transportation and warehousing management) (14., 36.) projects at Carnegie-Mellon University.

SUMMARY

I hope that these examples provide some substantiation of the belief that AI techniques can be useful in manufacturing. It is my belief that as the combinatorial complexity of part design, process design, and process execution continues to increase, AI will become as indispensible in the factory of the future as the computer is in the factory of the present.

REFERENCES

1.) Advances in CAD/CAM (Proceedings of the 5th International IFIP/IFAC Conference, Leningrad, 1982), T.M.R. Ellis and O.I. Semenkov (eds.), North-Holland (Amsterdam), 1983. (See Section IV. Artificial Intelligence in Design and Manufacturing.)

2.) Artificial Intelligence and Pattern Recognition in Computer Aided Design (Proceedings of the IFIP Working Conference, Grenoble, 1978), J.-C. Latombe (ed.), North-Holland (Amsterdam), 1978. (Numerous interesting articles, especially concerning electronic design.)

3.) Barrow, H.G., "Proving the Correctness of Digital Hardware Designs", Proceedings of the 3rd National Conference on Artificial Intelligence (Washington, D.C.), 1983, pp 17-21.

4.) Bennett, J.S. and Engelmore, R.S., "SACON: A Knowledge-Based Consultant for Structural Analysis", Proceedings of the 6th International Joint Conference on Artificial Intelligence (Tokyo), 1979, pp 47-49.

5.) Bennett, J.S. and Hollander, C.R., "DART: An Expert System for Computer Fault Diagnosis", Proceedings of the 7th International Joint Conference on Artificial Intelligence (Vancouver), 1981, pp 843-845.

6.) Brown, D.C. and Chandrasekaran, B., "An Approach to Expert Systems for Mechanical Design", Proceedings Trends and Applications (Automating Intelligent Behavior: Applications and Frontiers), 1983, National Bureau of Standards, Gaithersberg, MD, pp 173-180.

7.) Cuena, J., "The Use of Simulation Models and Human Advice to Build an Expert System for the Defense and Control of River Floods", Proceedings of the 8th International Joint Conference on Artificial Intelligence (Karlsruhe), 1983, pp 246-249.

8.) Davis, R., "Diagnosis via Causal Reasoning: Paths of Interaction and the Locality Principle", Proceedings of the 3rd National Conference on Artificial Intelligence (Washington, D.C.), 1983, pp 88-94.

9.) Descotte, Y. and Latombe, J.-C., "GARI: A Problem Solver that Plans how to Machine Mechanical Parts", Proceedings of the 7th International Joint Conference on Artificial Intelligence (Vancouver), 1981, pp 766-772.

10.) Dixon, J.R. and Simmons, M.K., "Computers that Design: Expert Systems for Mechanical Engineers", Computers in Mechanical Engineering, 2, 3, pp 10-18, 1983.

11.) Eastman, C.M., "Cognitive Processes and Ill-Defined Problems: A Case Study from Design", Proceedings of the 1st International Joint Conference on Artificial Intelligence (Washington, D.C.), 1969, pp 669-675.

12.) Elias, A.L., "Computer-Aided Engineering: The AI Connection", American Institute of Aeronautics and Astronautics, July-August, 1983, pp 48-54.

13.) Fenves, S.J. and Norabhoompipat, T., "Potentials for Artificial Intelligence Applications in Structural Engineering Design and Detailing", in Ref. 2.) above, pp 105-119.

14.) Fox, M.S., "Artificial Intelligence in the Factory of the Future", Proceedings of the ACM 12th Annual Computer Science Conference (Philadelphia), 1984, pp 29-38.

15.) Fox, M.S., Allen, B.P., and Strohm G.A., "Job Shop Scheduling: An Investigation in Constraint-Directed Reasoning", Proceedings of the 2nd National Conference on Artificial Intelligence (Pittsburgh), 1982, pp 155-158.

16.) Fox, M.S., Lowenfeld, S., and Kleinosky, P., "Techniques for Sensor-Based Diagnosis", Proceedings of the 8th International Joint Conference on Artificial Intelligence (Karlsruhe), 1983, pp 158-163.

17.) Fox, M.S., Smith, S.F., Allen, B.P., Strohm, G.A., and Wimberly, F.C., "ISIS: A Constraint-Directed Reasoning Approach to Job Shop Scheduling", Proceedings Trends and Applications (Automating Intelligent Behavior: Applications and Frontiers), 1983, National Bureau of Standards, Gaithersberg, MD, pp 76-81.

18.) Freeman, P. and Newell, A., "A Model for Functional Reasoning in Design", Proceedings of the 2nd International Joint Conference on Artificial Intelligence (London), 1971, pp 621-633.

19.) Genesereth, M.R., "Diagnosis Using Hierarchical Design Models", Proceedings of the 2nd National Conference on Artificial Intelligence (Pittsburgh), 1982, pp 278-283.

20.) Gini, M. and Gini, G., "Towards Automatic Error Recovery in Robot Programs", Proceedings of the 8th International Joint Conference on Artificial Intelligence (Karlsruhe), 1983, pp 821-823.

21.) Gini, M., Gini, G., and Morpurgo, A., "A Knowledge-Based Consultation System for Automatic Maintenance and Repair", in Ref. 1.) above.

22.) Grimes, L.E., Rychener, M.D., and Westerberg, A.W., "The Synthesis and Evolution of Networks of Heat Exchanges that Feature the Minimum Number of Units", Chemical Engineering Communications, 14, 1982.

23.) Grinberg, M.R., "A Knowledge Based Design System for Digital Electronics", Proceedings of the 1st National Conference on Artificial Intelligence (Stanford), 1980, pp 283-285.

24.) Hamscher, W., "Using Structural and Functional Information in Diagnostic Design", Proceedings of the 3rd National Conference on Artificial Intelligence (Washington, D.C.), 1983, pp 152-156.

25.) Henrion, M., "Automatic Space-Planning: A Postmortem?", in Ref. 2.) above, pp 175-191.

26.) Kelley, V.E. and Steinberg, L.I., "The CRITTER System: Analyzing Digital Circuits by Propagating Behaviors and Specifications", Proceedings of the 2nd National Conference on Artificial Intelligence (Pittsburgh), 1982, pp 284-289.

27.) Kim, J. and McDermott, J., "TALIB: An IC Layout Design Assistant", Proceedings of the 3rd National Conference on Artificial Intelligence (Washington, D.C.), 1983, pp 197-201.

28.) Latombe, J.-C., "Artificial Intelligence in Computer-Aided Design: The TROPIC System", Technical Note 125, Artificial Intelligence Center, SRI International, 1976.

29.) Le, M.H., Barnes, D.P., and Hardy, N.W., "Knowledge Based Error Recovery in Industrial Robots", Proceedings of the 8th International Joint Conference on Artificial Intelligence (Karlsruhe), 1983, pp 824-826.

30.) McDermott, J., "R1: An Expert in the Computer Systems Domain", Proceedings of the 1st National Conference on Artificial Intelligence (Stanford), 1980, pp 269-271.

31.) McDermott, J., "R1: The Formative Years", The AI Magazine, 2, 2, 21-29, 1981.

32.) McDermott, J., "Domain Knowledge and the Design Process", Proceedings of the 18th ACM/IEEE Design Automation Conference (Nashville), 1981, pp 580-588.

33.) Mitchell, T.M., Steinberg, L.I., Kedar-Cabelli, S., Kelley, V.E., Shulman, J., and Weinrich, T., "An Intelligent Aid for Circuit Redesign", Proceedings of the 3rd National Conference on Artificial Intelligence (Washington, D.C.), 1983, pp 274-278.

34.) Mitchell, T., Steinberg, L., Smith, R.G., Schooley, P., Jacobs, H., and Kelley, V., "Representations for Reasoning about Digital Circuits", Proceedings of the 7th International Joint Conference on Artificial Intelligence (Vancouver), 1981, pp 343-344.

35.) Nelson, W.R., "REACTOR: An Expert System for Diagnosis and Treatment of Nuclear Reactor Accidents", Proceedings of the 2nd National Conference on Artificial Intelligence (Pittsburgh), 1982, pp 296-301.

36.) Reddy, Y.V., Fox, M.S., Doyle, K., and Arnold, J., "INET: A Knowledge Based Simulation Model of a Corporate Distribution System", Proceedings Trends and Applications (Automating Intelligent Behavior: Applications and Frontiers), 1983, National Bureau of Standards, Gaithersberg, MD, pp 109-118.

37.) Rychener, M.D., "Expert Systems for Engineering Design: Experiments with Basic Techniques", Proceedings IEEE Design Automation Conference, 1983.

38.) Rychener, M.D., "Expert Systems for Engineering Design: Experiments with Basic Techniques", Proceedings Trends and Applications (Automating Intelligent Behavior: Applications and Frontiers), 1983, National Bureau of Standards, Gaithersberg, MD, pp 21-27.

39.) Shubin, H. and Ulrich, J.W., "IDT: An Intelligent Diagnostic Tool", Proceedings of the 2nd National Conference on Artificial Intelligence (Pittsburgh), 1982, pp 290-295.

40.) Stefik, M. and Conway, L., "Towards the Principled Engineering of Knowledge", The AI Magazine, 3, 3, pp 4-16, 1982.

41.) Stolfo, S.J., "Knowledge Engineering: Theory and Practice", Proceedings Trends and Applications (Automating Intelligent Behavior: Applications and Frontiers), 1983, National Bureau of Standards, Gaithersberg, MD, pp 97-104.

42.) Underwood, W.E., "A CSA Model-based Nuclear Power Plant Consultant", Proceedings of the 2nd National Conference on Artificial Intelligence (Pittsburgh), 1982, pp 302-305.

43.) Vesonder, G.T., Stolfo, S.J., Zielinski, J.E., Miller, F.D., and Copp, D.H., "ACE: An Expert System for Telephone Cable Maintenance", Proceedings of the 8th International Joint Conference on Artificial Intelligence (Karlsruhe), 1983, pp 116-121.

TECHNOLOGY

ARTIFICIAL INTELLIGENCE: Towards Practical Application
T. Bernold and G. Albers (editors)
Elsevier Science Publishers B.V. (North-Holland)

KNOWLEDGE PROCESSING EXPERT SYSTEMS

Peter Raulefs

Fachbereich Informatik
Universität Kaiserslautern
Kaiserslautern
West Germany

A short survey on the current state of the development and application of expert systems is given. It is argued that we are currently on the verge towards developing a second generation of expert systems if a number of open basic research problems can be solved. First generation expert systems exploiting currently available techniques from artificial intelligence will soon exhaust the expectations and market potential usually associated with knowledge processing and expert systems.

INTRODUCTION

Since the publication of the Japanese plans towards a fifth computer generation, considerable expectations have arisen about the coming of age of knowledge processing systems to supersede conventional data processing. Here, "knowledge" refers not only to propositional facts ('the GNP of Switzerland in 1983 is...."), but also to logical and empirically established relationships, procedures for solving problems in various application domains, as well as control knowledge in terms of tactics and strategies about how to make efficient use of factual and procedural knowledge.

The predominant architecture of expert systems for the different types of applications is outlined in Fig. 1:

(1) The INFERENCE MACHINE controls and executes all reasoning towards achieving the respective goals. Inferences are performed by the deduction and/or simulation system under guidance of the control system. Deductions and simulations are sequences of inference steps resp. state transitions according to rules resp. models supplied by knowledge sources.

(2) KNOWLEDGE SOURCES at least comprise a knowledge base to supply the inference machine. Factual knowledge might also be extracted from conventional data base systems. Other knowledge may be obtained from simulation models, as well as from other expert system at hand.

(3) The ACTUAL STATE MANAGER maintains intermediary results and (sub-)goals to be utilized in subsequent steps as well as information to be supplied

- for updating a knowledge source
- for providing the explanation system with information about what is going on
- for packaging and preparing information to be used by the knowledge acquisition system, or
- for preparing output to the output interface.

The inference machine will very often split up the overall task into specific subgoals to be attacked under some plan developed and maintained in the agenda.

(4) The KNOWLEDGE BASE MANAGEMENT SYSTEM (KBMS) manages both information flow between, and utilization of the various components of the actual state manager and the knowledge sources. The KBMS may itself be an expert system.

(5) The EXPLANATION SYSTEM is meant to keep users of the expert system informed about what is going on. This is usually required on several levels of detail or abstraction, adapting to the interest and competence of the user. It is mandatory that the explanation system provides explanations in an understandable way, e.g. by using natural language or graphics. Furthermore, the explanation system should be capable of answering queries such as

- "why" or "what for" a particular action has been taken by the expert system, and
- "how" some conclusion has been reached.

(6) The KNOWLEDGE ACQUISITION SYSTEM is used for bringing in additional knowledge to the knowledge sources. There are three principal modes for acquiring new knowledge:

- Interactive transfer of expertise: The explanation system is used to elicit the current capabilities of the knowledge sources so that experts, usually assisted by knowledge engineers, can identify gaps and deficiencies. The knowledge acquisition system then helps to input and incorporate new knowledge correcting and/or amending what is already contained in the knowledge sources.

- Knowledge compilation: There are two directions of compiling knowledge:

  Horizontal knowledge compilation consists in transforming knowledge represented in one way into another knowledge representation without changing its content.

  Vertical knowledge compilation consits in inferring "shallow" from "deep" knowledge as explained in Section on Current Research Activities.

- Learning: There are few and rather limited techniques for learning from specific cases and examples.

(7) The OUTSIDE INTERFACES provide communication between the expert system cases and examples.

(8) The EXPERT SYSTEM MANAGEMENT SYSTEM (XMS) serves as a central switchboard for supervising and operating all other subsystems.

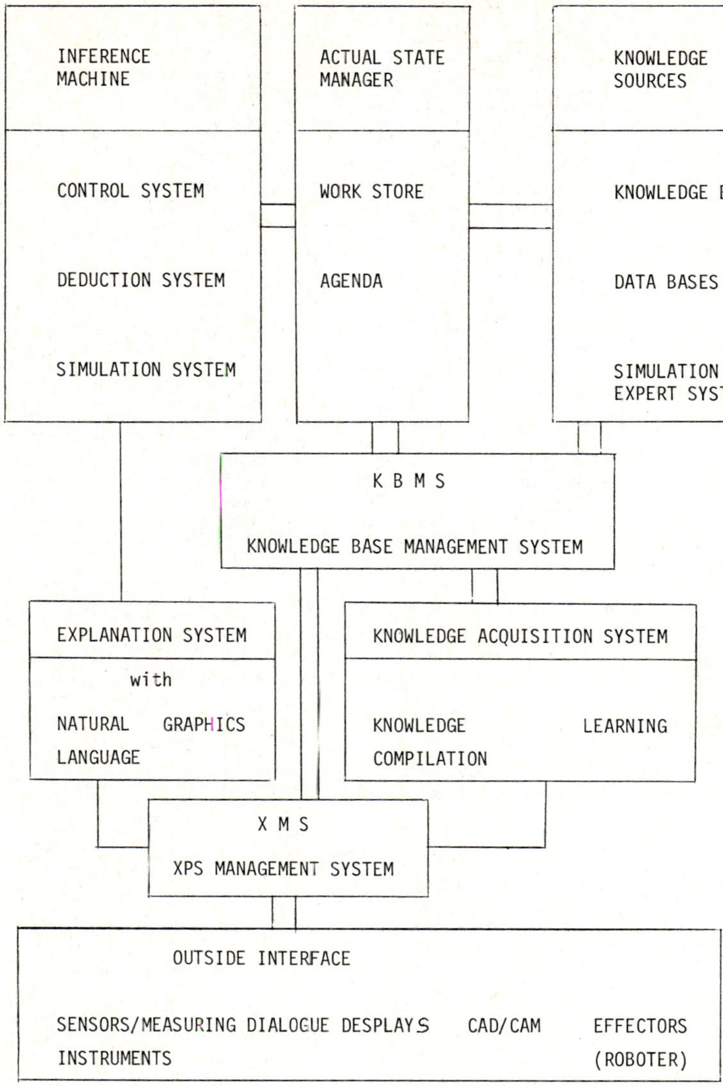

Fig. 1 Architecture of Expert Systems

CURRENT STATE OF APPLICATIONS

1. Overview

(1) INTERPRETATION of findings such as measurement data and sensory observations to obtain propositions about past, present, or future states of the system being considered. Specific goals of interpretation systems are

- identification and explanation of faults, i.e. falut diagnosis
- classification of findings into given categories.
- prediction of future developments.

(2) CONFIGURING actions or objects to achieve a particular goal. Configuring actions is usually called PLANNING and applies to planning e.g. robot actions, production schedules, etc. Configuring objects has successfully been applied to configuring computers, work places, production units, and various kinds of devices.

(3) CONSTRUCTING methods solve problems described in terms of intended functional behaviours. Such tasks have successfully been tackled for program construction, the design of electronic circuits and very simple mechanical devices.

(4) INTELLIGENT ASSISTANTS provide user guidance to complex systems, such as operating systems (examples: VMS, UNIX), software packages (example: MACSYMA for algebraic manipulations), and machine installations.

(5) TUTORING SYSTEMS help students to acquire a particular body of knowledge to be incorporated into their thinking structures.

(6) SHELLS (META EXPERT SYSTEMS) constitute tools for building new expert systems.

2. Particular Application Areas

2.1. Interpretation expert systems have successfully been applied to both biological and technical systems. Biological interpretation includes both medical applications, as well as topics such as assessing cultures, and diagnosing plant diseases. Medical diagnosis has long been one of the most widely pursued areas of expert system applications. In recent years, a major shift towards applications for signal interpretation and fault diagnosis in complex technical systems has taken place. Of particular importance appear expert systems for diagnosing and predicting faults in technical and chemical processes, where expert systems are also expected to provide guidance and planning for actions meant to repair or prevent faults. Such systems can be expected to play a major role in process control environments within a few years.

Depending on the intention associated with interpreting findings and sensory resp. measured data, interpretation expert systems are classified into

- diagnostic systems aimed at classifying faults, and determining causes of faults.
- interpretation systems (in a narrower sense) interpret findings by relating them to system states and functional behaviour w.r.t. a given system model.
- monitoring systems supervise continuous processes for early precognition of exceptional events to support suitable actions preventing them.

There are two basic modes for operating interpretation systems:

- interactive systems query the user about findings on the interpreted system, usually within a dialogue where the purpose of system actions (such as queries), explanations of how intermediate and end results are obtained, and clarification dialogues validating and substantiating user responses can be provided.

- embedded systems interpret findings directly obtained from the interpreted system.

Actually, embedded systems are usually operated in a mixed mode, as either sensory perceptions of a human operator are given in addition to measured data, or the system explains and clarifies its result to the user. Purely interactive systems are typically employed for consultations.

2.2. Configuring consists in

either - configuring components into assemblies which constitute mechanical or electronic devices.

or - configuring actions performing particular functions so that they combine to form some overall plan.

Both types of configuring problems pose the particular difficulty of compromising local decisions which global strategies, constraints and consistency requirements.

Component configuration is done in the economically highly successful expert system R1 resp. XCON for configuring DEC VAX and some PDP 11-series computers. Planning has been successfully tackled e.g. in the expert system MOLGEN which configures large genetic experiments which are highly complex because they include multitude of interacting individual experimental techniques.

Complex diagnostic systems employ planning for scheduling the order of particular investigations dependent on the dynamic state of finding a diagnosis. Furthermore, reparatures resp. therapy measures are being planned subsequently to obtaining a diagnosis.

2.3. Construction aims at devising procedures performing some given task. This problem has initially been considered for program construction from descriptions of an intended input-/output behaviour. Other domains are the construction of electronic circuits and mechanical devices.

Expert systems for program construction codify programming knowledge about

- algorithmic approaches towards computing particular functions, such as sorting.

- how to choose particular representations of data in the context of respective computational schemes.

- applying optimizing program transformations.

Applications towards constructing electronic circuits and mechanical devices are still in a rather preparatory and experimental stage. Construction in mechanical engineering requires specific support for the phases of problem and requirements analysis, as well as conceptional design preceeding material design as it is heavily supported by CAD/CAM-systems.

2.4. Intelligent assistants are part of the following system design:

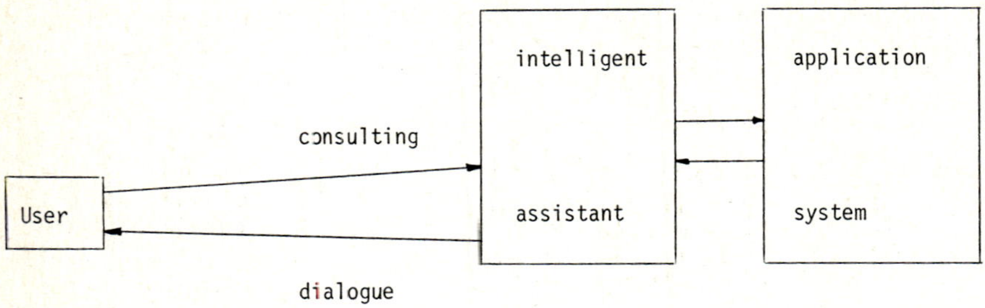

The purpose of an intelligent assistant consists in helping un or poorly trained users to utilize the capabilities of complex applications systems. This is particularly important if using such a system requires the selection of appropriate operations and parameters depending on the context of the respective situation. The user then needs to navigate through the respective options. Intelligent assistants (IA) provide help according to the following scenario:

(1) The user explains his goals and intentions to the IA.
(2) The IA analyses the intentions set forth by the user with respect to

- completeness: the IA tries to detect gaps and completes either by applying its own competence, or extracting the required knowledge from the user.

- consistency: the IA tries to detect unsuitable intentions, e.g. redundant or meaningless goals, and helps in correcting them.

- expedience: the IA provides help for optimizing solutions.

(3) From both the user's problem specification and its analysis obtained in (2), the IA constructs command sequences to the application system.

(4) All reactions coming from the application system are analyzed and interpreted by the IA. The results are explained to the user, who is also consulted about what to do next.

Typical existing IA have been developed as front-ends to complicated software systems such as

- operating systems (DEC VMS, Unix)

- data base systems

- algebraic manipulation systems.

IA helping to operate complex technical devices are still under experimental development, and have not yet reached a stage where they could be used in routine applications.

2.5. Knowledge-based tutoring systems have envolved from two directions:

- Existing expert systems have been extended towards tutoring systems by
  - using the explanation system for eliciting typical solutions.
  - supplying the knowledge base with paradigmatic cases for illustrating the major problem-solving techniques.

Experience with this approach has demonstrated that simply elicitating the usual knowledge contained in knowledge sources is insufficient, as such knowledge is meant for efficient problem-solving and often unsuitable for instruction purposes.

- Specific knowledge bases have been developed which present particular problem-solving techniques to students in a way which not only exhibits solution paths step by step, but do also allow to explore alternatives and justify why particular choices have been favored over others.

2.6. Shells, or meta expert systems have initially been deriving from successful expert systems by omitting their knowledge sources, and using the remaining components for constructing and interpreting new knowledge bases for different applications. The simplified schema

<expert system> - <knowledge sources> = <shell>

<shell> - <knowledge sources> = <expert system>

is however, strongly misleading: Expert systems beyond the prototype stage are optimized and tailored to their respective applications so that they do only support specific representation and reasoning mechanisms. Hence, they will not be suitable for different applications if at least slightly different such mechanisms are required. In particular it has often turned out to be fatal if specific knowledge representation and reasoning mechanisms have been enforced to represent a particular knowledge domain although some "artificial encoding" is necessary: As expertise is meant to be represented for subsequent machine processing, it is of utmost importance to keep the representation as "close" and "natural" to the domain of expertise as possible.

As a consequence, shells provide a carefully coordinated collection of tools supporting a variety of knowledge representations and reasoning schemes. A typical shell should include

- interpreters and (preferably)/or compilers for the major knowledge representations techniques such as logical, production-rule oriented, and object (frame)-based mechanisms.

- inference support for the respective knowledge representation techniques, including the major control mechanisms.

- a knowledge base management system (KBMS) supporting the above techniques for managing both dynamically elaborated knowledge and work store, as well as domain knowledge maintained in knowledge sources.

- tools for eliciting knowledge contained in knowledge sources, as well as for explaining
  - justifications and rationales of system actions ("why"-, "how"-, and "what for" - questions)
  - chains of reasoning on different levels of abstraction.

- tools to support the acquisition and modification of knowledge.

- tools providing basic functions and interfaces for building external interfaces (displays, sensors/effectors, data bases, etc.).

Clearly, existing shells only support these facilities on a rather limited scale. Admitting these restrictions, only very few shells have already undergone several design-application-evaluation-redesign literations necessary for developing mature products.

3. Assessment

Expert systems have currently reached the stage where

- specific isolated tasks can be successfully tackled if
  - the required domain of expertise is clearly defined and limited.
  - the knowledge built into the expert system is undisputed and generally agreed upon.
  - the knowledge required for the expert system to reach the expected level of competence is intelligibly accessible and can be represented without accounting for causal, functional, and structural relationships in the system being reasoned about.
  - the interface between expert system and environment is clearly confined to formalized man-machine interactions, input of measured and easily interpretable sensory data, and formalized commands to effectors.
- developments are primarily prototypes meant for exploring potentials and capabilities of expert systems.

Painful experience has amply demonstrated that merely building an expert system that meets its functional goals does by no means guarantee that it is acceptable both by economic and technical criteria unless the integration of the expert system into the application environment has been successfully achieved. A rule of thumb says that the development costs for a powerful expert systems are usually considerable less than the immediate costs for reorganizing the application environment and integrating the expert system into the reorganized system.

The currently predominant areas of application are

- *INTERPRETATION:*

(1) Since the advent of expert systems in the first half of the seventies, medical diagnosis has been most extensively been investigated as a field of application. This is due to the fact that medical diagnosis is an extremely diffuse domain in the sense that it primarily depends on judgmental and experiential knowledge, i.e.

it is extremely knowledge intensive, and

- diagnostic competence cannot be represented in a clearly structured theory, where multitudes of specific pieces of knowledge are concentrated in abstrations which can be precisely expressed and manipulated.

However, despite the relative abundance of projects developing medical diagnosis systems, none of them has really come to widespread use. This is a consequence of two phenomena:

- Fully developed medical expert systems have regularly reached a level of competence which exceeds that of highly esteemed specialists within narrow boundaries of specific domains. However, for such diffuse areas it is still an open problem to make expert systems clearly delineate their own capabilities to the user, so it is difficult to see whether solutions are based on solid competence or not.

This is rarely acceptable for a physician who wants to rely on such a system.

It is generally accepted that medical diagnosis expert systems could play a significant role if they incorporate enough knowledge covering both "ordinary" experiential knowledge to judge most of the routine cases, as well as highly specialized knowledge for working on rare and difficult cases. Furthermore, experiental, or shallow knowledge contained in current systems poses a severe limitation, as reliable diagnoses often require to include reasoning on deep knowledge accounting for pathophysiological and other functional relationships.

In summary, the prospects for having medical diagnosis expert systems ready for routine are

- poor unless it becomes possible to incorporate a wealth of medical knowledge which exceeds the amount currently contained in medical knowledge bases by orders of magnitude, and does include deep knowledge. Providing the mechanisms for this task poses crucial open problems for basic research.

- fair for applications to interpret findings on the basis of restricted, shallow knowledge. Examples are giving alerts in continuous patient monitoring for intensive care units and intelligent interfaces for systems involved in complicated medical examinations (such as ECG, EEG).

(2) Currently, there is a rapid increase in developments for technical applications in three directions:

- Fault diagnosis in technical systems, e.g. computer hardware, automobiles, electronic circuits, machines in manufacturing plants, and complicated devices such as electron microscopes. An initial target is to successfully diagnose most of the easily detectable faults, where travel and other labor expenses for service personnel often by far exceed the immediate costs of fault detection and repair. Expert systems operated remotely or on site can avoid much of these costs.
- Interpretation of measured signals and other sensors preceptions (e.g. findings based on sight or audition).
- Monitoring continuous technical processes as a combination of interpretation, fault diagnosis and prediction, and planning of appropriate actions for repair of prevention of faults.

CONFIGURING:

Expert systems for both component configuration and planning have successfully been developed and applied in domains where straightforwardly accessible and encodable heuristic knowledge is available:

- configuring large experiments in microbiology from multitudes of interrelated experimental techniques.
- configuring components of e.g. computers and production units.
- production planning.

Experience with such projects has demonstrated that configuration can be usefully tackled by expert systems if three conditions are satisfied:

(1) Sufficient complexity of the search space, i.e. the variety of components of actions to choose from is substantial enough to make combinatorial solutions unfeasible, especially when condition (2) is included.

(2) Sufficient constraint-complexity, i.e. composing components and/or actions requires to observe constraints such as

- ordering constraints (configuring one component/action establishes the preconditions for configuring another).
- compatibility constraints (one component/action destroys the options for choosing another).
- economic and technical feasibility constraints.

(3) Availability of heuristic knowledge.

- INTELLIGENT ASSISTANTS

are on the verge of experiencing a major breakthrough as soon as natural language interaction becomes technically feasible on the basis of natural language front-ends provided as tools for broad application domains. Economically, intelligent assistants open up completely new markets by making complex systems accessible and usable for untrained users.

- TUTORING:

Tutoring systems are currently entering a new era by realizing a cooperative paradigm for the computer-tutor/student-relationship: AI-techniques allow to deeply analyze gaps and deficiencies in the knowledge of students so that an intelligent tutor can individually respond to fill resp. correct them. However, much basic research remains to be done to develop techniques making this paradigm practical.

- SHELLS/TOOL KITS:

So far, expert systems have been developed custom-made for each task individually. Nevertheless, a general architecture with specific, not domain-oriented components as outlined in the 1.sect. has emerged. Considering the fact that companies mostly enter expert system development to gain experience with prototypes although there is a great shortage of personnel trained in AI-technology, tools and shells will definitely enjoy a substantial economic interest in the near future. However, it is doubtful to what extent currently available tools can already satisfy the expectations. Applying shells and tools is therefore not advisable unless help from experienced AI-engineers is available.

CURRENT RESEARCH ACTIVITIES

The weak spots of current expert systems include the following, particularly pressing technical deficiencies for which we outline research directions currently pursued to resolve them:

(1) Multiple Knowledge Representations. As knowledge representation techniques have evolved from expert system development in rather limited domains, there is increasing evidence that broader applications require single expert systems to utilize a multitude of knowledge representations simultaneously. Therefore, much research effort is currently aimed at maintaining and performing translations between different knowledge representations.

(2) Cooperating knowledge sources. Different sub-domains often call for using different knowledge sources. An interesting approach is to make use of them under the guidance of some knowledge based system itself. Other applications, such as diagnosis and repair planning, suggest to set up communities of cooperating expert systems which mutually consult each other.

(3) Deep reasoning. Current expert systems are severely limited in that they employ shallow knowledge, i.e. knowledge consisting of associating chunks of propositional with pieces of inferential knowledge without explicitly representing why and how this is related to the structure and function of the system being reasoned about. Representing and utilizing such deep knowledge opens up new perspectives: Currently, expert systems are "dumb" in the sense that they do not really "know" (i.e. can reason about) what they are actually doing. This often implies that they do nothing meaningful if unexpected situations come up. Deep knowledge will therefore open up considerably broader domains, where judgmental and experiential knowledge merely serves for extremely efficient inferences which would otherwise require extensive search when based on deep knowledge. Therefore shallow knowledge can sometimes be compiled from deep knowledge, and is therefore referred to as compiled knowledge, also. This is vertical knowledge compilation as briefly mentioned before. Expert systems incorporating both compiled and deep knowledge are currently being investigated towards developing a second generation of expert systems.

(4) User interfaces. The acceptability of expert systems for untrained users requires substantially improved user interfaces utilizing natural language and visual communication. Present research not only tries to improve on both of these communication channels, but also to integrate natural language with visual communication.

(5) Knowledge acquisition is the celebrated bottleneck in expert system development. Current research focusses on all three major approaches to provide more mechanical assistance for interactive expertise transfer, develop both horizontal and vertical knowledge compilers, and explore learning mechanisms.

In summary, we conclude with three theses:

I. Current technology for expert systems opens up a wealth of yet unexplored applications. However, this wave will fade out within a few years if it is solely based on systems incorporating only shallow, compiled knowledge.

II. To really exploit the potential of knowledge processing, substantial progress in basic research towards a second generation of expert systems employing deep reasoning techniques and utilizing deep knowledge is a crucial precondition.

III. Expert system technology will not come into widespread industrial use unless the major techniques are made available as easily accessible and usable software tools.

ARTIFICIAL INTELLIGENCE: Towards Practical Application
T. Bernold and G. Albers (editors)
Elsevier Science Publishers B.V. (North-Holland)

COOPERATIVE ACCESS SYSTEMS

Wolfgang Wahlster

Universität des Saarlandes
Computer Science Department
Saarbruecken
Federal Republic of Germany

In the next five years we can expect to find a variety of cooperative natural language (NL) interfaces to database systems, expert systems, operating systems, CAD systems and even text formatting systems. Although the general problem of getting computers to understand NL is far from being solved, the technology for limited NL access systems is available now and there is a large growing market for such cooperative interfaces to a wide variety of software. In the first part of the paper, we illustrate the capabilities for cooperative response generation implemented in AI systems. Then we briefly review the state of the art in NL interfaces to databases and expert systems. Topics covered include user modeling, the generation of eyplanations, mixed-initiative dialogs and knowledge acquisition via NL communication.

INTRODUCTION

Cooperative interfaces are developed with a view to increasing the accessability of valuable computer facilities, such as database systems (cf. King 1983), CAD systems (cf. Cullingford et al. 1982) and even text formatting systems (cf. Rich 1983). A further application area is that of natural language interfaces to expert systems. An example here is the system XCALIBUR (cf. Carbonell et al. 1983), an interface to the configuring system XCON. Yet another area involves cooperative communication with operating systems, such as VMS or UNIX. Examples are the AI system UC (UNIX Consultant, cf. Eilensky 1984) and the system Wizard (cf. Finin 1983) for VMS.

What knowledge and capabilities does a system require if it is to exhibit cooperative behaviour? First, it requires relevant conceptual and inferential knowledge: It must have a model of the person with whom it is to cooperate, and it must be able to understand the goals and the actions of this person and to adapt its own behaviour accordingly. Research on such interfaces concentrates on the one hand on problems of man-machine interaction; on the other hand, questions arise which are typical of artificial intelligence research, e.g., knowledge representation, knowledge acquisition and knowledge processing, as well as knowledge presentation.

THE GENERATION OF COOPERATIVE RESPONSES

I will now try to illustrate what is meant by cooperative behaviour in an interface by presenting several examples of such behaviour which have been realized in a number of AI systems in various parts of the world (see Fig. 1, cf. also Webber/Finin 1984, Bates/Bobrow 1984)

- Pointing out incorrect presuppositions
  - (1) **U:** `Did Mr. Jones pay the bill for our last delivery?`
  - (2) **C:** `No, we have not yet sent Mr. Jones the bill.`
  - (3) **S:** `No.` (→ misleading conclusion)

- Indication of discontinuities in the database
  - (4) **U:** `Is there a seat available on the flight to New York on August 8th?`
  - (5) **C:** `Yes, but from August 9th onwards, tickets are $200 cheaper due to the winter season.`
  - (6) **S:** `Yes.` (→ unfriendly response)

- Unsolicited justification of an answer
  - (7) **U:** `Is a long-term fixed money investment worthwhile at the moment?`
  - (8) **C:** `No, because interests are tending to rise.`
  - (9) **S:** `No.` (→ missing argumentation)

- Additional information on the individual conjuncts
  - (10) **U:** `Are Mr. Brown and Mr. Gray on a business trip?`
  - (11) **C:** `No, Mr. Brown is on a business trip but Mr. Gray is here.`
  - (12) **S:** `No.` (→ answer provoking follow-up questions)

- Unsolicited filling of the relevant deep case
  - (13) **U:** `Which colleagues are on business trips?`
  - (14) **C:** `Mr. Baker is in London, Mr. Miller in New York and Mr. Smith is in Japan.`
  - (15) **S:** `Mr. Baker, Mr. Miller and Mr. Smith.` (→ answer provoking follow-up questions)

- Offering to 'monitor' for information requested
  - (16) **U:** `Is there a seat available on the last flight from Munich to Hamburg?`
  - (17) **C:** `No, not at the moment, but I will put you on the waiting list and I will let you know if a passenger cancels his flight.`
  - (18) **S:** `No.` (→ unfriendly response)

- Using more specific quantifiers
  - (19) **U:** `Are you employing some researchers with a Ph.D., too?`
  - (20) **C:** `Yes, three.`
  - (21) **S:** `Yes.` (→ less cooperative response)

(U:= user, S:= conventional system, C:= cooperative system)

Fig. 1: **Forms of over-answering implemented in AI systems**

Let us begin with an example in which the system calls the user's attention to the violation of a presupposition. If the user asks the interface a question like (1) (see Fig. 1), and the system replies with (2), we can speak of cooperative behaviour. If you pose the same question to one of today's conventional information systems, you will probably simply receive the answer 'No'. This answer, however, is misleading, since an implicit assumption, or presupposition, on which the question is based is not fullfilled - namely that an invoice has been sent out to the client in the first place. In other words, the response of a traditional information system would give the user a completely false impression. A cooperative system must be in a position to call the user's attention to this sort of violation of a presupposition.

Another way in which a system can be cooperative is by pointing out a discontinuity in the database. Suppose, for example, you ask the system a question like (4), it would then be cooperative for the system to respond with (5).

Siklossy developed such a system several years ago: It searches the database systematically for such discontinuities, and when it determines that a small change might have substantial positive consequences for the user, it points this fact out, thereby over-answering the question(cf. Siklossy 1978).

We have investigated and implemented several further forms of cooperative behaviour in our own project. One of these involves the explanation of an answer. A system should spontaneously explain its own answers when such an explanation is likely to be useful to the user (cf Wahlster 1980). For example, if you ask an expert system for investment consulting a question like (7), it should not simply answer 'No', it should go on to add a justification like (8).

The part of a system which generates elucidations of this general sort is called an explanation component (cf. Wahlster 1981).

Still another strategy is to supply additional information about individual conjuncts within a question. If you ask a traditional information system a question like (10), the answer will be simply 'No'.

But one would generally like to know why this conjunction of statements is not true. It is therefore more helpful if the system replies with (11). That is, the system should make it clear which of the conjuncts is responsible for the falsity of the conjunction (cf. Wahlster et al. 1983).

A further possible stratey is to fill in deep cases in the semantic representation of a question. The purpose of this is to anticipate an obvious follow-up question by over-answering the original question. If the user asks, for example, a question like (13), the system can in principle interpret the question literally and supply just the names of these staff members (see 15) in Fig. 1). But it is in general more cooperative, given a question about a trip, to supply the destination of the trip as well (see (14), cf. Wahlster et al. 1983).

Yet another form of cooperative behaviour has been implemented by B. Webber and colleagues at the University of Pennsylvania (cf. Mays et al. 1982). It takes the form of an offer by the system to keep track of the future status of a condition specified by the user. If you ask a question like (16), the system should reply with (17).

This process is termed the monitoring of a condition: The system becomes active without further prompting as soon as the condition specified by the user is fulfilled.

A final possibility is the replacement of vague quantifiers which occur in the question by more precise ones. Suppose you ask a question like (19), the quantifier 'some' can then be made more precise if the system over-answers with (20). This answer contains much more information of course, than a simple 'Yes' (cf. Wahlster et al. 1983).

MIXED-INITIATIVE NATURAL LANGUAGE DIALOG SYSTEMS

Let us now look at the overall structure of systems of this sort (see Fig. 2). Such a system has, first, an analysis component which translates the natural language input into a formal semantic representation. This process is knowledge-based; the knowledge base contains general background knowledge, including a semantically oriented grammar and, e.g. a semantic network which encodes the relationships among the system's concepts. There is also knowledge which applies only to a particular domain of discourse; this includes domain-specific inference rules and the system's referential knowledge. Finally, part of the knowledge base contains so-called dialog knowledge. This includes a representation of the momentary thematic focus in the dialog, a user model which contains information about the user (cf. Wahlster 1984b), and finally an inference memory which enables the system to explain the reasoning underlying its answers.

The output of the analysis component is passed to an evaluation component. This component takes as input the semantic representation of the question and returns the semantic representation of an answer. It accesses not only the knowledge base sketched above but also external sources of data (e.g., a database) which belong to the back end system that the user is primarily interested in accessing. Finally, a generation component is required which translates the formal semantic representation of the answer into a natural language utterance suitable for output.

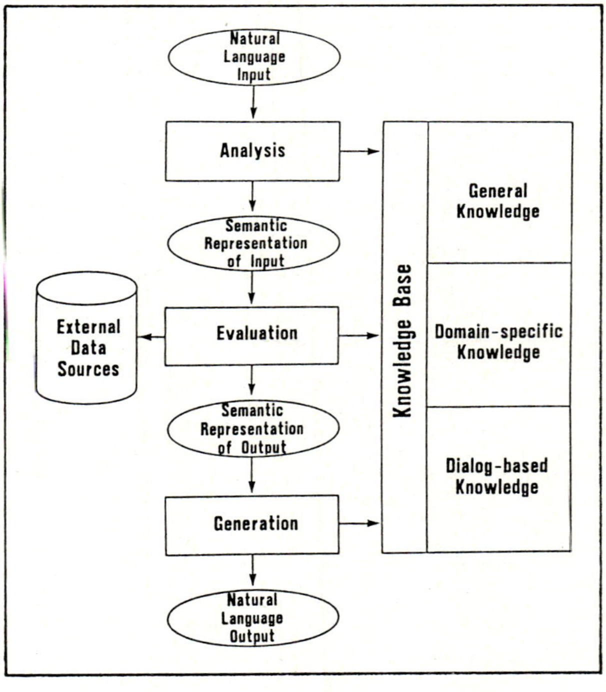

Fig. 2: **The overall structure of natural language dialog systems**

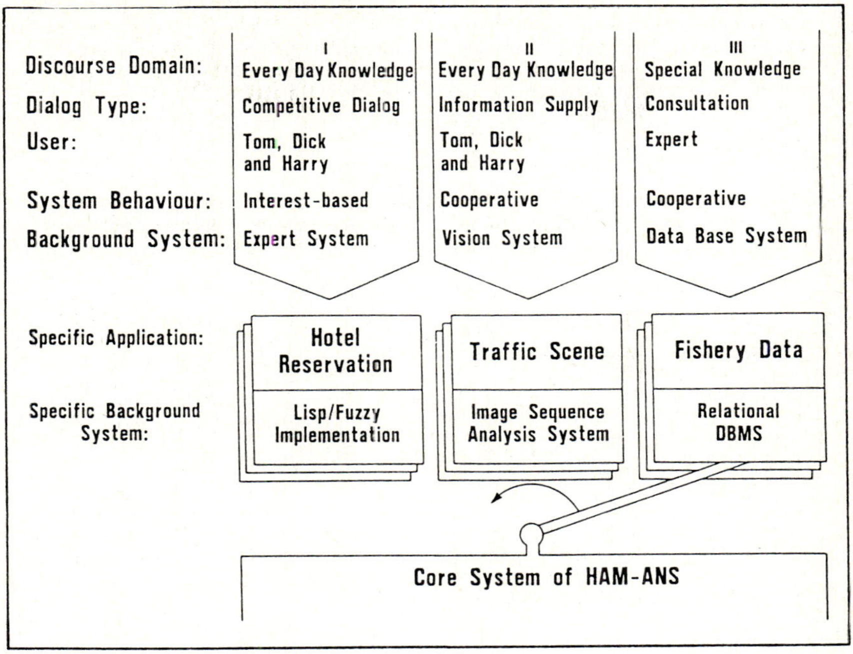

Fig. 3: **The discourse domains of HAM-ANS**

As an example of such a system, I would like to discuss briefly our own system HAM-ANS (cf. Hoeppner et al. 1983), with which it is possible to conduct written dialogs about several different domains of discourse (see Fig. 3). We have chosen both domains involving mainly everyday knowledge and domains which require specialized knowledge. As for the type of user who is given access to the system, we have chosen both laymen and experts. The system can be run in a mode in which its won interests are paramount in determining the form of its answers or in a mode in which its behaviour is purely cooperative. We have used the following dialog situations as case studies: The user can reserve a room in a hypothetical hotel; ask questions about a traffic scene which is being monitored by a vision system that analyzes image sequences; or query a relational database in which mass data about fishing expeditions are stored. An important point is that the system actually includes a switch, i.e. we can actually move from one application to another. For this to be possible, the structure of the system has to be so modular that only certain parts of the knowledge base need to be replaced to adapt the interface to an entirely different back end system.

One goal of our research is to have the system engage in mixed-initiative dialogs. That is, neither the system nor the user should retain the initiative all the time, asking questions to be answered by the other. Instead, in accordance with the turn-taking rules which govern dialogs between human speakers, the system should under certain circumstances yield the initiative to the user and then seize it again later. A clear case where this is necessary is the hotel reservation situation, where first the user calls a particular hotel and then the system takes the initiative by asking certain questions to determine which room seems most suitable. The user then has the opportunity to ask questions in order to evaluate the room which has been suggested. Finally, the system will try to regain the initiative by asking whether the user wishes to reserve the room or not.

Some of the challenging problems that the system has to deal with in the course of such a dialog involve the general topic of user modelling, which I mentioned above. Suppose for example, that the user asks a question like

(22) U: What kinds of chairs does the room have?

(23) C: There are several comfortable chairs in the room.

In order to generate an appropriate description of the chairs, the system must make some assumptions about the user's intended activities in the room (cf. Jameson/ Wahlster 1982). For example, if information has accumulated in the user model which suggests that the user might intend to entertain guests, it is reasonable to suppose that the user is particularly interested in knowing how comfortable the chairs are. The system should answer in such a case with (23).

As you can see, the system's behavious here is interest-based, i.e. guided by the system's own interest in renting the room.

The necessity of taking into account the user's desires becomes even clearer when we look at questions by the user which contain expressions that reflect a certain expectation. If, for example, the user, phoning a luxury hotel, asks

(24) U: Does the room by any chances have a TV?

(25) C: Yes, of course.

(26) S: Yes.

The system is justified in drawing certain conclusions on the basis of the occurence of the expression 'by any chance'. First, the user apparently would like the room to have a TV. Second, the user evidently is unaware that he or she is talking to a luxury hotel, since in such a hotel there is normally a TV in every room, so that it would be inappropriate to formulate the question so cautiously. In such a case, therefore, the system should not reply with (26), but rather with (25).

This more emphatic answer has the function of indicating that the user's uncertainty was based on an incorrect expectation, that the question in principle needn't have been asked at all.

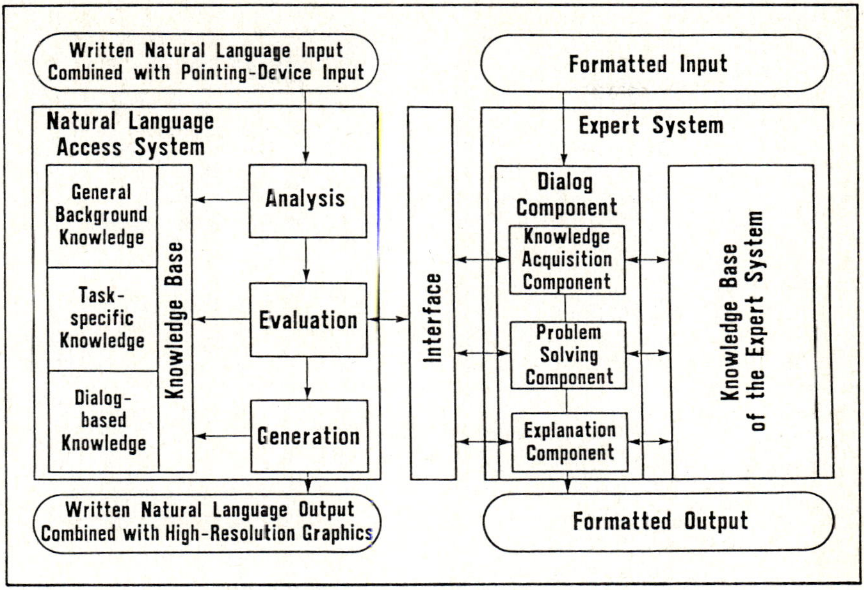

Fig. 4: **The architecture of an NL interface to expert systems**

INTELLIGENT INTERFACES TO EXPERT SYSTEMS AND DATABASES

An important application of cooperative natural language interfaces is to provide access to expert systems. The intelligent interface provides access to the inference component. The explanation component, and the knowledge-acquisition component (see Fig.4). The dialog component also makes it possible for both the user and the system designer to access the contents of the knowledge base directly. We have just completed the preparations for a system called XTRA (EXpert TRAnlator, cf. Wahlster 1984a) which is designed to give both the user and the expert access to a variety of expert systems and to be so adaptable that it can also be used to control a general expert system shell (see Fig. 5).

As you see in Fig. 4, we have two separate knowledge bases, one for the natural language interface and a second for the expert system. This separation of the knowledge bases makes it relatively easy to adapt the system for a new task: Only the task-specific knowledge needs to be replaced. The primary communication medium is natural language, typed in and printed out at a computer terminal. In addition, input may be supplied with the help of a mouse, and output may make use of high-resolution graphics.

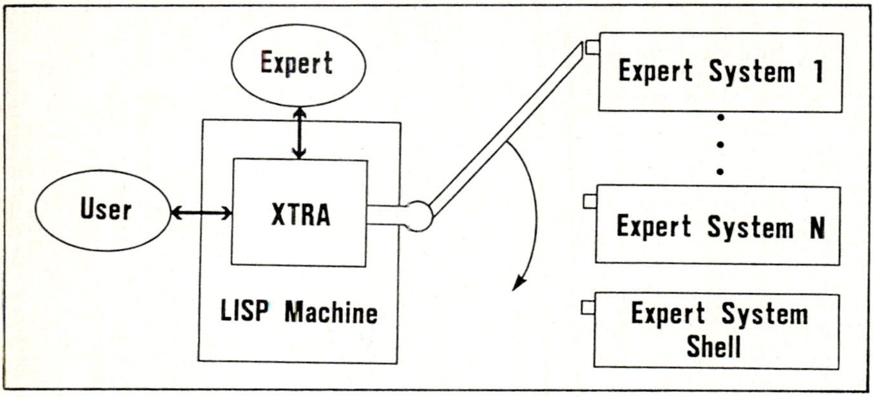

Fig. 5: **The adaptable access system XTRA**

To give an idea of the sort of dialog we are aiming at, Fig. 6 shows a hypothetical dialog with an interface which provides access to an expert system for fault diagnosis in a technical system. After the dialog sequence (27) - (28), the system must recognize in question (29) that the pronoun 'it'does not refer to the 'large number' just mentioned, but rather to the system disk. The user then asks a why-question (30), and the system provides an explanation like (31). The user's next question (32) presents a difficult problem for the analysis component. It must be recognized as an elliptical why-question which requires an iterative call to the explanation component, so that the system can respond with (33). The user then takes the initiative with (34), whereupon the system immediately recovers the initiative with (35).

Aside from expert systems, one of the most important commercial applications for cooperative access system at present is as front-ends to databases. In this case we have a neutral language interface which provides access to formatted mass data and a database management system, which handles all accesses and changes to the database. In the access system, knowledge is stored which would normally be possessed by an experienced user of such a database. This knowledge is stored in several different knowledge sources, which are managed efficiently by a Knowledge Base Management System (KBMS).

(27) C: Is the system disk reported to be bad?
(28) U: Yes, a great number of writing errors has been reported.
(29) C: Is it still write-protected?
(30) U: Why is the write protection relevant here?
(31) C: Because some disk tests will be started soon.
(32) U: Write protection for disc tests?
(33) C: Yes, because the operating system may be killed if the controller is bad.
(34) U: Then I'll start the disk test DISK-1 now.
(35) C: No, we'll start with DISK-2.

Fig. 6: Natural language access to an expert system for error detection in computer systems

(A) Explanation of interference-based answers:

(36) U: Is the bed fairly hard?
(37) C: I think so.
(38) U: Really?
(39) C: Its mattress is new.

(B) Explanation of conceptual knowledge:

(40) C: There are four seating accommodations.
(41) U: What do you mean by seating accommodations?
(42) C: A seating accommodation is a piece of furniture. The following kinds of seating accommodations are known: chairs and arm-chairs.

..... a seating accommodation has a seat, usually four legs and often a back-rest.

(C) Explanation of speech acts:

(43) C: May I book the room for you?
(44) U: Why do you ask that?
(45) C: Because I could offer you yet another one.

Fig. 7: Argumentative dialog sequences

Technology in this area has already advanced to the point where natural language interfaces databases can be implemented for personal computers. An example of such natural language interfaces is INTELLECT (cf. Eisenberg/Hill 1984), supplied by Artificial Intelligence Corporation, which runs on an IBM-PC XT and allows the user to query the system in English. This system provides access to the mini-database system dBase II, making use of the graphics package of VISICALC to produce as output a combination of natural language and graphics.

ADVANCED EXPLANATION COMPONENTS

I would now like to describe briefly some interesting developments in the area of explanation components (cf. also Wahlster 1981). These components are applied in a wide variety of AI systems, ranging from expert systems and instruction system to theorem provers, and deductive database systems. A few examples will give you an idea of the sorts of explanations which can be produced at present (see Fig. 7). The first type is the explanation of inference-based answers of the system. Suppose, for example that in the hotel situation the user asks a question like (36), and the system answers 'Yes', and the user then asks 'Really?', the system can explain its answer by a response like (39). What it has done is reveal a premise which it made use of in making the inference which led to the answer. Another type of explanation that is technically possible is the explanation of conceptual knowledge. If, for example, the system at some point during the dialog makes an utterance like (40), and the user would like to know exactly what is meant by 'seating accommodation' (see (41)), it is possible for the system to explicate this concept with a segment of text (see Fig.7). This text has not been stored in advance but is generated when required on the basis of the system's conceptual knowledge.

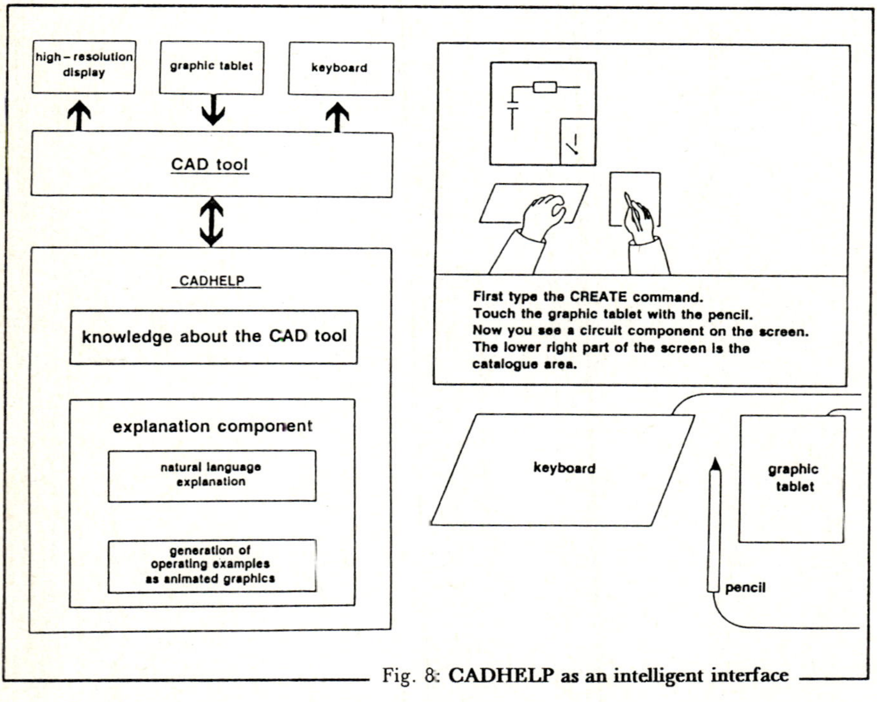

Fig. 8: **CADHELP as an intelligent interface**

A capability which has yet to be implemented is the explanation of speech acts. This will require considerable further research on speech act planning and recognition. For example, if the system asks a question like (43), and the user reacts with (44), the system should be able to supply an answer on a meta-level (see (45)).

I would like to conclude this discussion of explanation components with a description of an intelligent interface to a CAD system. The AI system CADHELP (cf. Cullingford et al. 1982) has the task of explaining a complex tool for computer-aided design whose hardware consists of a keyboard, a graphics tablet, and a high-resolution screen (see Fig. 8). CADHELP cooperatively adapts its explanation to the individual user. It may provide an animated graphics display in the upper half of the screen while generating in the lower half a natural language text which explains the various parts of this display. For example, it may state "The lower right-hand side of the screen is the catalog zone".

A particularly striking feature of this project is the fact that both the graphics display and the accompanying text are generated at run time on the basis of a semantic representation. Neither one is stored in advance, so that, e.g. a novice can be given a quite different explanation than an expert. Even in the course of a single dialog, if you ask the system twice about the same point, its second explanation will be very different from its first one.

CONCLUDING REMARKS

I would like to conclude my short survey by calling your attention to a new perspective in research on knowledge acquisition (see Fig. 9). Up to now the knowledge base of an AI system has in general been supplied by an expert with the help of an AI specialist. Attempts have been made to transfer at least some of the responsibility for knowledge acquisition to the system itself. The successful attempts have mainly taken the form of a component which elicits knowledge from the expert in dialog.

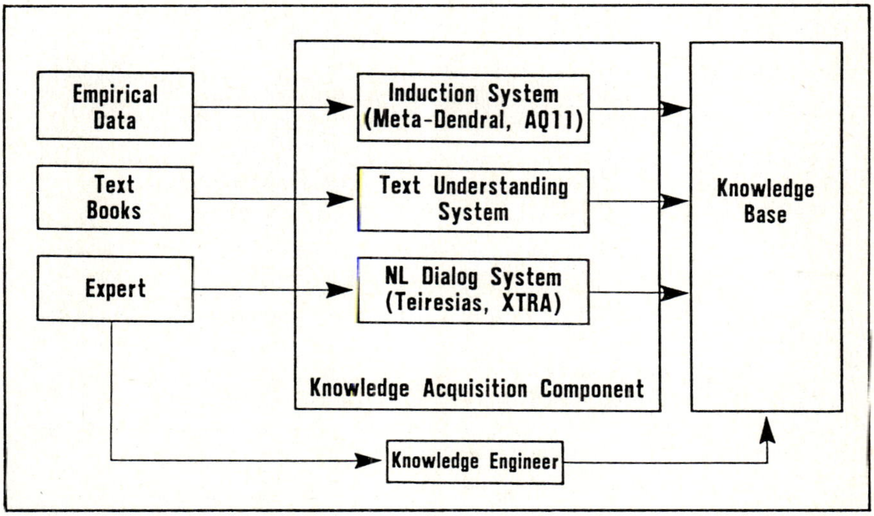

Fig. 9: **Modes of knowledge acquisition**

The system TEIRESIAS (cf. Davis 1982) is a well-known example of such a component. A more ambitious approach is to have the system extract knowledge from relevant specialist literature, i.e. to use a text understanding system to fill up the knowledge base. At the moment, this is still an unrealistic goal. Given the present state of the art, it is only feasible for a system to understand two or three pages of text on a very narrowly defined subject; it is not possible to process entire books. A still more ambitious approach is to have the system construct the knowledge base itself, applying inductive reasoning to observational data.

Finally, let me emphasize that current NL interfaces are a long way from having broad-based,universal language capabilities comparable to human dialog partners. People claiming that, with the advent of the first commercial NL interfaces such as INTELLECT, the problem of getting computers to understand NL has been solved, do the whole field of AI a serious disservice.

However, the technology for limited NL access systems is available now and there is a large growing market for such cooperative interfaces to a wide variety of software.

A commercial German language access system is presently not available, I am, however, currently coordinating a joint project, funded by the German Ministry for Research and Technology, in which companies like Nixdorf, Siemens and SCS together with academic research groups will develop a prototype of a product for German access to expert systems within the next three years.

REFERENCES

BATES, M., BOBROW, R. (1984): Natural Language Interfaces: What's Here, What's Coming and Who Needs it. In: Reitmann, W. (ed.) Artificial Intelligence Applications for Business. Nordwood: Ablex, pp. 179-194.

CARBONELL, J.G., BOGGS, W.M., MAULDIN, M.L., ARNIK, P.G. (1983): The XCAL-IBUR Project: A Natural Language Interface to Expert Systems. In: Proc. of IJCAI-83, Karlsruhe, pp. 653-656

CULLINGFORD, R.E., KRUEGER, M.W., SELFRIDGE, M., BIENKOWSKY, M.A. (1982): Automated Explanations as a Component of a Computer-Aided Design System. In: IEEE Transactions on Systems, Man, and Cybernetics, Vol. SMC-12, No. 2, pp.168-181.

DAVIS, R. (1982): TEIRESIAS: Applications of Meta-level Knowledge. In: Davis, R., Lenat, D.B.: Knowledge-based Systems in Artificial Intelligence. New York: McGraw-Hill, pp. 227-490.

EISENBERG, J., HILL, J. (1984): Using Natural-Language Systems on Personal Computers. In: Byte, January 1984, pp. 226-238.

FININ, T.W. (1983): Providing Help and Advice in Task Oriented Systems. In: Proc. of IJCAI-83, Karlsruhe, pp. 176-178.

HOEPPNER, W., CHRISTALLER, TH., MARBURGER, H., MORIK, K., NEBEL, B., O'LEARY, M., WAHLSTER, W. (1983): Beyond Domain-Independence: Experience with the Development of a German Language Access System to Highly Diverse Background Systems. In: Proc. of IJCAI-83, Karlsruhe, pp. 588-594.

JAMESON, A., WAHLSTER, W. (1982): User Modeling in Anaphora Generation: Ellipsis and Definite Description. In: Proc. of the first European Conference on Artificial Intelligence, Orsay 1982, pp. 133-138.

KING, J. (ed.) (1983): Special Issue on AI and Database Research. In: SIGART Newsletter, No. 86, October 1983, pp. 32-72.

MAYS, E., JOSHI, A.K., WEBBER, B.L. (1982): Taking the Initiative in Natural Language Data Base Interactions: Monitoring as Response. In: Proc. of the first European Conference on Artificial Intelligence, Orsay, pp. 255-256.

RICH, E. (1983): Users are Individuals: Individualizing User Models. In: Intern J. Man-Machine Studies 18, pp. 199-214.

SIKLOSSY, L. (1978): Impertinent Question-Answering Systems: Justification and Theory. In: Proc. ACM National Conference, pp. 39-44.

WAHLSTER, W. (1980): Towards a Computational Model for the Semantics of Why-Questions. In: Proc. of the 8th Intern. Conference on Computational Linguistics, COLING-80, Tokyo, pp. 144-150.

WAHLSTER, W. (1981): Natuerlichsprachliche Argumentation in Dialogsystemen. KI-Verfahren zur Rekonstruktion und Erklaerung approximativer Inferenzen. Heidelberg: Springer.

WAHLSTER, W., MARBURGER, H., JAMESON, A., BUSEMANN, S. (1983): Over-Answering Yes-No Questions: Extended Responses in a Natural Language Interface to a Vision System. In: Proc. of IJCAI-83, Karlsruhe, pp. 643-646.

WAHLSTER, W. (1984a): XTRA: Ein natuerlichsprachliches Zugangssystem zu Expertensystemen. In: Deussen, P. (ed.): Sonderforschungsbereich Kuenstliche Intelligenz, Univ. Karlsruhe, pp. 377-402.

WAHLSTER, W. (1984b): User Models in Dialog Systems. Invited Lecture at COLING-84, to appear in: Computational Linguistics 1984.

WEBBER, B.L., FININ, T. (1984): In Response: Next Stepp in Natural Language Interaction. In: Reitman, W. (ed.): Artificial Intelligence Applications for Business. Nordwood: Ablex, pp. 211-234.

WILENSKY, R., ARENS, Y., CHIN, D. (1984): Talking to UNIX in English: An Overview of UC. In: CACM, Vol. 27, No. 7, June 1984, pp. 574-593.

ARTIFICIAL INTELLIGENCE: Towards Practical Application
T. Bernold and G. Albers (editors)
Elsevier Science Publishers B.V. (North-Holland)

THE NEXT GENERATION OF ROBOTS: INCREASED FLEXIBILITY THROUGH THE USE OF SENSORS

C.W. Burckhardt

Laboratory of Micro Engineering
Swiss Federal Institute of Polytechnics
Lausanne
Switzerland

The robots which are installed today in industry (IR) are machines with mechanical limbs which can easily be programmed to carry out automatically a number of tasks.

Today, there are worldwide about 50'000 IR in operation, a number which doubles about every two years. Half of them are working in Japan and half of them are working in the automobile industry.

Switzerland, underdeveloped in the field of robots, has about 100 IR installed, many of them in precision mechanics. The largest robot installation is found at the company Conserves Estavayer S.A., linked to the MIGROS organisation, where seven robots manipulate packages of diary products in co-operation with a number of other automatic devices.

Elementary geometry tells us that six co-ordinates are required to pinpoint the position and orientation of an object in space. To move such an object from one place to another, we need a manipulator or a robot capable of co-ordinated movements of at least six axes. Each one of these movements must be powered by actuators (e.g. hydraulic or electric ones). At present, a lot of research and development work is oriented towards programming of robots and the introduction of languages. Although 90 per cent of today's operational robots use rather primitive languages, similar to the well known BASIC language, and are programmed from point to point.

The future belongs to robots capable of responding to orders of the type: take object X and put it to the place Y.

Robots, as one element of flexible automation, are employed in various branches of industry, from the manufacture of bulldozers to those involving microelectronics. Generally, small series, operation by hand is preferable, for very large series dedicated automation is more economical.

From another point of view, the robot can be considered as an extension of the computer so to say its arm in the physical world. But without sensory devices the robot can only carry out the orders given by its human operator. Only by the introduction of sensors can the robot gather information from its environment and only this can enable it to change its behaviour independently. The majority of present-day robots have no "intelligence". Indeed, how could they be intelligent if they receive no information on their environment?

It should be noted however, that all robots have a number of "internal" sensors which monitor the position and speed of movement of its limbs. In that way, the control mechanism is continuously informed on the actual state of the robot at any given time.

To a limited extent, there are applications today where robots are provided with some external sensory devices. There are e.g. devices to check dc-motor current, or position sensors which signal when the robot's gripper touches a certain point in space.

One example of an application is the stacking of objects (e.g. pallets) by a robot. In laying down an object, the robot feels the next object touching the first one and thus recognises the very moment when it has to detach its grip from the object it is holding.
Simple force sensors in electronic assembly are employed in a similar way. For example a robot is intended to insert a component in a printed circuit board. If the robot feels mechanical resistance when lowering the component vertically into position, it then knows that something has gone wrong. It could be that one "leg" of the component has missed its intended hole because it is bent or out of line, or because part of another component is in the way. If such things happen, a robot can interrupt the assembly process, eliminate the offending component and try again with another one. Light barriers are often employed to deal with such problems.

For arc welding, optical or inductive sensors are coming into use to track the edge of the part to be arc-welded and to supply the correct amount of welding material to be used.

There are already today a number of examples in industry where television cameras - more generally known as visual sensors - are used to pintpoint a machine part of which the position is only approximately known. T typical example in the automobile industry is the tracing of the hole in the car door in which the robot can then automatically install the door handle. The use of sensors allows thus to greatly improve the precision of industrial robots.

Common to all these applications is certainly the feeding of information from the environment into the control system of robots, but in their present use, the quantity of information transmitted from sensors is still very small.

If we return to the image of today's industrial robot as the arm of a computer, then we must compare it with a human industrial worker who is blind and has no sense of touch - who indeed has no organs of sense.

The actual aim of research laboratories all over the world is to equip industrial robots with organs of sense. Only when a robot (or a multiple robot assembly) is provided with serviceable sensory organs can it appreciate its environment and behave "intelligently". Although research along these lines has been pursued for many years, in some countries, its fruit has so far been scanty.

It was already proved, in principle already 15 years ago, that a robot equipped with organs of sense could behave intelligently, but models demonstrated in the laboratories worked extremely slowly and the means employed were unsuitable for industrial use.

Which are thus the sensors already known and installed? The following list gives a view of the most widely used sensors:

Force sensors: Such a sensor "feels" when a force works against a robot's movement- when its manipulating arm comes up against an obstacle, for example. It can also estimate the weight of an object it has grasped or dose the force needed for an assembly process. Such sensors are places in the "wrist" of a robot's arm, in its claw or in the base of the workbench.

Proximity sensors: These sensors signal the approach of a solid object and can be mounted at different positions on the moving parts of a robot.

Optical sensors: There are many optical sensors ranging from the simple light barrier to the visual sensors of the type of television "eye". More and more the CCD (charge coupled device) cameras are employed which, because of their small size and robust construction, can be installed direct in the robot's claw. In the future, visual sensors will be the most important components for keeping the robot in touch with its environment: the recognition of parts, checking of their position and size and their surface condition.

In the years to come, many new sensors for the robot will appear on the market. The many difficulties involving their use are varied and include in their essentials the following three points:

- The sensors must be small, light, reliable and robust - meaning above all shock-proof and insensitive to dust and moisture.
- Signals from sensors must be transmitted to the robot's control system.
- The robots control system, in other words its brain, must be able to extract the relevant information from these signals.

The greatest difficulty lies in the third point. How should be decided precisely on the relevant information to be used? A television eye gathers an enormous amount of information of roughly several millions of bits a second.

Even if we have actually enough hardware to cope with such quantities of information thanks to the continuous development in micro-electronics, the bottle-neck remains the software.

Only recently researchers realised that a new approach is necessary to resolve the problem of sensors for robots. The answer lies in applying the "artificial intelligence" concepts, especially in today's Expert System which are reaching maturity.

What can be expected over the next few years from the development of "artificial intelligence" summarizes as follows:

The computer which controls the robot should be able to elicit the relevant information from its sensors. Thus not all the signals received before the processing operation need necessarily be stored. The operator should be able to give his orders to the computer in a high level program language and, if they are not understood, he should be able to receive a question back from the computer. Finally, this dialogue should take place verbally.

This order, received together with information elucidated from the sensors, will permit the computer to work out the best strategy for the robot.

All the foregoing refers primarily to industrial robots. When can the robot be expected to be employed in daily life or in agriculture?

There are two reasons why robots are being used above all in industry:

The industrial scene is a very orderly one, compared with housekeeping or agriculture. The more disorder a robot has to cope with, the more "intelligence" is demanded of it.

Today, a robot is still an expensive device. Its price lies in the region of SFr. 100'000.--. A reasonable return on investment of such a device is only possible in certain industries. Prices must fall considerably if its use outside industrial operations is to become economically practicable.

ARTIFICIAL INTELLIGENCE: Towards Practical Application
T. Bernold and G. Albers (editors)
Elsevier Science Publishers B.V. (North-Holland)

VISION SYSTEMS: STATE-OF-THE-ART AND PROSPECTS

Bernd Neumann

Department of Informatics
University of Hamburg
Federal Republic of Germany

1. INTRODUCTION

Let me begin with a disclaimer: In this contribution I will not attempt a complete survey of existing vision systems. For this the reader is refered to the representative collection of articles edited by Pugh (PUGH 83) or any of the recent surveys (CHIEN and HARLOW 82, FU 83, KELLEY 83, PAU 84, PINSON 83, STIEHL and KRAFT 84). Nor does this contribution present systems under development in the laboratories. An excellent paper of Binford (BINFORD 82) is recommended to the reader interested in a critical analysis of major laboratory systems.

Bearing in mind the theme of this volume I shall discuss vision systems with respect to the following question: What can AI contribute to industrial vision systems? This may sound somewhat strange presuming that vision systems are AI products to begin with. I shall show, however, that a typical industrial vision system does <u>not</u> exhibit typical AI architecture. Major shortcomings and limitations of present systems can be traced to a design which may be improved by adopting a "knowledge-based" approach. It is shown that this may lead to systems with extended applicability and predictable performance. Furthermore the process of adapting a vision system to a new task may be facilitated by "configuration experts", i.e. expert systems guiding the configuration process.

In order to provide the layman with some background, the discipline of "Computer Vision" will be briefly introduced in the next section. The reader familiar with this field may safely proceed to the discussion of industrial vision systems in section 3. First, a broad range of applications is presented to demonstrate the versatility of the existing vision technology. Then an exemplary vision task - object recognition - is discussed in some detail. This leads up to a critical evaluation of today's systems. Although many limitations are dictated by the need of fast processing, and consequently point to a hardware bottleneck, there is also the need for methodological improvements. This is where an AI approach will be helpful.

In section 4 the notion of a knowledge-based vision system is introduced. It is shown that the use of suitable object models and model-based recognition techniques holds many promises with respect to adaptability and predictability of vision systems. While it is unlikely that efficient knowledge-based vision systems of large generality will be available in the near future, the underlying principles can be brought to bear on practical systems to some extent by employing configuration experts.

2. WHAT IS COMPUTER VISION?

Computer Vision had its beginning with the advent of fast digital computers after 1950. It was recognized early that visual data can be represented by numbers and thus be made the input of computer programs. The problem, of course, is how to process these numbers in order to obtain useful results. Right from the beginning the performance of the human visual systems set the mark. Selfridge proposed "eyes and ears for the computer" (SELFRIDGE 55). But for many years programs could only handle very restricted tasks, e.g. analysis of toy scenes composed of blocks (ROBERTS 65) or recognition of printed characters (FISCHER et al. 62). Tasks like the latter motivated the paradigm of "pattern recognition". This is a particular abstraction of a recognition task where an unknown object is taken to be represented by a set of numbers - the features - and the main problem is to assign it to one of a given set of classes using the features as a decision basis. Today a very well developed theory of Pattern Recognition is available for all recognition tasks which can be cast into those terms.

Computer Vision, in general, is more than an assignment problem - it requires methods much different from Pattern Recognition. In particular, features and classes proved to be insufficient notions for representing complex intermediate or final results. Today, the leading paradigm for Computer Vision is a multilevel, knowledge-based process which reconstructs and describes a real-life scene from projections. This view is also spelled out by the authors of one of the leading textbooks of the field (BALLARD and BROWN 82) who define Computer Vision as

> "... the construction of explicit, meaningful descriptions of physical objects from images."

Computer Vision is a well established field with a large fundus of methods.Yet much research remains to be done before technical systems can compete with biological vision systems. Various related fields are relevant for progress in Computer Vision:

- Electrical Engineering
- Computer Science
- Artificial Intelligence
- Cognitive Science
- Psychology
- Neurophysiology
- Mathematics
- Pattern Recognition

Computer Science and Artificial Intelligence are usually considered the parent disciplines of Computer Vision. But strong ties also exist to Psychology and Neurophysiology which provide valuable data and insights concerning biological vision. Although most computer vision researchers do not seek detailed correspondence with the human visual system, there is probably none who would not happily adopt a process from biological systems.

3. INDUSTRIAL VISION SYSTEMS

In this section I shall provide some information on existing industrial vision systems. Hopefully this will help the reader to form an opinion about what can possibly be done and what not. I shall begin by discussing major areas of applications, including examples selected from recent publications (ISIR 83, ROVISEC 83, PUGH 83).

APPLICATIONS

By far the largest number of applications are in the area of inspection (quality control). Vision systems are used to check for

- completeness (missing or excessive parts)
- geometry (shape, alignment, tolerances)
- material defects

Here are some representative inspection tasks handled by machines (the letters C, G and M indicate the objective according to the three possibilities mentioned above):

- drillings in automotive parts (C,G)
- keycap assemblies (C)
- flaws in castings or forgings (M)
- printed circuits, chips (C,M)
- labels and fill levels of champagne bottles (C,G)
- correct reading of gauges and instruments (G)
- surface defects of hot steel slabs (M)
- cleanliness of Coca Cola bottles before filling (C)
- packages of birth control pills (C)
- gap tolerances in car door assemblies (G)

Inspection tasks are particularly suited for machine vision since human workers tend to perform poorly on such tasks: Only a small fraction of the samples exhibits interesting faults, the overwhelming majority is flawless and quite boring. Hence attention deteriorates rapidly and errors result.

The second major area of industrial applications is robot position control, where vision systems cooperate with a manipulator to perform tasks such as object recognition, automatic assembly, or seam tracking for welding.

Here are some illustrative examples:

- pick-and-place from moving conveyor belts
- chip insertion into circuit boards
- iron coil recognition for crane control
- stacking and unstacking work pieces
- engine block location
- bolt position for car assembly
- collision avoidance
- pose refinement for electric motor assembly
- ore welding or sheet steel

Most of these applications have been realized by adapting a general-purpose vision system to the particular task. The keycap assembly system (in PUGH 83) is a notable exception. It can only inspect keycap assemblies.

From the available reports it is difficult to assess the labour (and cost) which went into the adaptations. My personal experience suggests that, as a rule, more is required than setting certain parameters, for example: arranging the illumination by trial and error or even reprogramming the system software. This is one of the major shortcomings of present-day vision systems: They may require considerable efforts from human experts before they perform satisfactorily at a particular task. There are about fifty brands on the market from which to choose today. A recent survey can be found in (KINNUCAN 83).

METHODS

A typical industrial vision system is shown schematically in Fig. 1. It consists of lighting equipment for controlled illumination of the object of interest, a sensor to pick up the image, a preprocessing unit for image transformation and fast feature extraction, a postprocessing unit for complex computations and decision making, and finally a user interface for interaction with a human operator. Using the task of object recognition as an example, I shall now briefly describe these components in some detail.

Illumination plays a critical part in most applications. It is the essential means to make a vision task manageable with present-day technology. In fact, industrial vision has been defined as "computer vision with controlled illumination". For object recognition, one typically tries to produce a clear contract between object and background, e.g. by backlighting.
But there are also more sophisticated illumination techniques, e.g. structured light which can be used to extract 3-dimensional object properties. To this end laser techniques have also been developed.

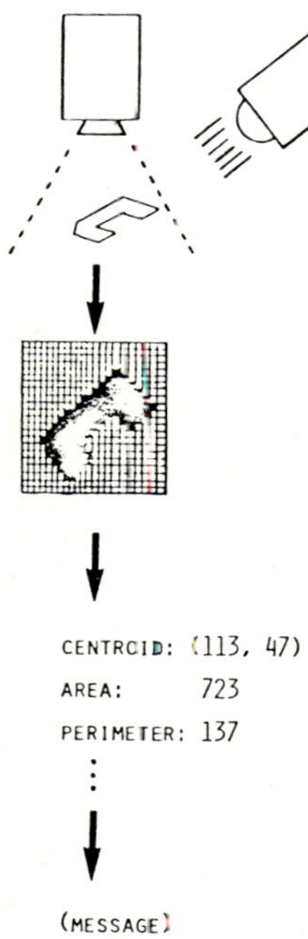

- Illumination
  - Backlighting
  - Flash
  - Infrared
  - Structured Light
  - .
  - .
  - .
- Sensor
  - TV-Camera
  - Solid-State Matrix
  - .
  - .
  - .
- Digital Image
  - 64 x 64 ... 256 x 256 Pixel
  - 2 ... 256 Greylevels
- Preprocessing
  - Fast Feature Extraction
  - Using special hardware
- Postprocessing
  - Complex Features
  - Object Recognition
- User Interface

Fig. 1: Components of industrial vision system

There is a variety of sensors available, ranging from TV-cameras to solid-state devices. The latter ones are extremely rugged and can be built as small as a pack of cigarettes. After digitization the sensor output is a field of numbers, called the digital image. Each number represents the brightness ("greyvalue") of a picture element ("pixel"). Typically, industrial vision systems use digital images of a size between 64 x 64 and 256 x 256. Greyvalues are quantized into up to 256 greylevels. For ease of processing, however, most systems abandon greyvalue information very early by thresholding, thus all further processing is based on a binary (i.e. black-and-white) image. Threshold selection is a critical step if slight variations of object or illumination properties cause radically different binary images. This can often - but not always - be avoided by a judical choice of illumination and background. It cannot be ruled out that binarization is altogether inappropriate - these tasks call for greyvalue processing which is usually more complex and costly.

The preprocessing phase encompasses operations which can be carried out very fast, often using dedicated hardware. For binary images these operations usually belong to a standard set which is listed below. The output is a description of the black (or white) image regions in terms of feature values.

Binary image processing:

smoothing, shrinking, expanding

connectivity analysis

computation of features
- total area
- number of holes
- perimeter
- centroid
- longest and shortest diameter
- axes of equivalent ellipse
- compactness (area/perimeter^2)
- enclosing rectangle
- polar signature

If interesting image regions cannot be extracted by binarization, greyvalue processing is in order. Below are some of the operations used by the few existing greyvalue systems. (The repertoire of laboratory systems is much larger).

Greyvalue processing:

filtering

- averaging
- subsampling
- median filtering

edge analysis

- gradient value and direction
- local gradient maximum
- grouping of contour elements
- straight line fitting
- blob extraction

While preprocessing operations have to cope with large pixel arrays, the input data of all ensueing operations have small or moderate volume. Hence postprocessing is rarely time-critical and can be carried out by general-purpose microcomputers. The main task at this stage is classification of image regions by comparing the features with prototype descriptions. Most systems use the nearest-neighbour decision rule, i.e. decide for the prototype which is closest in feature space. Some advanced systems permit "relational" object descriptions involving more than a single image region. In this case classification is based on the relational match paradigm which calls for structural comparison of descriptions. In any case, the success of the classification step depends on the similarity of the unknown object - described by its image features - with prototype descriptions given to the system in a "learning" phase.

This is - in short - how a typical industrial vision system performs object recognition. In this simplified presentation I cannot do justifice to all systems on the market, particularly not to those which are specialized for a narrow range of tasks. For example, systems performing quality control using Xray images may very well require processing steps which are quite different from the steps described above. Our "typical vision system" is exemplary in the sense that it reflects the architecture of the majority of system dealing with the general task of object recognition.

LIMITATIONS

The performance of present-day industrial vision systems is quite limited in the sense that there are many potential applications which cannot yet be realized. In most cases the cause is a combination of task complexity, time requirements and costs.

Hence cheaper and faster hardware will continue to push the limits and open up new fields of application. But this sort of progress will not cause the qualitative jump needed to overcome troublesome limitations arising from the currently employed methods. What are there methodological limitations?

First, there is the use of binary images. Low background contrast, variable illumination and variable object surface properties may cause highly varying binarization results. Hence all these factors have to be controlled to secure reliability. If anything changes, e.g. if the conveyor belt gets dirty, malfunctions are likely.

Second, let us examine the features which are used for recognition. Most of them are global with respect to an image region and thus are sensitive to local degradations, e.g. region deformations due to partial occlusion or imperfect binarization. Hence a correct classification may be jeopardized although a large part of the region is in perfect shape. This could be improved by employing descriptions based on local features, e.g. contour pieces embedded in relational structures. Such systems have the virtue of "graceful degradation", however, at the cost increased complexity. So far, few systems use relational descriptions.

Virtually all existing systems can only recognize planar shapes. This means that three-dimensional objects can only be recognized, if the image has features matching those of a prototype image. Since, in general, an object may have an unlimited number of different projections, there must be as many prototypes if it is to be recognized in all views. This is, of course, prohibitive and care must be taken than an object is always seen in one of a limited number of perspective views.

In summary, industrial vision systems of today have restricted applicability. As a consequence of the methods used, it is difficult to predict the performance when task parameters change. Expert knowledge and sometimes trial-and-error is required to adapt a system to a new task. In the next selection it will be shown that these problems may be eased to some extent by using an AI approach to vision.

4. AI APPROACH

In Order to assess future developments and potential improvements of existing vision systems we now take a look into the labcratories There are several characteristics which distinguish laboratory systems from an industrial vision system. To a large extent these characteristics are typical for present-day AI research, hence it is appropriate to speak of an SI approach to vision.

First, most laboratory systems tackle tasks of considerable generality. (This does not mean that they actually achieve generality - see BINFORD 82). Many of the restrictions of industrial vision tasks mentioned earlier do not apply to experiments carried out in the laboratory. For example, there are systems dealing with 3-dimensional shapes, analyzing scenes with shadows, recognizing partially occluded objects, etc. Hence, there exist methods which will improve the applicability of industrial vision systems.

If there is a single characteristic of AI system from which industrial vision would benefit most, it is the knowledge-based architecture. This is, of course, a trademark of AI systems. Knowledge-based processing calls for an explicit representation of all static information pertinent to a given problem. In the context of computer vision this means primarily that all information must be made explicit which links the image to physical reality. This information is often called "image information knowledge". Fig. 2 illustrates the image formation process. A ray of light leaves the light source, reflects from the object surface and is picked up by the sensor. From the physics of this process we know that the resulting image depends on each of the following components.

Object: shape
surface properties
position and orientation

Illumination: spectral characteristics
reflecting surfaces
position and orientation

Sensor: resolution, sensitivity, etc.
position and orientation

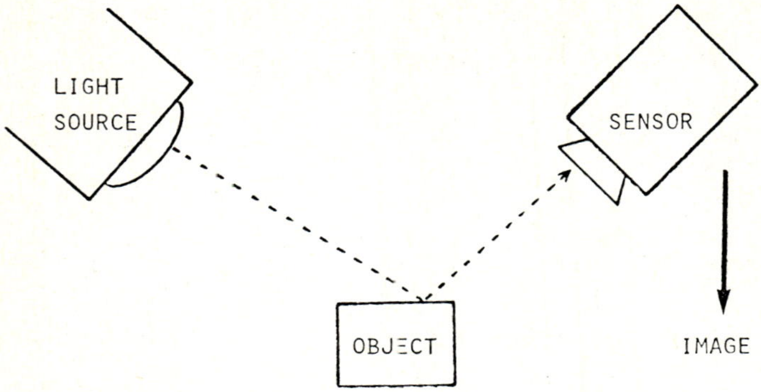

Fig. 2: Image formation process

Hence each image is an encoding of various properties of the physical reality, and image analysis processes must be set up accordingly. In a knowledge-based architecture this is achieved by using explicit representations of these influencing factors. In other words: Knowledge about illumination, sensor and object characteristics is kept in a data-base which can be easily accessed and modified. This has several consequences.

First, prototype objects are represented by strictly object-inherent properties:

- 3-dimensional shape (incl. tolerances)
- surface properties (reflectivity)
- range of possible positions and orientations

Hence, different from todays industrial vision systems, prototypes are not represented by image features which have the disadvantage of also encoding illumination and sensor properties.

This makes object representations independent of other tasks components, improving the adaptability of vision systems to new tasks. It also paves the way to using CAD/CAM models for vision tasks, eliminating the process of "learning" prototypes.

Secondly, the effect of a particular choice of sensor or lighting equipment is coded in such a way that changes may be made easily without heavy reprogramming. This will certainly facilitate the adaptation to new tasks.

A third advantage concerns unwanted changes of sensor, illumination or object properties which are quite characteristic for an industrial environment. Using knowledge-based image processing the effect may be precalculated to a considerable accuracy. Hence the performance of vision systems becomes more predictable.

Unfortunately the knowledge-based approach sketched out above also adds considerable complexitiy. In view of the time-constraints omnipresent in industrial applications such a system will presently be too slow by orders of magnitude. However, some of the advantages of a knowledge-based architecture may be achieved without waiting for faster hardware. For this I suggest an expert system approach to vision system configuration.

Configuration experts are software tools which guide a human user in choosing system components, setting parameters and making decisions occuring in a system configuration task. A well-known example is XCON (formerly R1) developed for the configuration of VAX computer systems (MCDERMOTT 82). For computer vision, a configuration expert has the objective of supporting vision system adaption to new tasks. Thus it should contain expertise of the kind which is presently required from human experts (and makes the configuration task a costly process). As for the expert system with a high-level knowledge-based program which would be slow but could be used as a simulation tool and as a source from which fast solutions can be compiled. Simulation of a vision system is within reach: The hard part is generating realistic synthetic images based on image formation knowledge. This can in fact be realized with advanced Computer Graphics methods. The second feature - compilation of fast programs from high-level specifications - does require considerable research. But in my view, this is a feasible and necessary way to bring AI methodology to bear on industrial vision system performance.

5. SUMMARY

In this contribution I have tried to answer the question: What can AI contribute to industrial vision systems? Reviewing the present capabilities of industrial vision systems I discussed several methodological weaknesses resulting from a simplistic approach dictated by time and cost constraints. In consequence, todays vision systems are limited in many ways and often lack good engineering virtues, e.g. a predictable performance at a new task.

The discussion of potential - and expected - improvements focussed on two major contributions of AI research: a knowledge-based approach to image analysis and an expert system approach to system configuration. It was shown that the development of such systems will lead to extended applicability, improved adaptability, predictable performance and a potential integration with CAD/CAM.

6. REFERENCES

Ballard and Brown 82
Computer Vision
D.H. Ballard, C.M. Brown
Prentice Hall, 1983

Binford 82
Survey of Model Based Image Analysis Systems
T.O. Binford
International Journal of Robotics Research, Vol. 1, No. 1
1982, 18-64

Chien and Harlow 82
Automated Visual Inspection: A Survey
R.T. Chien, C.A. Harlow
IDEE PAMI Vol. 4 No. 6 (1982) 557-573

Fischer et al. 62
Optical Character Recognition
G.L. Fischer, D.Y. Pollock, B. Radack, M.E. Stevens
Spartan, Washington, D.C., 1962

Fu 83
Robot Vision for Machine Part Recognition
K.S. Fu
in: D. Casasent, E.L. Hall (eds.) Robotics and Robot Sensing
Systems, Poc. SPIE Vol. 442, 1983, 2-14

ISIR 83
Proc. 13th International Symposium on Industrial
Robots and Robots 7
North Holland, 1983

Kelley 83
Binary and Gray Scale Robot Vision
R.B. Kelley
in: D. Casasent, E.L. Hall (eds.), Robotics and robot Sensing
Systems, Proc. SPIE Vol. 442, 1983, 27-37

Kinnucan 83
Machines That See
P. Kinnucan
High Technology Vol. 4 No. 4 (1833) 30-36

McDermott 82
R1: A Rule-Based Configurer of Computer Systems
J. McDermott
Artificial Intelligence 19 (1982) 39-88

Pau 84
Approaches to Industrial Image Processing and Their
Limitations
L.F. Pau
Electronics & Power, February 1984

Pinson 83
Robot Vision: An Evaluation of Imaging Sensors
L.J. Pinson
in: D. Casasent, E.L. Hall (eds.), Robotics and Robot Sensing Systems, Proc. SPIE Vol. 442, 1983, 15-26

Pugh 83
Robot Vision
A. Pugh (ed.)
Springer Berlin/Heidelberg/New York 1983

Roberts 65
Machine Perception of Three-Dimensional Solids
L.G. Roberts
in: D.T. Tippett et al. (eds.), Optical and Electro-Optical Information Processing, MIT Press, Cambridge, Mass., 1965, 169-197

ROVISEC 83
Proc. 3rd International Conference on Robot Vision and Sensory Controls
IFS Publications, 1983

Selfridge 55
Pattern Recognition and Modern Computers
O.G. Selfridge
Western Joint Comp. Conf. 1955, 91-93

Stiehl and Kraft 84
Sichtsysteme fuer Industrieroboter
H.S. Stiehl, H.R. Kraft
HMD 115, 1984, 65-89

ARTIFICIAL INTELLIGENCE: Towards Practical Application
T. Bernold and G. Albers (editors)
Elsevier Science Publishers B.V. (North-Holland)

SUMMARY OF THE DISCUSSIONS

Expert Systems and Knowledge Engineering

The main topic in the discussion was the usefulness of the application of Expert Systems. Two different viewpoints of a fruitful application of the new technology were proposed:

The first was based on the meaning, that those new systems would assist human experts to free them from their routine jobs, and let them concentrate on the more difficult ones, at the same time expanding their expertise. A further function might be the possibility to preserve through such a system the Know How of a human expert and make it available at all times. Another reason promoting these systems would be the time saving factor with training students in the field. This could partially be done with tutor systems attached to the Expert System.

The opposite view was, that integration of the Expert System in the daily routine work, as e.g. in a hospital, would be difficult. But the usefulness of those systems might be to distribute knowledge, which is beyond systems that support in diagnosing rare and exceptional diseases, which the physicians are not used to diagnosing.

Further topics centred on the main problems of future research: Not hardware would be the problem, but cost effective tools for building Expert Systems, which would support various levels and kinds of knowledge representation. Especially tools to support the process of knowledge acquisition.

Robotics and Intelligent Interfaces

The central statement was that the application of the new technology of Natural Language Processing would be first used to facilitate the access to existing software such as operating systems and classical databases. Thereby the application of todays techniques of Artificial Intelligence would allow the use of such very costly systems more intensively. Such interfaces would be producible with the present Know How in Artificial Intelligence only for limited domains of discourse. One trend might proceed as the development in the field of Expert Systems as to come to shells for Natural Laguage Interfaces.

In such shells only the domain dependant knowledge would have to be added. This would reduce the enormous effort of constructing such interfaces. For the extension of the domain of discourse and for their interface to other systems such as vision systems, many basic research problems will have to be solved.

A further topic concerned the range and usefulness of robotics application in production. A qualitative improvement, such as with techniques of Artificial Intelligence, might lead to a decrease of the batch size which in turn could make small series, produced by robots, profitable.

Günter Albers

APPLICATION

ARTIFICIAL INTELLIGENCE: Towards Practical Application
T. Bernold and G. Albers (editors)
Elsevier Science Publishers B.V. (North-Holland)

ARTIFICIAL INTELLIGENCE IN A LARGE-SCALE ENTERPRISE - THE EXPERIENCE OF DIGITAL EQUIPMENT CORPORATION

Brian Rees

European AI Marketing
Digital Equipment Corporation
Petit-Lancy
Switzerland

INTRODUCTION

The press has given a lot of exposure of Artificial Intelligence in the last few months. With their natural tendency towards sensationalism they have possibly gone too far. Artificial Intelligence, like any new technology, is essentially neutral. It is what gets done with it that counts. Whereas we do expect Artificial Intelligence technologies to usher in some major advances over the next few years and decades, we do think that some comments have either been somewhat rash, or have failed to point out the timescale of some of these developments.

Today we would like to show you how Artificial Intelligence could make a significant contribution towards solving various business problems and some of the challenges that this new technology presents.

Artificial Intelligence is a new technology. It is not just a new product or a development of an existing product but a step in a completely new direction in computing. DIGITAL now has not just a manufacturing and engineering organisation in place to deal with Artificial Intelligence issues, but also a marketing team to meet the challenges that we know need to be faced by the computer industry and the application of this new technology in solving business problems.

This presentation deals with the experience that DIGITAL has made with Artificial Intelligence, specifically as it relates to expert systems.

New technology should be introduced to improve productivity. However, it does not necessarily follow that the introduction of new technology into any area will automatically lead to increased productivity. Studies and experience have shown that careful analysis of potential applications is required before implementation.

This introduction of any new technology also needs to be weighed against other factors. (Organisation, people needs etc.) In many cases the use of a new technology is an alternative to some other method of solving the problem.

AI A SCIENCE

Artificial Intelligence in its 'pure' form is a science. It begins by trying to understand human intelligence, so that this understanding can be used for the development of a computer system which embeds intelligence.

There is a division in the AI community which reflects two positions. One is the pure 'scientist' who feels that unless we understand a great deal more about learning and the way we think and can put this into computer systems, we do not really have AI. The other camp, (the technologist who drives a Porsche,) believes that we have learnt enough to be able to implement useful systems now.

The 'Theorists' want 'deep' systems - systems which understand a great deal about general knowledge and can be applied liberally to almost any problem. The 'pragmatists' select a specific problem and apply todays AI tools to create a useful system now.

The 'Theorists' want 'deep' systems - systems which unterstand a great deal about general knowledge and can be applied liberally to almost any problem. The 'pragmatists' select a specific problem and apply todays AI tools to create a useful system .these are called 'shallow' systems. 'Deep' system work is still at the research stage.

Here we will be talking more about the approaches used by the Pragmatist. The question then needs to be asked "Why do we need 'reasoning' computers?" There are several answers:

To understand the difference between a conventional computer and one that incorporates Artificial Intelligence let us first define intelligence. There are a number of definitions, here is one: -

"Intelligence is the capacity to apprehend facts, propositions and their relationships and to reason about them."

This definition from Ed Feigenbaum at Stanford University admits the existence of both knowledge and the procedures which manipulate the knowledge.

Conventional computers can have huge data bases but, because of the limitations of sequential programming and the primitive structure of these data bases, no real "reasoning" can be carried out.

In the terms of procedures, 'reasoning' implies an open and flexible approach to solving problems. Conventional programming systems are predictive in nature. (E.g. they encapsulate a specific set of steps which represent a solution to a problem.) Artificial Intelligence programming on the other hand, incorporates a general set of 'rules' which may or may not apply to the specific problem in hand, but represent a 'dynamic' programming solution.

One of the main reasons that DIGITAL began to develop an Artificial Intelligence capability was the clear recognition that conventional programs where not capable of handling the increased complexity of some of our business problems.

Major Areas of Artificial Intelligence

There are many areas where a "reasoning" ability, (or knowledge based programming,) on the part of computeres is the only way further progress is going to be made in automating work. The principle areas are: Robotics, vision, natural language, speech and expert systems.

We see Robotics as being the foundation stone of production automation, (for example manufacturing,) thereby creating a modern 'slave system'. There are some significant advantages to having robots in production work, not least those processes which constitute an environment which is hostile to human beings.

Vision refers not only to the ability to see, but also to the processing of images, patterns etc.. General usage of robots for example, will only become really feasible when a robot is able to recognise what it is that it is handling. This is more complex than might be imagined. (It involves 'seeing' the object and also recognising' what it is exactly - the application of knowledge to the task.)

Natural language, the ability to communicate effectively whith people, will become increasingly important as computeres become cheaper and powerful enough to be used in every office and home. In fact natural language is the key to making the computer an 'integral part' of human existence, allowing the ordinary man to contribute in a more significant way to our society.

Speech will be applied similarly to natural language in providing effective man/machine interface. Here the difference between 'recognition' techniques in conventional programming systems and AI 'knowledge based' programming is very clear. Recognition of some elements of speech as expressed in short commands is possible with conventional programming, however, to be able to cope with continuous speech a major problem arises since many words which sound the same have different meanings depending on the context that one is talking about.

Expert systems will be mainly concerned with "capturing expertise" and making this expertise generally available on computers.

STATE OF THE ART

Robotics is still in its infancy. For example, when a robot has to pick up an item and place it elsewhere, if the object is only slightly displaced, then today the robot is faced with some major problems in recognising this difference and adjusting its actions accordingly. We need to make robots more 'knowledgeable' of their environment. Future robots will have to be able to better sense their environment and apply some 'intelligence' to their processing.

Vision will contribute a great deal to the efficiency of robots but is still at the research stage. However, some security applications, (fingerprints and voice recognition systems,) are already being built today.

Some natural language systems are available today. Instead of having to write a database query in computer language, it is now possible to access data through a number of simple instruction such as "Get me the number of customers who have bought a VAX-11/780 this week". This is tranlsated by the natural language processing software into a machine-recognisable query form, thus relieving the user of the tedious task of having to learn the computers language in order to be able to use the machine. These systems are not particularly robust since they are not 'deep' systems and as such do not handle queries which are not part of the 'context' of the problem at hand. They need to be designed specifically for a well defined and bounded problem.

Speech is being used in toys and is available today in the form of tools. (a good example here is our DECtalk product.). This is currently limited to speech generated output from text files. The problems associated with speech recognition, especially for continuous speech are still the subject of intensive research. (Once again connected with the problems of putting more knowledge into recognition.)

One area of AI technology that does appear to be successfully usuable today is expert systems. Developing these systems seems to still require significant computer programming expertise, but it is a technology which is being used more and more.

In general the state of the art is that people understand some of the basic techniques of knowledge based systems, the next step is to be able to build these systems easily and also to impart more 'knowledge' into them.

EXPERT SYSTEMS

Artificial Intelligence as it relates to expert systems is of the most immediate importance to the business world.

Once again Ed Feigenbaum:

"An expert systems is an intelligent computer program that uses knowledge and inference procdures to solve problems that are difficult enough to require significant human expertise for their solution. The knowledge necessary to perform at such a level, plus the inference procedures used, can be thought of as the model of the expertise of the best practioners in the field."

This quote should give you an indication of some of the pitfalls in expert systems development and usage. For example: If you put 'bad' knowledge into the expert system, it will be a 'bad expert'. Also if you do not have any expertise, don't expect to be able to build a useful expert system.

Effectively, expert systems are knowledge-based systems that encapsulate some 'expertise' i.e. an expert's knowledge.

The goal is to construct an Intelligent processing system, that has the capability to behave as an 'expert' in a given field. An important consideration is that the expertise has to be transferred from a human being into the computer system. Easier said than done, but nonetheless a necessary investment.

A number of systems which are considered to have expertise embedded in them have been developed over the past 20 years or so. Figure 1 shows how the time in man years required to develop such an expert system has been reduced substantially. Also most of these systems were large for their day, today, systems of similar complexity can be implemented relatively quickly, however, it still takes substantial resources.

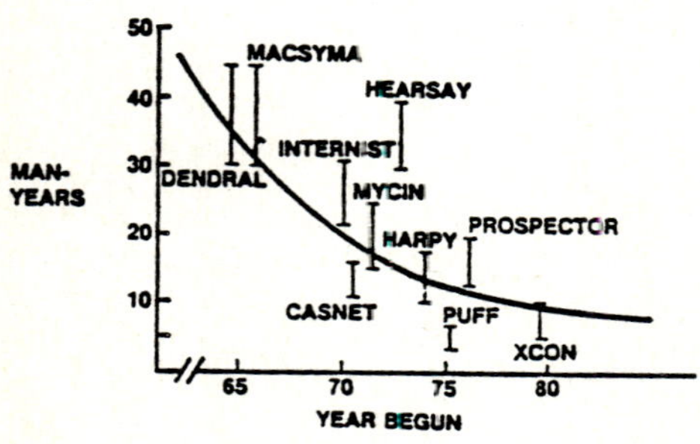

Figure 1: Historical Developments of Expert Systems

XCON

A practical example of a successful expert system is that developed by DIGITAL for its own use and designated XCON (eXpert CONfigurer). This system configures VAX-11 and some PDP-11 computers.

DIGITAL provides computer equipment to its customers on a 'a la carte' basis, this means that a very large number of computer configurations are possible. It is not clear that every configuration requested by a customer will work successfully. The traditional process that we used to verify the feasibility of a configuration was done through the use of Technical Editors. For reasons of streamlining production techniques and also reducing the number of 'badly' configured systems we developed an expert system which assists in the job of configuration for all but the most complex customer configurations.

Given a customer's order, XCON determines what substitutions and additions need to be made, (if any,) to build a complete and functional computer system with the best possible performance.

Because systems are based on customer specifications, computer configuration at DIGITAL is time-consuming and complex. It used to take a configuration expert about 25 minutes to manually put together a system. Multiply this by tens of thousands of tailored orders a year and the time problem becomes enormous.

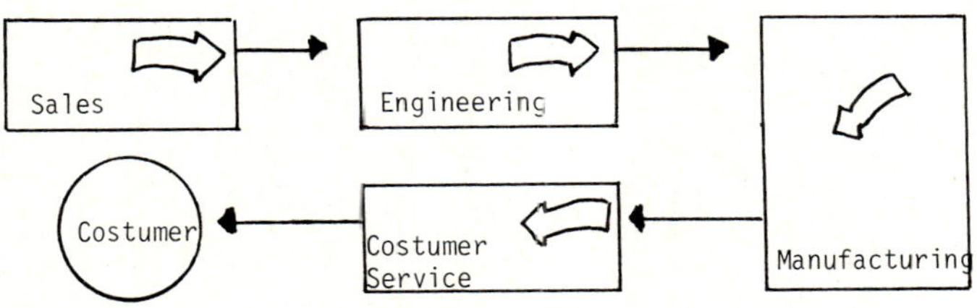

Figure 2: Expert Systems assisting configuration of DIGITAL Computer Systems

XCON is an on-line system that has been growing for five years. The output sheets from this expert system are used by manufacturing to assemble the computer system. Further developments have been made to make this expertise available to both sales-people and also field service people who install the system at the customer site.

XSEL is the Expert Sales assistant part of this program and XSITE is for the field service group to assist in site planning.

XCON has been integrated with other expert systems and will eventually become part of a "knowledge network" to integrate sales, engineering, manufacturing and field service.

DIGITAL'S CHANGE TO AN AI BASED APPROACH

DIGITAL, in fact, made three unsuccessful attempts to automate the computer configuration process with tradtional software techniques before settling on a rule-based Artificial Intelligence approach.

Programs based on conventional techniques ran into difficulties because they could not deal with the ill-defined knowledge structure of the configuration problem, nor could they keep pace with DIGITAL's continual product and engineering changes.

In many fields, business activities and problem-solution requirements are also subject to change. Conventional programs are not able to meet this challenge.

The essential difference between a conventional approach and the Artificial Intelligence approach is the way in which knowledge is stored. Artificial Intelligence technology requires the saving of not just factual data, but the 'meaning' or relationsship between different objects.

The programmer of a traditional system needs to predict with certainity every possible situation that the program will have to handle, changes to the way that the computer processes information have to be inserted at a very precise point in the code. Expert systems techniques on the other hand allow the programmer to make a single change in the rules to have the correct result. (A general rule to substitute a new peripheral in every case where a retired product has been configured.)

Currently expert systems are mainly built using 'production system' technology.

The dynamic programming of modern expert systems technology can be represented by a 'chain' of CONDITIONs and ACTIONs. A given status or 'context' of a problem is matched to a condition in the program which causes an action that in turn gives rise to a new condition that 'produces', (hence the name production system,) another action and so on.

It is this continuous, dynamic, "self-modifying" aspect that sets Artificial Intelligence techniques apart from conventional programming methods. Using "rules of behaviour", the A.I. system "reasons" out its own course of actions, based on the status of the problem being worked.

THE ISSUES OF IMPLEMENTING AN EXPERT SYSTEM

At DIGITAL, the implementation of expert systems has lead us to a definition of the pieces required in order to be able to build and use and expert system as part of the practical application of Artificial Intelligence effectively: -

1. Select the right problem

2. Identify an expert with the necessary expertise

3. Create a knowledge engineer

4. Create effective management for the development and introduction process

5. Acquire the tools - hardware, software and services

1. Problem Selection

Problems that are traditionally solved by computers are generally fairly well understood. (E.G. payroll, airline reservations.) Conventional techniques work well on problems which can be expressed 'arithmetically'. At DIGITAL we have discovered that the sort of problem that can best be solved through expert systems technology are those that need to be addressed from a business point of view, and are the sort of problem that people with some specialised expertise find relatively easy to solve. (E.g. require the application of intelligence/knowledge.) The problem should be in an area in which there is an expert available.

2. Identification of an Expert

It is necessary to identify at least one, if not several, experts. DIGITAL found that in a given area there may well be a number of experts who, when brought together to encapsulate their knowledge, reflect divergences of interpretation. There may be a problem in getting them to work together harmoniously as they usually work independently.

In some cases the experts are 'prima donnas', it may be very difficult to work with them. Expertise may also not reside with the person or group you might expect. Another facit is that you may assume that experts get their expertise from a book or from some form of formal training, this does not need to be true, some of the most successful experts habe developed their own methods of doing things which go against 'the book'.

3. Creation of a Knowledge Engineer

The knowledge engineer translates the work methods of the expert into a computerised system. There are perhaps only 500 to 1000 Artificial Intelligence researchers in the world today who can recognise where an expert system could be useful and then continue to implement. This presents a real difficulty in developing and implementating your own expert system. DIGITAL itself is running an intensive program to develop its own knowledge engineers. It is, however, not absolutely essential to have Artificial Intelligence "thoroughbreds" as there may well be a "creative" programmer in your MIS team already. This is the sort of person that we find adapts well to the problems associated with implementing expert systems.)

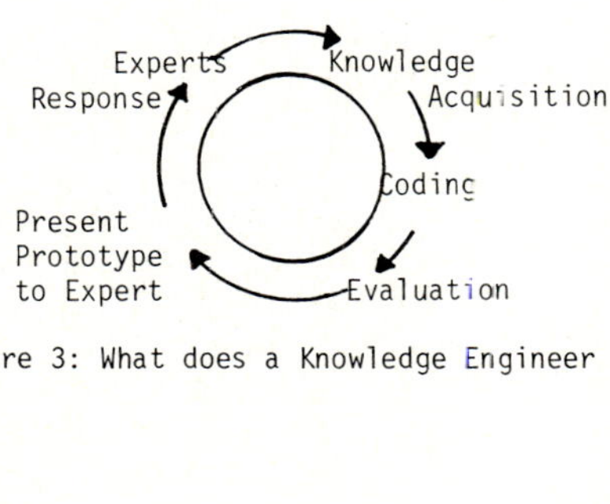

Figure 3: What does a Knowledge Engineer do?

A knowledge engineer needs a selection of special talents: to be a highly competent programmer, systems analyst, psychologist and diplomat - bearing in mind that he will have to deal with independently-minded experts. A knowledge engineer needs to be able to work in a very special way - participative design. This means that after talking to the expert, the knowledge engineer encodes some rules, verifies them together with the expert and modifies them as required. A closed feedback loop of implementation.

4. Management of Expert Systems

Artificial Intelligence is really just a new technology, the management of this technology is of major importance. The implementation of an expert system will not succeed without the whole-hearted commitment of upper level management. The development and installation of an expert system needs to be constantly monitored and controlled. It is possible that first attempts will not be crowned with success. Perhaps because when a problem is addressed in this way, the problem itself changes. This would have to be explained to upper management but if they are involved from the beginning, they will accept program changes and initial setbacks more readily.

Although the usage of protoyping has become fairly widespread in recent years, it is important to understand the time needed to develop a working protoype expert system compared with a typical MIS development program. An expert system can already be useful and usable at the 60% to 70% completion level. This short initial development cycle is possible because the knowledge engineer is sitting with the expert and designing the system as they go along. Once the system reaches this level, it can immediately be made available to the expert himself, so he can use it as a supporting tool. in many cases, the idea is not to replace the expert but rather to enhance his capability by giving him a computer that can handle his mundane tasks. The computer would be making 'recommoncations' that the expert verifies and makes the final decision. In a few years we expect to see expert systems technology progress so far that the expert is able to insert new rules into the system and further enhance its usefullness.

Another important benefit coming from this fast protoyping is that the system is able to show a hint of its potential usefulness before a lot of resources have been committed. A project which is clearly not going to produce the required return on investment or capabilities can be stopped after having used a relatively small amount of resources. There is another aspect as well. Once one system of this type has been completed, a number of other possibilites magically appear whereby extension of the encapsulated knowledge can be usefully provided to other individuals or organisations within your company. DIGITAL's example here is that XCON, a system designed to improve our manufacturing process, has been expanded to allow salesmen to produce a tailored computer system for customers with all options - on-line. Indeed this approved configuration can then be passed to the field service engineer who uses the information in his preliminary site installation planning.

Because this is a new technology, there is a tendency to concentrate on the task of actually encapsulating the knowledge. Whilst it is important to be kept up to date on the progress of the expert system, this is not the only measure of succes. A number of key questions will need to be asked. What will this new system mean in terms of organisational changes? How will it affect the people now doing a certain job that you hope to enhance with the expert system? How do they react? Are they going to cooperate if they feel that their job is in danger? It is important to focus on understanding and addressing the changes which will occur when the system becomes operational.

5. The Tools - Hardware, Sofware and Services

Almost all Artificial Intelligence research in the world has been carried out on DIGITAL computers. DIGITAL is perhaps closer to appreciating what is required than any other computer company.

The hardware needs to have a large virtual address space VAX's. There will be run time systems based on the VAX architecture which will be both very cheap and reliable. It will be possible to carry out development on large VAX computers and then migrate the completed expert system down into a smaller desk-top VAX. One of the most important criteria for computer systems used to develop and deliver AI capabilities, is to have a strong, stable architecture.

Over the next few years, DIGITAL will be in a position to supply all the basic tools necessary for AI development, but it is the customer who decides what type of work will be enhanced by these new technologies. An advantage of using DIGITAL software is that the user has access to the wealth of software already available on DIGITAL computers.

Afters these basic tools, DIGITAL expects to be able to offer some of the software that addresses productivity in specific applications. These will in all likelyhood be fairly specific to the area of knowledge of the company that developed the programs, especially if the program is based on expert systems technology. (For example, if a bank develops an expert system in, say, investment consulting, then we will find that the design is related to the way that particular bank operates.) Other products which we see emerging, such as natural language query systems will be less specific.

Further development will probably be into generic applications in the area of general business problems. We don't expect these solutions to have an Artificial Intelligence label. Perhaps a spread sheet program that is more intelligent. It would be bought because it has better functionality, not because it is Artificial Intelligence.

Gradually we see a shift in the computer industry towards symbolic programming as compared to the more conventional numeric programming. Oddly enough, although computers until now have mainly been programmed to do numeric calculation, inherently they can deal more effectively with symbolic computation.

SERVICES

DIGITAL does not just supply the Artificial Intelligence building tools, but has a Europe-wide, in-depth service organisation operation which for AI related products will be centred in Valbonne, France. The service organisation serves both as the means of giving customers full support as well as allowing feedback on evolving customer requirements in the area of Artificial Intelligence products.

BUSINESS DECISION

Anyone considering establishing an expert system should consider four important points:

1. Are the resources available to establish such a system?

2. Can it be integrated effectively into the business operation?

3. Would it take more effort to up-date and maintain the system than it would for a human assitant to do the task?

4. Is it worth it in terms of ROI?

SUMMARY

In summary, we can say that Artificial Intelligence is important today because of its implications for tomorrow. We expect Artificial Intelligence technology to enhance todays systems, to build on the data bases to turn these into knowledge based systems. This process needs to be evolutionary and not revolutionary.

It will leed to a re-examination of the existing organisational structures to take advantage of the potential offered by Artificial Intelligence and the products that will be coming onto the market shortly.

By starting carefully defining the problem/opportunity you wish to address Artificial Intelligence technology can be most effectively incorporated into your organisation. In general Artificial Intelligence technology should be used where there is a problem looking for a solution, not where a solution is looking for a problem.

It is in the area of expert systems that the most immediate and rewarding investment of time and effort will be made by the business world.

It should also be noted that in many cases Artificial Intelligence tools can increase productivity within your existing MIS department purely because these tools, if understood are more productive. Researchers developing Artificial Intelligence software were always aware of the need for better software engineering tools. This is one of the reasons why most implementations of Lisp have debugger for example.

Artificial Intelligence is not a replacement for the expert but a tool that will enhance his capability and availability, leading perhaps to a more efficient business and some new market opportunities for your company.

ARTIFICIAL INTELLIGENCE: Towards Practical Application
T. Bernold and G. Albers (editors)
Elsevier Science Publishers B.V. (North-Holland)

EXPERT SYSTEMS IN SERVICES SECTORS: USE OF EXPERT SYSTEMS IN SIX SAMPLE CASES

Daniel Sagalowicz

Technical Advisor
Framentec/Teknowledge
Monte Carlo
Monaco

As has already been reported to you in these proceedings, expert systems and in general knowledge systems have many advantages. In this paper we will expand on six such advantages:

1) Solve problems that thwart data processing techniques
2) Preserve professional expertise
3) Distribute expertise
4) Fuse multiple sources of knowledge
5) Convert knowledge into a competitive edge
6) Alter business common sense and perception

We can distinguish the use of expert systems into 3 areas: Industrial, service and management. In the industrial area, typical uses of expert systems are for scheduling, product planning, quality assurance, maintenance, process control. In the service area, the use of expert systems corresponds to automation of routine advice, standardization of service, quality control, knowledge worker productivity, access to computer systems and training. In the management area, the use of expert systems corresponds to syndication of corporate culture, communication of strategic goals, organizational memories, managerial coordination, strategic planning, information fusion, decision making. As indicated in figure Nr. 1, the difficulty of creating knowledge systems increases from industry to service to management. This is mostly due - we think - to the fact that we, as engineers, understand better the industrial sector than the management sector.

WHAT KNOWLEDGE SYSTEM CAN DO

1. SOLVE PROBLEMS THAT THWART DATA PROCESSING TECHNIQUES
2. PRESERVE PERISHABLE EXPERTISE
3. DISTRIBUTE EXPERTISE
4. FUSE MULTIPLE SOURCES OF KNOWLEDGE
5. CONVERT KNOWLEDGE INTO A COMPETITIVE EDGE
6. ALTER BUSINESS COMMON SENCE AND PERCEPTION

I personally do not think that there are real technical difficulties which are in one are harder than in the other. On the other hand, at the same time, the difficulties increase from industry to management, the payoffs also increase from industry to management. So far, most of the expert systems have been in the industrial area. We think, that the next "batch" of expert systems will be in the service area.

We are now going to explain 6 cases that correspond to the 6 advantages of expert systems mentioned previously. The first one corresponds to a computer manufacturer, who has problems with delays due to errors at the installation. That computer manufacturer first would try to improve the technical training of the sales personnel which turns out to be extremely difficult, then would try to check whether minor mistakes have been made by sales personnel. This turns out to be extremely difficult by traditional data processing techniques. Therefore, this computer manufacturer turns toward technology of artificial intelligence in general and of knowledge systems in particular to enter the orders and verify them automatically. In that case, the knowledge bases are composed of engineering configuration rules, local installation rules, manufacturing and inventory rules, and delivery rules. The purpose of such a system is to aid marketing information orders, validate or correct errors, give feed-back to the sales people, generate planning information for manufacturing. The lesson to be learned from this first case, the computer manufacturer case, is that knowledge engineering can solve problems of great economic value which resist solution by other methods.

The second case we would like to present is the case of repair of a major engine. The main problem is that when a manufacturing organization sells large engines in very small numbers, very few maintenance engineers can handle that kind of line competently. Moreover, if those engines have been in existence for a long time, it may be the case that the maintenance engineers are about to retire themselves. The solution involves a knowledge base composed of diagnostic rules, therapy rules, documentation rules. The purpose is then to centralize the company's knowledge of maintenance, to speed central diagnosis and repair, and to generate a report on breakdowns automatically. This is well within the current technology of knowledge systems. The main lesson of this particular case is that knowledge engineering can capture and preserve perishable expertise.

The third case corresponds to a company specializing in oil exploration. One main problem in oil exploration, among many, is the incidence of drilling incidents what is known as dragging incidence or sticking incidence. These incidences can delay drilling by several hours, sometimes several days, sometimes several weeks and cost the company large amounts of money. To help solve those kinds of incidences, it is possible to develop knowledge systems whose knowledge base is composed of geologic information rules, drilling history rules and drilling analysis rules.
The lesson of such a case is that, with such knowledge systems, companies can syndicate their knowledge to sustain growth and avoid delays.

The fourth case corresponds to building cost overruns. When analyzing construction cost overruns, one can notice that engineering errors account for about 80 % of these overruns. Of these, 10 % are errors of commissions and 90 % are errors of omissions. To solve this, a knowledge system could be developed with cost factor rules, regional validation rules, delay rules, and design rules. Such a system could be used in many areas which correspond to building, for example: manufacturing, construction, tooling, staffing, and so on. In those areas, typically, many experts cooperate toward one main goal. In this case, knowledge engineering enables the organization to combine and apply the expertise of many different specialists.

The fifth case is a typical ECG analysis program, where the goal is to increase market share by improving slightly the performance of a measure intrument. One such way to improve is to package a medical expert with every instrument so as to include that medical expertise as part of the instrument. Such a system would have a knowledge base composed of patient history rules, statistical analysis rules, disorder rules, anomaly rules. It would provide the advantage of combining medical expertise with processing skills, and could produce a report to be given directly to a medical doctor. Such a system could achieve - roughly - a performance of 85 % of a medical expert. The lesson of such a case is that knowledge engineering can convert expertise into a competitive advantage.

Finally, case number 6 corresponds to a geology company. The goal is to improve the number of the analyses that are acceptable to customers. Apparently, in many cases, 5-10 % of the analyses performed by geology companies are refused by customers, and an expert geophysical engineer is used to mediate complaints and authorize write-offs. These write-offs correspond to heavy losses for a geology company. The idea is to develop an expert system that would use the expertise of this geophysical engineer. Such a system would include collection analysis rules, instrument characteristics rules, and anomalous performance rules. It would enforce the company quality procedures, it would validate data calibration and ranges, it would rationalize anomalous results. The lesson of this case is that the capacity to engineer knowledge would alter the management's perception of business reality. Often, what management sees as problematic facts of life, turns out to be a possible task for knowledge engineering.

The lesson that corresponds to all these 6 cases is that the situations that instigate knowledge engineering initiatives, are as follows: organization requires too many skilled people to recruit or retrain. Problems arise that require almost innumerable possibilities to be considered, third for excellence requires a scope of knowledge exceeding reasonable demands on human training and continuing education, fourth, problem solving requires several people because no single person has the needed expertise. Finally, the company's inability to apply its existing knowledge effectively now causes management to work around basic difficulties.

ARTIFICIAL INTELLIGENCE: Towards Practical Application
T. Bernold and G. Albers (editors)
Elsevier Science Publishers B.V. (North-Holland)

OFFICE AUTOMATION:
A FIELD FOR APPLIED ARTIFICIAL INTELLIGENCE

Henry Thompson

Department of Artificial Intelligence
University of Edinburgh
Rank Xerox
Switzerland

I. INTRODUCTION

Two things about the title of this talk need to be explained - What does Office Automation have to do with Artificial Intelligence, and why "Applied" Artificial Intelligence? The answer to the first question is in fact "Not much - yet". Which ties in with the answer to the second question . 'applied' in this case means the tools and techniques which have developed within AI for exploratory computer program development. What I want to do in this talk is argue that the domain of Office Automation, like many other domains, can profit greatly by adopting these tools and techniques, and evolving from the admittedly limited amount of 'intelligence' which they bring to bear on the problem towards more elaborate kinds of Artificial Intelligence approaches.

To do this I will first distinguish a bit more carefully between these two facets of AI, and give a few thoughts to the vexed question of what intelligence is anyway. Then I will pursue at some length the distinction between the kind of program development environments which have emerged from AI and the more familiar, more traditional ones which have their origins in commercial and scientific computing. Finally I will come back to the distinction between AI environments and AI systems, and argue for an evolutionary approach to getting from one to the other.

II. INTELLIGENT SYSTEMS VS. DEVELOPMENT ENVIRONMENTS

Most of the papers of these proceedings are concerned with Artificial Intelligence proper - the construction of computer systems which embody substantial amounts of human expertise in a particular problem area. One might think that the application of theoretical AI to such practical problems is what is properly meant by the phrase "Applied Artificial Intelligence." Without getting involved in fruitless linguistic and philosophical debate, what I want to suggest is that this is to narrow a view of AI, because it is founded on too narrow a view of intelligence. In particular I want to argue that the most immediately exploitable results of theoretical AI are almost incidental to its main thrust, namely the programming environments it has built as necessary tools.

But what is intelligence then? Whatever else it may be, one thing which I think is immediately understandable is that the more of it something has, the easier it is to deal with. The more intelligence some system, whether human or machine, has, the less you have to tell it in the course of some cooperative effort.

Consider the task of trying to find a particular entry in a particular personnel file, over the telephone. Consider how different that task would be in terms of difficulty if you were speaking to a child (See the big box in the corner, with the drawers?. Count one, two, three, the fourth drawer,...); a file clerk from the wrong dpartment (the filing department (the filing cabinet in the corner, the drawer market 'personnel', the file headed 'Employee addresses', ..); the personnel manager (Maxwell's home address, please). As your interlocutor is more intelligent, and knows more about the task domain, the effort involved in getting the job done decreases. Now getting a computer to do a task for you is much like getting a particularly narrow-minded and willful child to do it, and so the task of building a system, any system, can be seen as an attempt to increase the intelligence of the host computer to the point where it can be used without too much inconvenience.

But therefore one can build a system for any problem domain, one must first build a system for system building - that is, a program development environment. Building AI system is a particularly difficult kind of system building, and as the scientists who do AI are typically computer scientists as well, a lot of the effort in AI over the years has gone into building the tools they needed for their kind of system building, a kind of system building that turns out to be rather different from the kind supported by the more traditional program development environments, a kind of system building which is arguably more appropriate for the kind of problem we confront in the Office Automation domain.

Just what is the difference between these two different kinds of system building - these two different views of what programming is all about?

III. PROGRAMMING: PROBLEM SOLVING OR IMPLEMENTATION?

There are two essentially different kinds of programming - programming as implementation and programming as problem solving.

In the first, the focus is on implementation from explicit, detailed specifications. In the second, it is on experimental exploration of a problem space via computation.

Growth of ambitions with respect to the kind of task which can be tackled computationally has led to a dramatic growth in the relative prominence of the second type of use.

Two different types of programming langtages have envolved to meet the needs of these two different types of programming:

- languages which are modular, strongly typed, highly redundant, specification oriented, with a compile-link-load style of use, with origins in computer science, "closed", for coders

- languages which are flexible, untyped, growth oriented, with an interpreter-based style of use, with origins in artificial intelligence, "open", for scientist-programmers

We will call the first the "Early Binding" languages, because thex require crucial decisions about program structure to be made early in the programming process. Examples of this sort of language are Pascal, Ada[1] and Modula.

We will call the second the "Late Binding" languages, because they allow the programmar to defer decisions about program structure as long as possible. Examples of this sort of languages are Lisp, Smalltalk and Prolog.

[1]Ada is a trademark of the US DoD

Let's look at the points which distinguish these two sorts of programming language one at a time. Of course, in what follows I am exaggerating the clarity and precision of this distinction for the sake of argument - none of the languages cited above exhibit all and only the named characteristics. The points made below define the end points of a scale, along which languages may be differentiated.

III. A Overall language structure

Early Binding Languages: Central notion of interface, to divide and protect, giving rise to rigid module structure and redundant specification of constraints, and reducing bandwidth of communication necessary between collaborators.

vs.

Late Binding Languages: Homogeneity, lack of over boundaries, with concomitant increase in bandwidth of communication required.

III. B Typing

Early Binding Languages: Strong typing, enforced at design and construction time - follows from previous point.

vs.

Late Binding Languages: Virtually no typing, allowing decisions to be deferred until in the midst of things - encourages or even demands automatic storage allocation and deallocation (garbage collection). May require subsequent constraint to improve efficiency.

III. C Specification vs. Design

Early Binding Languages: Demands complete, accurate specification before programming starts. Module and interface structure dependent on specification. Inimical to subsequent changes in organisation.

vs.

Late Binding Languages: Expects under-determined, envolving, and/or nonexistent specifications. Expects and supports changes in organisation as well as detail.

III. D Style of use

Early Binding Languages: Editor, Compiler, Linker, Runtime typically distinct systems, with the expected frequency of cycling around the loop being fairly low. Encourages pre-construction of entire systems.

vs.

Late Binding Languages: Editor and Interpreter or Incremental Compiler typically thoroughly integrated, with expected frequency of alternation very high. Encourages patchwork style of development, defining core and leaving periphery until later.

III. E ORIGINS

Early Binding Languages: Origins in commercial and scientific computing, where problem was and is to take well understood algorithms and processes and efficiently and robustly implement them.

vs.

Late Binding Languages: Origins in artificial intelligence, where problem was and is to explore a poorly understood phenomenon with computational tools, building frameworks to investigate hypotheses.

III. F ACCESS TO SYSTEM

Early Binding Language: Protects the system from the user, enforces a strong distinction between the two. Appropriate to batch or time-sharing.

vs.

Late Binding Languages: Makes the system available to the user, does not distinguish between the two. Encourages customisation, fully embedded sublanguages. Uniform representation of programs and data facilitates programconstruction programs, program manipulation programs (c.f. Masterscope). C.f. also Programmers' Assistant, CLISP. More appropriate to single-user machines.

III. G USERS

Early Binding Languages: Related to style of use, access issues.

Meant for use by programmers, with little or no knowledge of subject domain, working to specification.

vs.

Late Binding Languages: Meant for use by experts in the subject domain, as a vehicle for their ordinary scientific activity.

In the time available such a summary as this is necessarily lacking in detail - for a more thorough discussion with particular exmphasis on the exploitation of powerful single-user workstations by systems built on Lage Binding Languages see (Sheil, 1983).

IV. THE INCREMENTAL APPROACH TO AUTOMATION

I hope that by now the overall point about AI and Office Automation has begun to emerge - that Office Automation is just the sort of poorly understood domain which demands the Late Bincing style of investigation. Attempts to rigourously define a specification for an office oricessubg task, implement it in Early Binding style, and then install and use it have had very little success - we simply don't understand the nature of the task well enough. What I believe is necessary is to treat Office Automation as a domain where the addition of expertise to computer systems must be pursued incrementally, by experts in the domain, using the kind of program development environment I have been calling Late Binding.

What this means is viewing the problem as one of providing better machine assistance to the human worker, rather than fully automating his/her task. From this perspective existing systems such as spreadsheet tools for accountants, document preparation systems and electronic mail systems are all good first steps in the right direction. What is needed is to recast them in a flexible development environment, so that experimental modifications and enhancements can easily be made. Then the user of such a system who says"That's the third time today I've performed that sequence of operations - let's see if we can't automate that" will be in a position to do just that, and before long a true AI system will emerge. An excellent example of this approach is given in (Newman and Mott, 1983), and a number of other articles illustrative of my points here can be found in the Design of User-Friendly Systems and Programming Environments sections of the collection in which that article appears (Degano and Sandewall, 1983).

So, in conclusion, I have tried to point out two complementary ways in which the fruit of work in Artificial Intelligence can be brought to bear on the problems of Office Automation - by adopting the Late Binding style of program development, and by using it to build systems in the office which allow for an incremental shift of function from the user into the systems.

REFERENCES

Degano, P. and Sandewall, E. (Eds.) 1983. Integrated Interactive Computing Systems. North-Holland

Newman, W.M. and Mott T. 1983. Officetalk-Zero: An Experimental Integrated Office System. In Degano, P. and Sandewall, E., editors, Integrated Interactive Computing Systems. North-Holland.

Sheil, B 1983. Power Tools for Programmers. Datamation: 131-144, February.

ARTIFICIAL INTELLIGENCE: Towards Practical Application
T. Bernold and G. Albers (editors)
Elsevier Science Publishers B.V. (North-Holland)

REQUIREMENTS ON EXPERT SYSTEMS AS SEEN BY AN INSURANCE COMPANY

Christian J. Jenny

'Zurich" Insurance Company
Zurich
Switzerland

INTRODUCTION

Insurance Companies and AritICial Intelligence (AI), strange bedfellows or a promising love affair? Can AI find a way into the apparently conservative world of insurance where - as lore would have it - only very conventional systems are in use?

Insurance companies are typical commercial systems users. COBOL, IMS, CICS are the tools of their trade, not micro electronics, robotics, high-tech cybernetics - at least at first sight. In reality things are quite different. Insurance companies are presently considering - and in many instances already implementing - some of the most modern system concepts. The imperative need to reduce costs, the accelerating pace of application changes due to business flexibility, the management of large and ever growing networks of branch-offices and agencies and the high interdependencies of their data structures have created a need for modern system technologies, such as on-line, real time data processing with down-loading of activities to lower ranking nodes in network, personal computing, shared data bases, 4th generation languages, etc.

What then would be the applications for Expert System. Probst and Bonzon (1) give the following definition:

"An Expert System is a system consisting of a knowledge base (comprising a data base of facts as well as a base of logical rules) and a control program, which may be called inference engine, using the knowledge base for logical deductions".

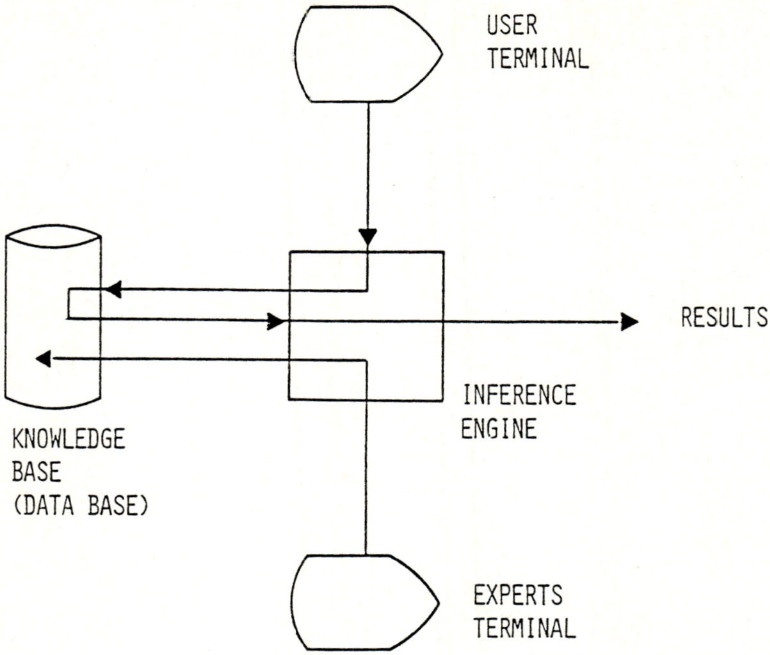

FIG. 1: BASIC ELEMENTS OF AN EXPERT SYSTEM

Potential profits for ES in insurance treatment to some extent by this exposé:

- Improvement of quality
- Increased development productivity
- Increased application flexibility
- Manpower reduction in underwriting
- Individualization of products
- Handling highly complex products

- Improved system controls
- Improved management controls

THE ENVIRONMENT

Requirements and targets for Expert Systems can only be appreciated if the surrounding environment is somewhat known. As an example, let us consider the "Zurich" Insurance computing center, shared by three Swiss companies of the "Zurich" Group: Alpina, Vita and "Zurich". The center operates in 3 shifts, providing computing services for all production and test runs. Each of the three companies has its own program development department, developing all application procedures and programs to its individual needs. The total portfolio of production programs exceeds 4,000.

Presently installed are two IBM 3081 of 14 and 15 MIPS with one of the 3081s to be upgraded to an IBM 3084 (approx. 26 MIPS). On-line storage comprises and excess of 70 GB, not including a Mass-Storage System for storage back-up operations.

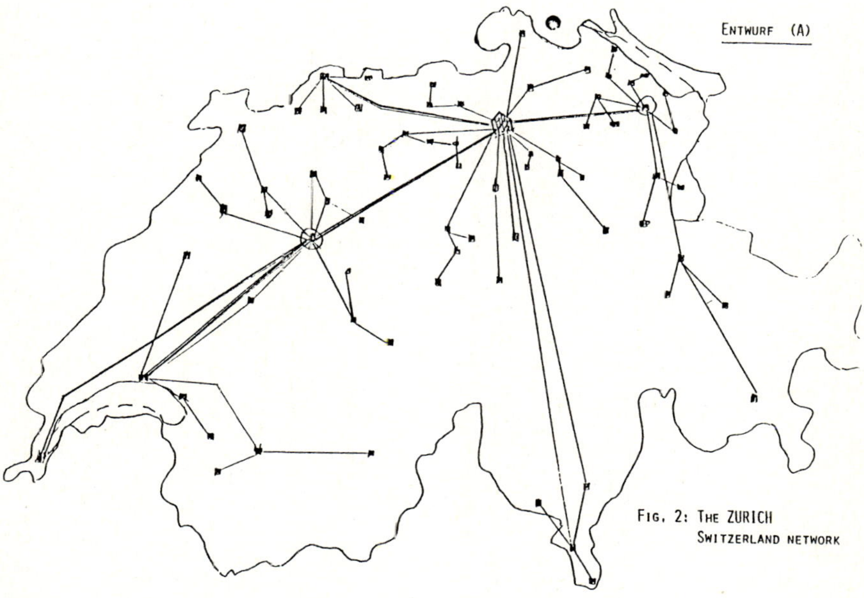

FIG. 2: THE ZURICH SWITZERLAND NETWORK

A network of 9.6 kb and 48 kb leased lines interconnects all Swiss branch offices and agencies of the three companies (each agency conducting business of one company only). The network is formed by 3 linked stars with major hubs in Zurich, Saint Gall and Berne, interconnecting in excess of 1,000 terminals of the IBM 3270-type (Fig. 2).

Complexity of operations can be appreciated when considering the "dynamics" of such an installation. Installed computing power has grown from 1.2 MIPS in 1977 to presently 29 MIPS and is estimated to exceed 100 MIPS by 1987. Installed on-line storage has increased from 6.8 GB in 1977, to today's 70 + GB and should at least double that by 1987. Daily transactions have risen from 18,000 in 1977 to 300,000 in 1984 and will topple 600,000 in 1987. These figures reflect an exponential growth of the computing facilities with all accompanying problems of large and fast growing systems.

Data bases (VSAM and IMS) number in excess of a hundred and are highly interdependent (Fig. 3a). All data base accesses must follow strict dependency rules. Batch operations do not execute at random, but follow the strict rules of a precedence network (Fig. 3b).

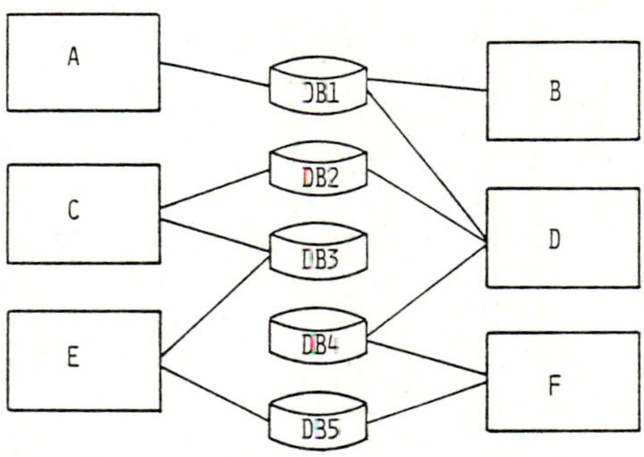

FIG. 3A: PROGRAMS A...F INTERCONNECTING DATA BASES DB1...DB5

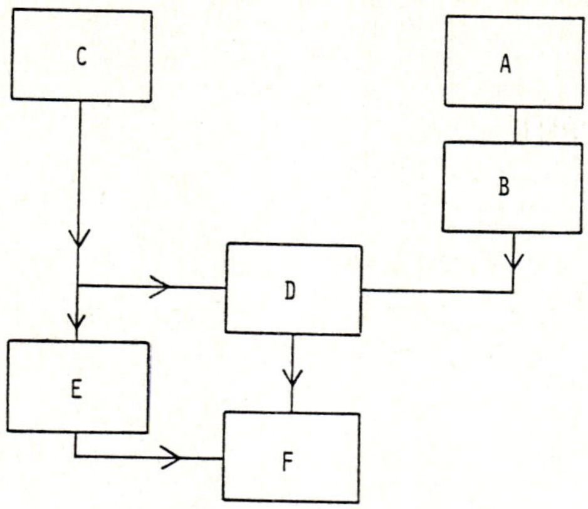

FIG. 3B: A PRECEDENCE (SCHEDULING-) NETWORK FOR BATCH EXECUTION (BASED ON FIG. 3A)

Automatic procedures are mandatory to ensure correct and efficient execution schedules. Any irregularity, such as failure of a procedure, causes major changes in the precedence network, requiring immediate operator action. Moreover, data base interdependency places severe conditions on newly developed applications, as they must consider all existing limitations.

APPLICATIONS AND THEIR DESIGN CRITERIA

Insurance systems comprise a set of functions specific to a distinct business area (such as household, motor vehicles, business casualty, etc.) and implemented on a central facility (Fig. 4).

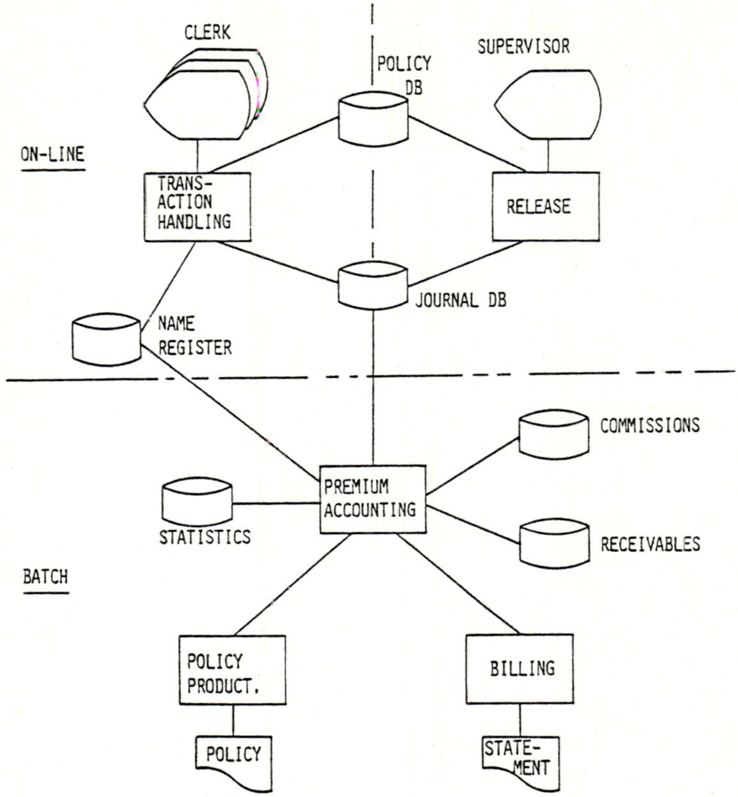

FIG. 4: STRUCTURE OF INSURANCE APPLICATION

On-line: - Transaction handling

. Contract data entry

. Underwriting (tariffing, plausibility checking, policy-recording, journalling)

. Name and address entry

- Policy data release

Batch: - Premium accounting

- Billing

- Policy production

- Recording for statistics, commissions, receivables

Note the separate on-line functions "Transaction handling" and "Policy data release". Insurance business procedures require distinct operations for underwriting and release (sign-off) of an underwritten contract, one being conducted by a clerk, the other by a supervisor.

Typical for large and often complex procedures is the splitting into an on-line and an off-line part. Although there is a trend towards increasing on-line processing, response time requirements, systems utilisations and integrity considerations demand a batch (or background) portion which can be executed asynchronously with the on-line operations. Most batch processing is relegated to second shift, leaving first shift to real-time processing and third shift to data saving and reorganization operations.

Besides of the listed functions, there are other insurance functions not tied to a specific business area:

- Commission accounting
- Name and address register handling
- Claims adjustments
- Claims payments
- Statistics and business controls
- Receivables

All these functions are executed centrally. A further set of functions does not necessarily depend on a central facility:

- Planning
- Investments and real estate
- Reinsurance
- Agency accounting and bookkeeping
- Personnel salaries and informations
- Sales support
- Office automation

Major criteria in the design of application procedures and program are (by priority):

- Functionality and operability (quality)
- Data integrity (quality)
- Program integrity (quality)
- User guidance (human factors)
- Response time (human factors)
- Minimization of disk-accesses (production costs)
- Minimization of CPU cycles (production costs)
- Design standards (development costs)
- System utilization (production costs)
- Change flexibility (development costs)
- Maintainability (development costs)

This exposé asserts that expert system may facilitate some of the above criteria and could contribute substantial assistance in meeting their goal.

POTENTIAL USE FOR ES IN INSURANCE SYSTEMS

Consider the design criteria given in Section 3. ES could be applied towards improvement of quality, human factors, development costs etc. Other potential use of ES would facilitate insurance applications which could not be realized otherwise.

Applying ES towards quality

Operability: ES applied toward operations, making it simpler, easier and providing immediate operator assistance, could be major use for handling emergencies in the machine room in on-line and batch-environments. Problems with procedure failures (Section 2, Fig. 3b) could be attended either by operator guidance or fully automatically realizing the precedence network. Similarly, communications network breakdown-recovery could be handled without operator intervention. Rerouting algorithms would be improved by learning techniques based on previous performance.

Applying ES towards integrity

Data integrity is a major source of concern. Plausibility checks are at present far from sufficient. Although much of the information needed for exhaustive testing is available within the date base network, only little is used, due to the lack of making intelligent decisions. For example: should automobile-comprehensive accept an insurance application for a 3-year old vehicle of SFr. 70'000.--, when the same person carries a household fire insurance of only SFr. 25'000.-- and a life insurance policy for less than SFr. 50'000.--? Although quite possible, an intelligent system would ask the operating clerk, whether given figures are really correct and to please supply particulars.

One way to improve program integrity is the generation of better application test procedures. Another AI discipline, program proving, falls of course in this category as well, but only Expert Systems are considered. Expert Systems can provide "difficult" cases, searching for traps that have already been recognized in part during unit tests of single programs.

Applying ES towards human factors

As an example, consider user guidance by means of ES. Casual users can be lead through carefully worded, elaborate procedures, whereas an experienced user is best served by scant requests, providing only a minimum of guidances. Intermediate cases are to be handled as needed.

Applying ES towards systems development productivity and costs

Development cost arises to a large degree through change requests and maintenance. Industry-wide estimates show cost of maintenance and application changes to consume 30 % to 50 % of the DP development budget. Abonneau (2,3) claims a reduction to only 7 % by utilizing knowledge-based systems where changes are mostly accomplished by altering data in the knowledge base instead of changing or rewriting an application program.

New insurance applications

Insurance products, as provided by a general insurance company, are mass products. However, many instances arise, where specially tailored coverage must be provided for uncommon risks with a complex set of requirements. Here, general insurance system do not suffice, thus necessitating manual acquisition and underwriting procedures. Although often adequate, it could be of great advantage to provide assistance to an agent through Expert Systems. For instance, knowledge based on previour acquisitions and on damage reports could be employed for guidance.

REQUIREMENTS

The thesis put forward by this exposé is that insurance systems are large and complex, fast growing with severe on-line demands, putting increasing strains on hard- and software and are to be implemented to a large extent on central facilities due to their interwoven data base structure (Fig. 3a). Hence, it is mandatory that the introduction of any new systems techniques, such as Expert Systems, which cause an increase of power and storage demands, must be paralleled by architectural measures for keeping requirements to a manageable level. Off-loading, distributing, front-ending, personal computing, etc. must be made available to the same extent as resource demands increase.

For example, no purpose would be served by reducing development and maintenance costs (see Section 4.4.) by means of Expert Systems and at the same time increasing demands on computing and storage to off-set any gains.

Summarizing potential requirements for expert systems deduced from the described environment and its applications, results in the following recommendations:

(1) Apply ES to non-central computing facilities first, although potential gains may be nominal (personal computing).

(2) Apply ES to new insurance applications (Section 4.5) before tackling productivity and costs.

(3) ES may have a great impact on human factors (Section 4.3): make use of intelligent terminals (personal computers as user interfaces) for implementing ES.

(4) Similar to (3), apply ES to plausibility (Section 4.2.) by use of intelligent terminals.

(5) Ensure architectural measures to counteract increase in system demand and complexity due to ES.

(6) Do not attempt ES implementations without carefully estimating processing and storage requirements. Do consider influence on system complexity.

(7) Off-load ES whenever possible.

And above all, ES is a technology almost entirely new to the insurance environment. Minimize risk by first applying it to small, high structure (i.e. well defined) projects with good project management (4).

(1) A.R. Probst, P. Bonzon, "L'Emergence des Systemes Experts", OUTPUT, No. 3, 1983, Goldach, Switzerland

(2) C. Abonneau, "Application Development Productivity", European GUIDE, November, 1980.

(3) C. Abonneau, "Application Development Productivity; knowledge-based systems", European GUIDE, July - August, 1981

(4) F.W. Mc Farlan, "Corporate Information Systems Management", Richard D. Irwin, Inc. Homewood, ILL., 1983.

ARTIFICIAL INTELLIGENCE: Towards Practical Application
T. Bernold and G. Albers (editors)
Elsevier Science Publishers B.V. (North-Holland)

CURRENT WORK ON EXPERT SYSTEMS AND NATURAL LANGUAGE PROCESSING AT SIEMENS

Georg Eibl

Siemens AG, Central Technology Division
Corporate Laboratories for Information Technology
Munich
Federal Republic of Germany

PRELIMINARY REMARKS

I am very grateful for the opportunity to give you a short overview of the activities in Applied AI within SIEMENS. The theme of this conference is:

> Artificial Intelligence - Information processing at the threshold of practical application?

The organizers of this meeting and some managers in industry and administration still put a question mark behind that statement. They probably argue that the field is dominated by scientists oriented to basic research, with little successes in practical applications. On the other side, one was already able to read several years ago:

> AI - out of the lab, into the workplace.

The following short description of AI projects within SIEMENS will show you that AI applications are appearing in many and diverse fields.

PROJECTS

1. Expert Systems for Demonstration

Last year an expert systems' group was established within the Corporate Laboratories for Information Technology (3). For that purpose a short-, middle- and long-term strategy with the assistance of Standard Research Institute International and Prof. Raulefs (University of Kaiserslautern) was defined.

We presented the following three experimental expert systems at the Hannover Fair 1984:

ABDIA (see fig. 1)
FOX (see fig. 2)
EXKUSE (see fig. 3)

One of the main objects for the development of these expert systems was to become acquainted with the AI principles, methods, tools and the new soft- and hardware environment.Besides these training purposes, the system mainly serve for demonstration. In parallel we have started with the development of an expert system for the configuration of an operating system for real-time application. However, it is still too early to report on this inhouse application.

ABDIA: Abdominal Diagnosis	
Domain of Application:	medical diagnosis of acute abdominal diseases
Tape of Systems:	rule-based expert system with explanation capabilities
Methods used:	mixed backward- and forward chaining of production rules, probabilistic reasoning
Implementation:	INTERLISP-D

Figure 1

FOX: Photography Expert	
Domain of Application:	consulting an amateur photographer in choosing appropriate equipment for a certain photographic motive
Type of System:	frame- and rule-based expert system
Methods used:	forward-chaining of IF-THEN-rules, mechanisms for property inheritance, access-oriented procedure invocation, constraint propagation
Implementation:	LOOPS

Figure 2

EXKUSE: Experimental Kitchen Design System	
Domain of Application:	Kitchen Design
Type of System:	object-oriented
Methods used:	Interaction-oriented
Implementation:	LOOPS and INTERLISP-D

Figure 3

2. Knowledge-Based Resource Planning System (RP)

For the last six years an office system, Computerservice for Secretary and Management, has been in operation at Siemens. About a hundred secretaries, managers and subject experts have been using this system daily. The Computerservice comprises text processing, electronic, mailing and filing, and a database containing designing information for R&D projects.

In the framework of this office system this RP will be developed with the aim of supporting finance and personnel planning for R&D projects. The planning process requires the cooperation of a large group of subject experts and management stretching over a period of many months. The RP should make the planning process transparent to all persons involved. Above all, the user should be in a position to evaluate data spontaneously and adapt the data to his particular problems.

Our RP was, and hopefully will further be sponsored by the Commission of the European Communities. Together with

Compagnie Internationale pour l'Informatique-Honeywell Bull (F)
Laboratoire de Marcoussis (F)

our company participated in the ESPRIT Pilot Project No. 15 within the workplan 3.1 (Knowledge Information Management System). Fig. 4 shows the technical goals and the realisation.

This ESPRIT project is designed to investigate key areas of information processing such as knowledge representation, inferencing techniques and human computer interfaces (1).

KNOWLEDGE-BASED RESOURCE PLANNING SYSTEM

Technical Goals

Architectural extension of office systems to achieve:

- a uniform, robust and natural human interface
- user instruction about organizational facts
- control of complex office processes in a distributed system
- adaption of office systems to organizational changes

Realization

Implementation and evaluation of a prototype in the domain of Resource Planning (RP)

- analysis of the RP-procedure
- development of office demantics
- engineering of a RP-knowledge base
- realization of cooperating agents
  - to supervise and control the office process
  - to interact with an instruct human users

Figure 4

3. ISAR: An experimental System for Fact Retrieval

Formal languages for fact retrieval are very common today. Yet, opinion differs greatly concerning the suitability, realisability, reliability and efficiency of natural language interaction with data bases. This stems from an obvious lack of know-how and experience.

The system mentioned here in short was developed for the purpose of study and to demonstrate the possibilities and problems involved in natural language access to data using a serie of AI aids and techniques. However, the main aim was directed at a row of practical questions. For instance, we were interested in how robust and efficient certain linguistic analysis methods are, in the possibility of increasing knowledge interactively, in dialogue modelling (such that the user is not overloaded with questions by the system for example) and in the possibilities of automatic evaluation. In other words, we were searching for a pragmatic solution to restricted natural language dialogue. These types of dialogue as they occur when confining oneself to the extraction of information common to DB's today can be regarded as suitable and appropriate.

What we most certainly did not aim at was to model possible advanced forms of human understanding and behaviour or to attempt to find answers to the many problems which still exist in linguistic oriented AI-systems today. Neither did we strive for an extensive coverage of linguistic utterances.

Originally, we only intended to build a kind of preprocessor for an existing data base system with a formal data manipulation language (however without further contents specialization). Later, however, the linguistic processor programmed in Interlisp was complemented by a modelled fact retrieval system in the same programming environment operating on different types of data. Figure 5 shows the rough outline of ISAR.

ISAR's adaptability stems mainly from the fact, that, without fundamental changes to the language processor, questions and demands covering totally different areas of application can be dealt with. An important prerequisite for this and especially for the input of new information is the capability to process input sentences containing unknown words (new to the system) correctly.

The user of such a system should be able to put his questions to the system via the keyboard in every-day German. At the same time, he should not have to bother himself too much with a restricted format, reserved notation and implementation-specific system characteristics. He should however be sufficiently familiar with the particular subject field and also the contents of the data base. If natural language data manipulations of this kind is to be at all worthwhile, it is also important that the subject field be well-structured by way of distinctive classes of objects and that reference can be made to specialist jargon using an exotic grammar or special set phrases.

We experiment with ISAR using geographic, demographic and economic data on countries of the world (including information on the most important rivers, lakes, mountains) as well as personal data and astronomical information on the planets(2).

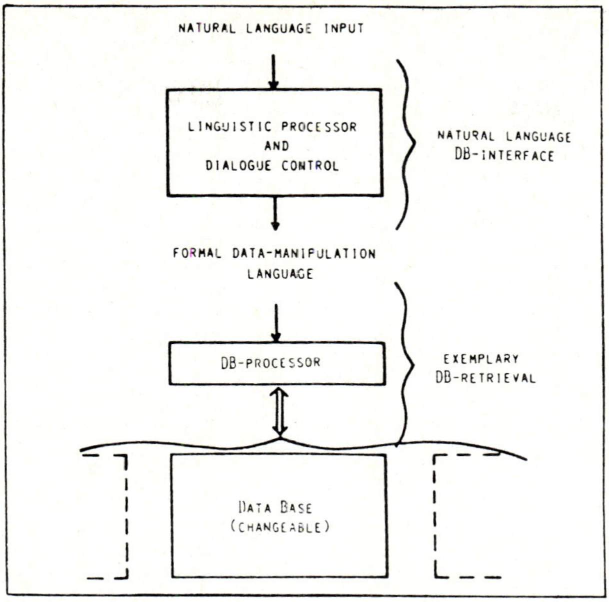

Figure 5

4. TINA: Text Content Analysis

This project aims at developing a variety of linguistically based processes and methods which support the automatic preprocessing of natural language data, be it word lists, titles, abstracts or essays, and permit the extraction of special factual information for texts in natural language.

In TINA we are neither striving for overall global solutions to the problem of text-understanding nor are we trying to provide ad-hoc solutions to special and unique problems occuring in subfields. On the contrary, utilizing techniques from the field of artificial intelligence, we are concentrating rather on linguistic methods and procedures developed with respect to real world information processing We have been working on a set of procedures and modules which can be easily linked together so that a variety of applications can be maintained, for e.g. text-analysis, information retrieval, natural language interface to data bases - in several languages, with large volumes of data, and last but not least, with short response times.

Two examples of this approach are a mophological and a syntactic retrieval tool:

A) MARS: Morphological Analysis for Retrieval Support (4)
Goal:

In free text search, the searcher is not independent of the real shape of word occurring in the data base. If "electricity" is being sought for words like "electrical", "electric" or even "Electricity" will not be found. Information retrieval systems used today have only mechanical aids for these problems: the searcher can use truncation (right, left, middle, depending on the special IRS) to cover a broader variety of tokens. These methods are generally imprecise in that the retrieval results often include useless information.

MARS is based neither on graphemes nor on strings but provides linguistic aids for this problem: It builds up a reference system over the words of a given data base (for our purposes, we used the word list of the Food Science Technology Abstracts (FSTA)), using the word stems as indicators pointing to the token the stem occurs in.

The method MARS uses is one of morphological decomposition. Each word of the input file is decomposed into its morphological components to find the stem of the word; e.g. "electrically-heated" will be decomposed into "<electric> ally - <heat> ed" (with the two stems in brackets).

The decomposition needs a list of the morphemes of both the common language and the special purpose language it has to deal with. The list consists currently of about 7500 entries for English. The decomposition also requires an automaton to specify which morphological categories can follow which other ones. Special constraints are applied if there is more than one decomposition result.

The decomposition handles about 96% of the input words correctly (even in this extremely difficult application area of chemistry); it decomposes about 80 words per second. The system is in use for English, German and Spanish; other languages can be included.

MARS architecture:

To build up the inverted file of the stems, the following steps are necessary:

- remove non-linguistic elements such as figures etc. from the file
- decompose the remaining words and extract the stems from the decomposition (The Food Science Technology Abstracts included 36000 words).
- invert the stems by building up a pointer system to the token the stem occurs in.

For the retrieval, MARS uses a program system with the following principle functions:

- analysis and decomposition of an input word (as in the analysis part)
- search the inverted files with the stem(s) resulting from the de-decomposition and display all tokens existing in the word list.
- posibility of marking the word(s) in which the user is interested to use these in his search.

MARS has no direct access to a database. It is an offline system used in the preparation and formulation of search questions.

Results:

A searcher using MARS is independent of the actual form of the word he wants to retrieve. He is free to choose the form of any word he wants to search with. He will retrieve all linguistically related words (and not only the words including identical strings).

He can define certain kinds of synonyma and (at least in the case of the FSTA) is informed about the occurences of every word (how often it occurs in titles, in abstracts etc.). He can also analyse compound words and decide how much and which of the stems he wants to search with and how the sets of tokens should be interrelated. He, of course, will also find stems which are part of compound words. Tests have shown that a significant improvement of the retrieval results could be obtained.

B) COPSY: Context Operator Syntax (7)

Goal:
The goal of COPSY is the automatisation and optimisation of a free text search of titles, index phrases or any other short texts which consists of expressions or noun phrases, i.e. combination of meaningful words. Traditional search systems work on single, syntactically isolated words.

Method:
COPSY analyses a search query, extracts the syntactic structure and converts it into a normalised form. This form is matched with normalised forms of documents in the data base in order to obtain a ranking of the output documents. It is important to note that it is the normalised form which is used for matching and not the original input form. This means that documents containing the phrase "markets for butter" will be found even if the query was "butter markets". The output from COPSY is a list of ranked documents based on syntactical phenomena in search questions and objects.

Application areas:
COPSY can replace traditional search methods using ADJACENT and NEAR operators, which are mechanical means for handling phrases, in special applications. The searcher no longer needs to build up sophisticated search strategies by calculating "distances" of words and so simulating natural syntax. He enters a search question in natural language without having to manipulate the question any further.

COPSY may be used as a post search filtering tool: It can rank objects offered as output by a traditional information system according to the degree in which they are relevant to the search question. For certain applications it may also be used in a stand-alone mode. A research goal is the integration of a tool such as formulating queries in a language which is not identical with the language of the documents stored in the data base (e.g. search questions in German, documents in English).
Searching abstracts and full text using more syntactic information could also be tempting long-term goal for an enlarged COPSY.

5. SPICOS: Siemens - Philips - IPO Continuous Speech Recognition, Understanding and Dialogue Research Project

Siemens has considerable experience both in acoustic signal processing and in linguistic analysis of documents and database query. This has led to a number of applications such as highly efficient word recognizers or linguistically oriented information retrieval software.

We recently decided to integrate some of this know-how into a research project with the goal to develop an experimental system with the complete set of functions of speech understanding systems, like

- phonetic-acoustic analysis
- linguistic analysis
- document database
- blackboard architecture for hypothetical recognition results
- dialogue control
- speech synthesis

Because of the precompetitive research character of the project we are cooperating with other research groups both from industry and universities, with Philips (International) BV as the main industrial partner.

We will concentrate mainly on speech understanding levels above the acoustic level, using linguistic and domain-specific knowledge (and suitable knowledge representation techniques), and on an integration of the different levels. To experiment with the system we will use a documentation database where the user can interact with the system in spoken natural language dialogues.

Firstly, the system will try to recognize the question acoustically. Then the result of the analysis will be checked liguistically and transformed into a database query which then will be executed. The query result will be transformed into a natural language answer and either displayed or the screen or processed as a speech signal. (See figure 6)

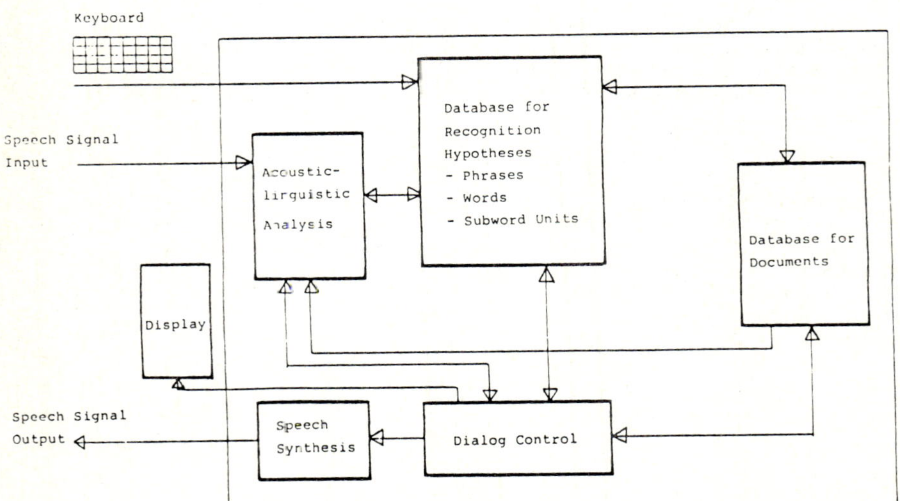

Figure 6 Rough Outline of SPICOS

6. METAL: Maschine Translation System

Siemens Language Services had long seen the need for operable Maschine Translation (MT) systems. The goal was to have available in-house an MT system which would be able to translate monotonous texts (such as operating manuals for telephone systems) at such a quality level that the posteditor can greatly increase his usual output.

After various experiences with MT systems and systems claiming to be MT systems, Language Services decided to utilize the many years of research expended in the USA and, since 1979 in cooperation with the Linguistic Research Center (LRC) of the University of Texas, to develop a system which takes practical aspects of a translator's work into account. The LRC MT system includes a translation program METAL, as part of a suite of programs designed to automate the complete process of translating technical texts. It is a language-independent system. During the first phase, it is intended for translations from German to English (5,6).

METAL is modular in multiple ways. For example, programs and linguistic analysis procedures are strictly separate so that one can be modified without affecting the other. Thus, for several types of texts, different grammars can be invoked without any change in the programs.

Language-independence of a system is especially useful if often the same source texts have to be translated into several target languages at the same time. Since the analysis of the source language is by far the most costly step it would be uneconomical not to use it more than once. If 80 % of the machine time has to be spent on the analysis of the German source text, a lot of time and cost can be saved if this same analysis intended for the translation into English can be used for the translation into e.g. Spanish and Arabic as well.

METAL is embedded in a text processing environment which automatically reconstitutes the original text format with all tables, graphs etc. after the translation process. That is especially crucial in technical documentation. It saves the step of having to reinput everything and to restructure the translated text.

A spelling corrector decreases the number of mistranslations that are due to errors in the source text. If the system is unable to analyze a sentence with a minimum level of certainty, it produces a terminology list as output. The posteditor is called upon to translate the sentence (instead of possibly having to sort through "garbage").

The quality of MT systems has often been measured in percentage points. The figures usually refer to the number of "correct" words or sentences.
Such a scale is of course highly questionable. During the experimental stages, the METAL German-English systems has so far reached a correctness level of between 40 and 80 % of "sentences". It is no secret that the present state of the development could be improved upon. METAL will not replace the translator but it will probably change his job description.

SUMMARY

In conclusion it should be mentioned that an AI-Center within our Corporate Laboratories for Information Technology is in plan for 1984. Its topics will be

* support of rapid prototyping
* developing and testing of new AI tools
* education
* know-how transfer to our operating groups
* inviting guest researchers, faculty members and graduate students.

I am convinced that the establishment of this AI-Center is therefore an additional indication that SIEMENS would actually no longer put a question mark at the end of the title of this conference.

REFERENCES

/1/ COMMISSION OF THE EUROPEAN COMMUNITIES: Preparatory Information Package for the Proposed European Strategic Programme for Research and Development in Information Technology. 84/2086/TFTI-III, p. 59-60

/2/ LEHMANN, E.: ISAR - ein experimentelles deutschsprachiges Faktenabfragesystem. In J.W. SCHMIDT (Hrsg.), Sprachen für Datenbanken. Informatik-Fachberichte 72, Springer, Berlin etc. 1983, p. 11-25

/3/ LEHMANN, E.: Expertensysteme - Ueberblick über den aktuellen Entwicklungsstand (1983). Internal Report. To appear as report of the Federal Department of Research and Technology of the Federal Republic of Germany.

/4/ NIEDERMAIR, G.Th.; THURMAIR, G.; BUETTEL, I.: MARS: A Retrieval Tool on the Basis of Morphological Analysis. To appear in: Proceedings of the 3rd Joint BCS and ACM Symposium (1984)

/5/ SLOCUM, J.; BENNETT, W.S.: The LRC Machine Translation System: An Application of State-of -the-Art Text and Natural Language Techniques to the Translation of Technical Manuals. Working Paper LRC-82-1, July 1982

/6/ SCHNEIDER, T; Some Notes on Machine Aids for Translators. Aus META, 4/83

/7/ SCHWARZ, C.; Freitextrecherche - Grenzen und Möglichkeiten aus der Sicht der Informationslinguistik. In: Nachrichten für Dokumentation, 33/6, 1982, pp. 228-236

ARTIFICIAL INTELLIGENCE: Towards Practical Application
T. Bernold and G. Albers (editors)
Elsevier Science Publishers B.V. (North-Holland)

COMPUTER ASSISTED SYNTHESIS PLANNING - A PROJECT OF THE CHEMICAL INDUSTRY

Willi Sieber

Project CASP
Sandoz AG
Basle
Switzerland

In pharmaceutical research we have to synthesize typically 10'000 potential active compounds before we eventually can market a single one of them. This means that we have to design the same amount of syntheses. It is therefore important to have an information system to assist the planning process.

If an organic chemist enters industrial pharmaceutical research he additionally to chemistry has to learn a lot about pharmacology and medicine. It is hard for him to keep his personal knowledge up to date with the rapid advancements of science. This is the point where our expert system will support him.

In the following I would like to explain the practical procedure. The chemist is sitting in front of a computer terminal for graphics in his lab. He can draw a chemical structural formula on the display with a light pen. He has a menu of commands that can be activated with the lightpen. The commands are DRAW, RUBOUT, MOVEATOM, SHIFT, C N O P S for atomtypes and so on. When the structural formula is completed he can store it in a file and use it later on for different purposes.

The structural formula is a worldwide understandable form of communication among chemists. Even in japanese or russian literature the formula looks alike. This is an advantage over other types of expert systems that are dependent on more or less clearly defined expressions in a specific language.

The chemist will typically first do a retrieval job checking if his structure is worldwide known among the 7.5 million registered structures from Chemical Abstracts Services (an american organization that collects and summarizes all chemical publications worldwide). He can also check if it is known within his company (unpublished confidential results). All those informations will give him the necessary background to decide if it could be worth to work with that structure as a potential pharmaceutically active compound.

With other program systems he can generate threedimensional conformations of his structure and compare it with known active compounds (molecular modelling). He can also look into the potential drug metabolism i.e. how the compound gets degraded in the human body by enzymes. With the synthesis planning program he can generate potential synthesis paths and during the real lab synthesis other computer programs can help him to characterize the produced materials analytically by comparing his data with facts from former analyses of similar compounds.

Let's go back to the methodology of synthesis planning. The structural formula represents the compound we would like to have at the end of our total synthesis. Syntheses are carried out stepwise. In the lab a starting material is treated with a reagent and thereby converted to a product.

This product after purification will be the starting material for the next synthesis step and so on.

The synthesis planning methodology has to look at the total synthesis in reversed order. We define the final product (synthesis target) and are asking what synthesis steps could lead to it (precursors). A reversed chemical reaction is called a transform.

The chemist at the computer terminal will activate the command PROCESS to get a first generation of transforms and precursors. They are represented symbolically by the synthesis tree. The branches represent transforms and the nodes represent precursors (chemical structures).

He will now go through the alternative proposals and rate them as useful or useless. He can look at the precursor structures and corresponding literature references for the transforms. Those references provide also some information about reagents, solvents, reaction time and temperature. There is eventually more detailed information available on microfiche or in the original literature.

The chemist will now select the best proposal from the first generation and use the PROCESS command again to produce a second generation therefrom and so on. All Precursor structures are also automatically looked up in a catalog of starting materials that are commercially available.

A typical session at the computer terminal lasts for 1 to 2 hours. The chemist has to rate some hundred precursors of several generations. He can make a few hardcopies of the most significant results or finally get a plotted output of all proposals with references. He can also save the synthesis tree in a file and continue his work at a later time.

Why is this an expert system? Is'nt it just a substructure search system ? To answer these questions we have to look closer at the knowledge represented in a transform.

The main key for a transform is a substructure i.e. a pattern of a few atoms and bonds. This would be sufficient for a reaction retrieval system. But our transforms are similar to subroutines, they contain also reasoning and decisions about the scope and limitations of a reaction. This is the specific expert knowledge for each reaction. It is represented in a special programming language ALCHEM, that permits to use expressions like ATOM, BOND, RING, ALPHA, BETA, CIS, TRANS, STEREOCENTER and so on.

The program statements are qualifiers that determine if the reaction is useful, uncertain or useless with respect to molecular constraints. They deal with the reaction conditions and make a rough prediction of the yield. Such a transform is typically 1 page of references and 2 pages of qualifier statements.

How is the transform library built and maintained? At the beginning we could incorporate the classical knowledge from collective textbooks. Our lab chemists extracted the relevant constraints and representative examples. The programming in ALCHEM was done by a few specialists using the text editor, compiling, testing, documenting as usual.

Later on we had to scan the current chemical journals to cover the modern methods and to update the classical reactions.

This is done in the following manner. First we have to check if a so called "novel" reaction is new for our transform library or if it is a variation of an already existing transform. This is simply done by PROCESSing an example from the publication.

To facilitate the generation of transforms we can use a sort of preprocessor. It permits to draw the reaction graphically. It asks for the expert knowledge in a dialog. From those informations it creates the transform. However, some complex qualifiers have to be added with the editor.

Today several lab chemists are directly submitting new reactions from the current chemical literature with that procedure.

Let's summarize what computer assisted synthesis planning can do for the chemist. Without it he has to go to the library and try to figure out how syntheses of similar compounds were carried out in the past. Another way is to combine the reactions he knows from his personal experience. The library work is tedious because there is no general way of classification of reactions and chemical structures, there is no index for structural formula except for molecular formula. Chemical nomenclature can be used in different ways.

The synthesis planning program knows many times more reactions than the chemist. It is unbiased and can generate new proposals that have never been carried out so far but are reasonable according to the expert knowledge. While rating the proposals he encounters many reactions he did not know and because he has to make a selection he is forced to judge them.

Finally some remarks about the history of computer assisted synthesis planning. In 1967 Corey and Wipke had the first program at Harvard University already with all graphics capabilities. Shortly after the first publication other groups followed at several universities. The chemical industry was interested but soon figured out that an expert library of chemical reactions is very labor intensive. Our company and other european companies decided to collaborate and started with Wipke's SECS program. We are exchanging regularly within our group. Another group of companies is working with Corey's LHASA program. The elegant graphical handling of chemical structures in those programs influenced many other scientific applications.

ARTIFICIAL INTELLIGENCE: Towards Practical Application
T. Bernold and G. Albers (editors)
Elsevier Science Publishers B.V. (North-Holland)

A CASE STUDY OF THE DIPMETER ADVISOR DEVELOPMENT

Robert L. Langley

Etudes et Production Schlumberger
Montrouge
France

The Dipmeter Advisor as a case study was presented by Smith and Baker (1) at the Seventh International Joint Conference on Artificial Intelligence in August 1983. This discussion follows a similar format of Smith and Baker, and it is an update of that work based on our experience with the program since the transfer from research to engineering in January 1983.

INTRODUCTION

The Dipmeter Advisor project was started at Schlumberger Doll research in 1987. During the second half of 1982, the Dipmeter Advisor program was rewritten on the XEROX 1100 (Dolphin) and the Dolphin based version of the program was transfered from Schlumberger Doll Research to Schlumberger Interpretation Engineering for testing and evaluation. A six month engineering evaluation was begun in January 1983 to determine to what extent the program could be used to meet the needs of the field organization. Since August 1983 the system has been undergoing modifications by engineering (Etudes et Production Schlumberger near Paris, France) as a final preparation for release to selected field test sites for a more complete evaluation.

THE PROBLEM

Making measurements inside the borehole is one of the main services that Schlumberger provides to the oil industry. In a wireline logging operation a number of logging tools are lowered into the well drilled by the oil company client. Computerized surface equipment record the data from the logging tool as the "sonde" (measurement section) is moved past the geological formations penetrated by the drill bit. A wide variety of logging tools are lowered into a wellbore to obtain the information needed by the oil company client. One such logging tool is the dipmeter which makes micro-conductivity measurements simultaneously around the wellbore from electrodes that are on four pads that are 90 degrees apart. With modern Schlumberger dipmeter tools, vertical data samplings are made only 0.1 inch apart and they raw data are recorded on magnetic tape for subsiquent processing and analysis. "Dip" or tilt of the various formations penetrated by the borehole is computed by combining inclination, orientation and caliper measurements with displacements computed from correlations of the variations in conductivity measurement from each of the pad electrodes.

Figure 1 from (2) shows the lower portion of a dipmeter sonde containing the caliper section and measurements sensors. The caliper arms press the sonde electrodes against the wellbore wall during the axquisition of the data needed to compute the dip of the formations penetrated by the drill bit. Analysis of processed dipmeter provides information as to the location and the geometry of the hydrocarbon "traps".

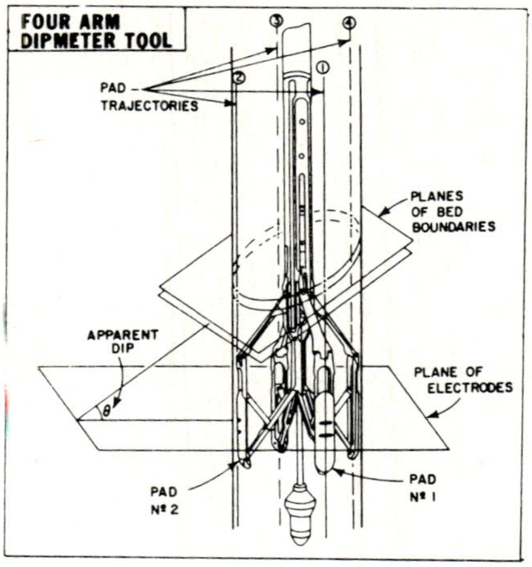

Figure 1 after Gilreath 1976

Figure 2 shows the arrow (tadpole plot made from the computer processed raw data for analysis by a dipmeter interpreter. On an arrow plot the dip magnitude and azimuth are represented as a "tacpole".

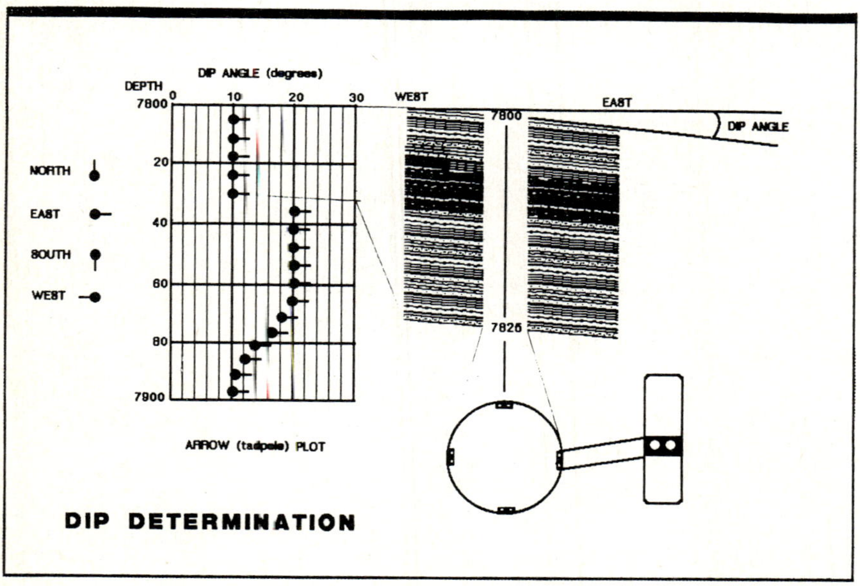

Figure 2

The interpretation of the processed dipmeter data is a highly skilled art and only a few have the skills necessary to do the job well. The Dipmeter Advisor is an attempt by Schlumberger to develop a system to address the problem of dipmeter interpretation.

THE DIPMETER ADVISOR SYSTEM

The system is made up of our central components: (i) a number of production rules partitioned into sets according to function: (ii) an inference engine that applies rules in a forward-chained manner; (iii) a set of feature detection algorithms that examine dipmeter and other log data; and (iv) a menu driven graphical user interface that provide features such as smooth scrolling of log data and user directed data manipulation capabilities.

Conclusions are stored as instances of one of 65 token types, with approximately 5 features/token, on a blackboard that is partitioned into 15 layers of abstraction. There are 90 rules and the rule language uses 30 predicates and functions. The rules have the familiar empirical association flavor. A sample is shown below.

IF:

- there exists a delta-dominated, continental-shelf marine zone, and
- there exists a sand zone intersecting the marine zone, and
- there exists a blue pattern within the intersection

THEN:

- assert a distributary fan zone

  top - top of blue pattern

  bottom - bottom of blue pattern

  flow - azimuth of blue pattern

To facilitate the interpretation process, interpreters group dips into patterns (figure 3 from Gilreath and Maricelli (3).

GREEN PATTERNS: The dip is constant with changing depth. Green patterns often reflect structure.

RED PATTERNS: Dips whose magnitude increase with increasing depth. Such patterns are usually the result of deposition on a sloping surface, hence the alternate name "slope pattern".

BLUE PATTERN: Dips whose magnitudes decrease with increasing depth. These patterns are often termed current bedding because of their association with deposition by river or ocean currents.

Feature detection algorithms are used to identify red, blue and green tadpole patterns for association with gedlogic features in the rule application phases.

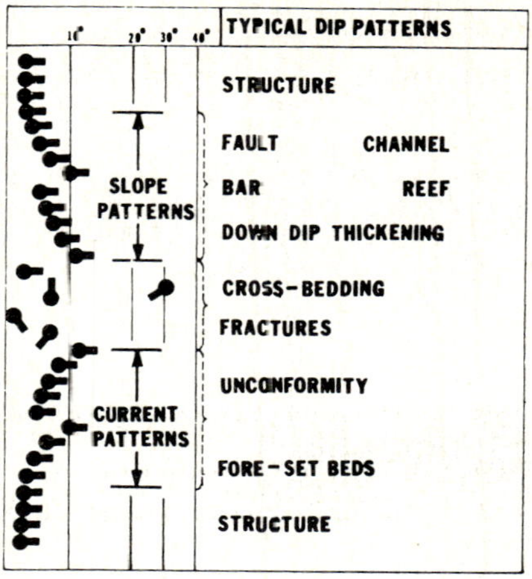

Figure 3 after Gilreath 1964

The functionality of the graphical interface is illustrated by figure 4 showing the Dipmeter Advisor screen during a processing session. Conclusions from the processing are shown in the form of tokens in the lower left portion of the screen. The tokens can be expanded to provide additional information about the conclusions in the form of smaller windows or shading of data on the screen. At the end of each phase the user can add to, modify, or delete conclusions reached by the program before going to the next step (phase). The Options menu provide facilities for making Azimuth-Histograms or other types of data enhancements to aid in the interpretation.

After the user is satisfied with the conclusions from a phase, the Exit Phase option is chosen and then the Available Phase menu (figure 5) becomes available to the user. The 11 available phases direct the user in a logical sequence that leads to an interpretation of the data. The following is a description of the phases that are now in the system.

INITIAL EXAMINATION: The user can examine the available data and formulate his ideas and overall impressions before any processing is started.

VALIDITY CHECK: Zones where the data may be questionable are identified during this phase.

LITHOLOGY DETERMINATION: The program identifies lithology by using cutoff values on a lithology indicator curve.

GREEN PATTERN DETECTION: This is the first step in the structural interpretation. In this step tadpoles are identified that have similar dip magnitude and azimuth over an interval.

STRUCTURAL DIP ANALYSIS: The green patterns identified in the previous step are filtered and merged to determine intervals of constant structural dip.

PRELIMINARY STRUCTURAL ANALYSIS: Rules are applied in zones where changes in structural dip are occuring to identify structural features (e.g. faults).

STRUCTURAL PATTERN DETECTION: To further characterize structural features, the system examines the dipmeter data for red and blue patterns near the features.

FINAL STRUCTURAL ANALYSIS: The system applies a set of rules that combines information from previous phases to refine its conclusions about structural features (e.g. strike and type of faults).

DEPOSITIONAL ENVIRONMENT ANALYSIS: The system applies a set of rules that draws conclusions about the depositional environment. For example, if told by the human interpreter that the depositional environment is marine, the system attempts to infer the water depth at the time of deposition.

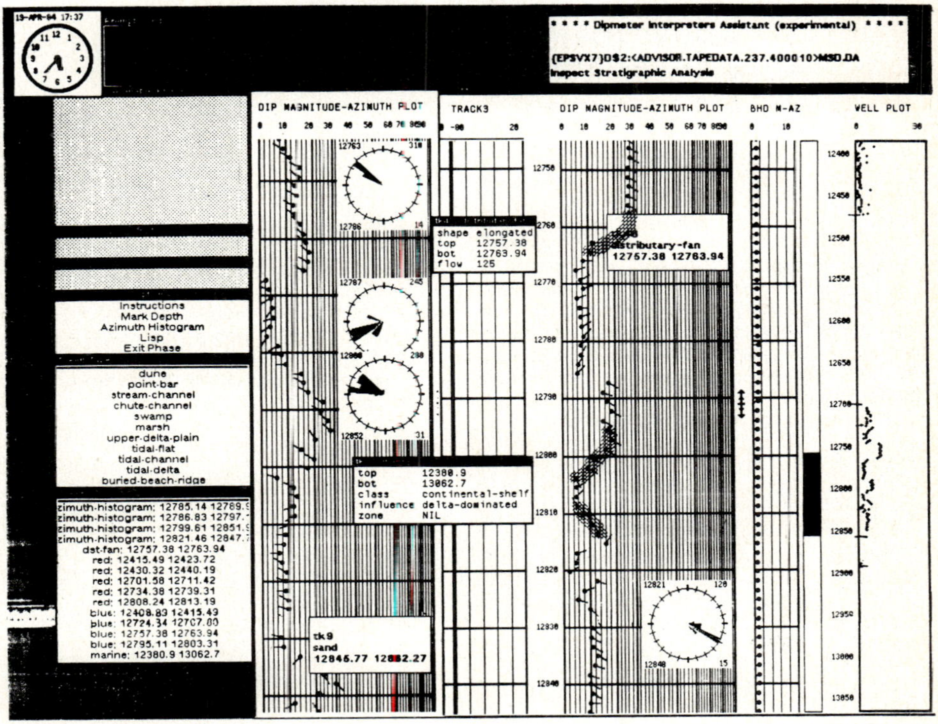

Figure 4

STRATIGRAPHIC PATTERN DETECTION: The system examines the dipmeter data for red, blue and green pattern in intervals where the depositional environment has been identified.

STRATIGRAPHIC ANALYSIS: Conclusions from the three previous phases are used to arrive at an interpretation of the stratigraphic features.

In the present system four phases use "rules" written on the basis of the interactions with the expert interpreter. The remaining phases do not use rules, but utilize more conventional algorithmic components.

Available Phases

End Session
Initial Examination
Validity Analysis
Lithology Analysis
Green Patterns
Structural Dip Analysis
Preliminary Structural Analysis
Structural Patterns
Final Structural Analysis
Depositional Environment Analysis
Stratigraphic Patterns
Stratigraphic Analysis

Figure 5

ENGINEERING EVALUATION OF DIPMETER ADVISOR

The engineering evaluation of the system was done during the first six months of 1983. It was realized that answers obtained from the interpretation of dipmeter data are often expressed in non-quantitative terms and there are often disagreement even among the experts. This led to the question at the beginning of the evaluation as to how the answers from the Dipmeter Advisor should be evaluated. The problem of answer variability, and other questions relating to interpretation procedures, how other (non-dipmeter) data was used in the interpretation, experience factors, etc., led to the conclusion that the dipmeter interpretation specialists themselves should be an important part of the evaluation. As a result, the evaluation was not just of the Dipmeter Advisor, but was also of dipmeter interpretation within Schlumberger.

The evaluation of the system by engineering revealed the following (i) dipmeter interpreters are in real need of a flexible system for interactive data manipulation such as the one in the Dipmeter Advisor; (ii) the production rules in the system are difficult to evaluate, even by dipmeter interpretation experts, without actually trying the rules on their data; (iii) and knowledge from multiple dipmeter experts and experts from other disciplines such as geology are important for further development of the system.

ENGINEERING DEVELOPMENT

The main (short term) effort in the development of the "engineering prototype" Dipmeter Advisor has been directed toward adding additional non-AI graphics data manipulation facilities that are useful to the dipmeter interpreter. The improved graphics for the system developed in engineering along with the remainder of the system developed by Schlumberger Doll Research are currently being installed in selected field test sites where a more complete evaluation of the AI part of the system will be done by "local experts".

THE FUTURE

The engineering Dipmeter Advisor development is being done at a time when improved borehole data acquisition hardware tools are greatly increasing the amount and the quality of the data that is useful in providing geological interpretations to our clients. Future (long range) developments of the system will be directed toward: (i) including new knowledge about dipmeter interpretation gained from our experience with new borehole data acquisition hardware; (ii) and merging of the Dipmeter Advisor System into a more comprehensive geological interpretation scheme now being called the Geological Advisor. The Geological Advisor will also have as inputs other Schlumberger AI systems such as LITHO.

ACKNOWLEDGMENTS: The initial design and development of the current graphics for the Engineering version of the Dipmeter Advisor was done by Bob Young (now at SDR). Graphics software developed at SDR by Tony Passera provided a good starting point during this development. The porting of the Dipmeter Advisor to the current system by Reid Smith at SDR was a major step in the realization of a field version of the system. Reid continues to provide valuable support to the project. Jose Lun (EPS Interpretation Engineering) is developing software improvements for the system as the needs are identified during evaluation. Al Gilreath (the initial expert) and several other dipmeter experts have contributed greatly during the engineering evaluation.

REFERENCES

(1) R.G. Smith and J.D. Baker, The Dipmeter Advisor System: A Case Study in Commercial Expert System Development. "Proceedings of the Eigth International Joint Conference on Artificial Intelligence, IJCAI, August 1983, pp. 122-129.

(2) J.A. Gilreath, The Dipmeter, Schlumberger Publication C-12000, 1976

(3) J.A. Gilreath and J.J. Maricelli, Detailed Stratigraphic Control Through Dip Computations. The Bulletin of the American Association of Petroleum Geologists, Vol 48, No. 12, Dec. 1964 pp. 1902-1910.

ARTIFICIAL INTELLIGENCE: Towards Practical Application
T. Bernold and G. Albers (editors)
Elsevier Science Publishers B.V. (North-Holland)

FF: A NIXDORF EXPERT SYSTEM FOR FAULT-FINDING AND REPAIR PLANNING - AN OUTLINE DESCRIPTION

Stuart E. Savory

Department E05
Nixdorf Computer AG
Paderborn
Federal Republic of Germany

The purpose of this paper is to describe the pragmatic NIXDORF expert system (FF) for general purpose diagnoses as used with a knowledge base for troubleshooting the NIXDORF 8832 fault-tolerant computer in a commercial online environment and generating corresponding repair plans which do not endanger the running fault-tolerant system. The repair plans are automatically tailored to the capabilities of the person performing the repair, and provide natural language output via self-contained automatic translation into different languages (eg: english and german).

INTRODUCTION

The Nixdorf Fault-Finder (FF) is a very simple Expert System shell, using a directed graph to represent the dependencies between classes of (hardware) faults and their causes. An optional database of constructional dependencies also enables the completely automatic generation or repair instructions (for the hardware) once a fault has been localised. Multiple simultaneous faults are covered by the model, as are mixed-initiative dialogues. Elementary graphics outputs are also provided, to shorten the amount of explanatory text needed. The shell also supports dialogues in multiple languages. (e.g. english and german).

FF thus enables the user to make consistent, thorough, fully-documented, consequent analyses of all faults occurring in the device(s) described in the knowledge base(s) attached to FF. The FF shell is independant of the knowledge-base and is thus re-usable. It is the task of the expert to declare the particular knowledge which is interpreted by the FF shell.

The performance, quality and accuracy of the expert system depends solely on the quality and accuracy of the knowledge provided by the expert. The shell itself drives a user interace which has been deliverately kept very simple, both to make it easier for the casual user to use and learn, and also to ensure its portability between knowledge bases. With minor adaptations it even supports spoken output (via linear prodictive coding), and inputs via single keystrokes, thus enabling a simple pusbutton telephone to be used to provide remote access to the knowledge base. A special interface allows one to generate a full and consistant narrative documentation of the knowledge base. After (or instead of) a consultation, one just types in the command"document".

The expert system is based on ideas developed at SRI (/GAS 81/) and at Imperial College (/HAM 82/), which I expanded and implemented to provide the functioning expert system described herein.

USERS-VIEW OF THE FAULT-FINDER

This section describes the user interface to the FF fault-finder system. The FF expert-system is a method of helping you (the user) to find faults in any chosen system. It consists of two parts.

The first, and most obvious part is the knowledge base, which knows about the faults in the particular device you are going to diagnose. This knowledge base has been built up by an expert in the domain of this particular problem. Thus it is as if you had that expert at your beck and call to help you analyse the faults any time you need help.

The second and less obvious part is the socalled Expert System Shell (XPS). This is the "thinking" and "explaining" machine which interprets the knowledge base provided by the expert, and which controls the dialog of the expert system with you, the user.
This Shell has the great advantage of re-usablility. It is independent of the particular knowledge base and problem that you are analysing. This means that once you have learnt how to use this dialogue interface, you can use it to analyse any problem for which experts have provided a knowledge base.

This paper outlines this Shell and is thus independent of any particular knowledge base. However, for the purpose of having examples which can be widely understood, most of the examples will be from a very small and simple knowledge base about the Nixdorf 8832 fault-tolerant computer which is where Nixdorf have put the system to practical use.

As a user, you can also use FF as a training tool for the problem-domains described in the available knowledge bases. You can do this simply by stepping through simulated case studies of your choice whilst using the experts system's explanation facilities as a teaching aid. Alternatively, the "document" interface allows you to generate a full and consistant narrative documentation of the knowledge base.

1. The Expert System driven Dialog

The expert has constructed the knowledge base into a tree (or bush) of interrelated faults distinguishable by symptoms at each branching point. An example tree is shown below.

```
                         TOPFAULT

         -----------------------------------------------
      A         B        C                D          E
   ---|---   ---|---                 -----|-----

  A1   A2   B1   B2                       D1        D2
               ----|----           ----|----------

            B21    B22             D11 D12 D13 D14
                                   -----|-----

                                   D121   D122
```

When you start the consultation, the FF system will identify itself first. (This is to enable the knowledge engineer to cure any bugs in the expert system by knowing which version you are using).

The expert system will then ask you whether the symptom for the top fault is present. You may answer "yes" or "no". The FF system will then analyse each fault (in the example above named A through E) in turn to remove all your help (to collect data, or perform an action) it will ask you a question, or describe an action for you to present, FF will descend in the tree, analysing faults on the faulty branch recursively.

The expert system is delivered with a simple knowledge base for you to experiment with whilst learning the user interface.

If this were all there were to FF, it would hardly deserve the name "expert-system". However, we have provided a number of other facilities in the dialogue to help you. These are described below, and include:

- The ability to ask "why" if you don't understand.
- The ability to ask for a "status" report.
- The ability to ask for "help" if you get lost.
- The ability to give the system a "hint" to change its focus or context.
- The ability to input in different languages (english, german, etc.).
- The ability to provide synonyms as answers.
- The ability to ask what "answers" are possible.
- The ability to preview the "causes" of any fault.
- Automatically generated narrative knowledge base documentation.
- Elementary graphics output for simple sketches.
- Analytic summaries of all runs of FF.

You can ask any of these questions at any time before continuing the dialog. The way in which you, the user, can interrupt the system's question-posing and take control of the dialog in order to pose questions of your own is described below. Although there may appear to be a lot of functions available at first sight. I have nevertheless kept this interface quite simple to make it easy for you to learn how to use it.

2. Explanation Functions

2.1 Help

If you can't remember what the ansers are that the XPS system expects from you, just type in the word "help" in reply to any question. The XPS will then display to you your options, together with their abbreviations and alternative spellings etc. (c.f. Alias below), and will then repeat the question (thus you never have to remember what the original question was).

You don't have to type in a particular reserved word each time, since they mostly have alias values (e.g. instead of "yes", you may type just "y" etc. You can get a list of all alia by typing in "help" as described above.

2.2 Why

If you don't understand why the XPS is asking you a particular question, just answer the question with the word "why". The XPS will then give you an appropriate answer depending on the context of the dialogue. After the XPS has provided an explanation, it will repeat the original question, so that you don't have to remember what the question was. If you need further explanations, continue answering with "why", and you will get different explanations due to the changing contexts, since the explanations refer to the last fault mentioned in the previous explanatory text. Finally the XPS will say that it has no further explanation to offer since its repertoire is exhausted. At this point you should answer the (re-asked) original question.

2.3 Status

At any time you can ask the XPS what the current status of its knowledge is, i.e. which faults have been corrected or are incorrigable, or are known to exist, or are still unanalysed. You can do this by simply asking for the "status" as your answer to any question.

2.4. Answers

At any time you can ask what the possible indivisible faults are that the knowledge base knows about. To do this you just ask for the "answers". All faults which cannot be broken down into finer detail will then be listed out.

2.5 Causes

At any time that the system asks you a question, and you are not quite sure of where it is trying to get to, you can ask it what the causes of the fault are, whose symptom you are being asked about. You can do this just by typing in the word "causes". If there are no further causes, because the question refers to an indivisible fault that you can repair, the system will say so. If on the other hand there are one or more causes of the (logical) fault, or there are multiple choice answers to a test question, then the system will list them out for you. This is to help you to have a better understanding of the structure of the knowledge in the system. Subsequently the system will repeat the current question for you.

3. User Initiatives

Normally the XPS makes consistent, thorough, fully-documented, consequent analyses of all faults occurring in the device(s) described in the attached knowledge base, by tracing through ALL of the possible faults with the dialogue driven by the XPS. However, in order to speed the analysis of single-fault problems, or of high-priority faults, it is possible for you to take the initiative in the dialog by using the function "hint" as described below.

3.1 Hint

Normally the XPS makes consistent, thorough, fully-documented, consequent analyses of all faults occuring in the device(s) described in the attached knowledge base, by tracing through ALL of the possible faults, with the dialogue driven by the XPS. However, you may have a flash of inspiration and realise what the most likely cause of the problem is. You can then take over control of the dialog by typing "hint". The XPS then lists out the possible basic faults, together with their abbreviations, and asks you which fault you believe is the cause of the problem. You may then state (the abbreviation for) your belief, and will be instructed how to correct it. Next, the system will check whether the top-fault has now also been repaired (i.e. that the repaired fault was the only one present) by enquiring about the top-fault. If this is also now repaired then the XPS can abort the consultation successfully, otherwise the XPS continues with the thorough and complete multi-fault analysis.

4. Constructional knowledge base for Repairs

The knowledge base to enable repairs to be made holds constructional, relational and generic data about the system to be repaired. The knowledge is declared as PROLOG clauses, being divided into the nine types shown and explained below (for electromechanical devices only). This first example list is in alphabetical rather than logical order:

```
cable (rpc-cable, smc-drive, smc-rpc-panel, smc-rpc-slot).
clamped (rpc-cable).
holds (safety-detents, smc-crive).
is-a-sort-of (smc-drive, telescope-mounted).
is-safe (screwed-cable).
makes-safe (mains-switch, rear, mains-cable).
obstructs (smc-drive, rear, rear-door).
opening-tool (door, a-key, unlock).
posn (rpc-cable, upper-left, left, peripherals-chassis).
```

4.1 Generic knowledge

Generic knowledge is independant of any particular piece of hardware, that is, it can be regarded as being generally true. Nevertheless, the delaration of the name of a particular generic object (class of object-types) has the effect of "reserving" that name and assigning it a very specific meaning. The class name must be unique within the knowledge base.

The two predicates currently used are shown in the example below. The predicate name states the implied action, i.e. open or close. The first parameter names the generic object type (e.g. the class of doors). The second parameter names the tool used to perform the action on the named object class. If the tool is declared as "your-hand" then it will be automatically omitted from generated instructions. The third parameter is the imperative form of the particular verb used with the tool on the object, and replaces the generalised notion of open/close.

Examples:

```
opening-tool (door, a-key, unlock).
closing-tool (switch, your-hand, switch-on).
```

It is necessary to separate opening-from closing-tool for the same object because the tool may be different (e.g. something may be unglued using a solvent, and reglued using a glue), and the verb will most certainly be different (e.g. switch-off vs. switch-on).

4.2 Assignment to generic classes

Having generic classes of objects as described above is not sufficient, each specific object must be associated with its generic type (class name).

Examples:

```
is-a-sort-of (main-switch, switch).
is-a-sort-of (smc-drive, telescope-mounted).
```

The first parameter is the specific object name, and the second parameter is the name of the generic class of the object-type as described in the previous section. The specific object name must be unique within the knowledge base. If the object is a replacable one (FRU) then the name must be the same name as is used for the type two fault in the diagnostic part of the knowledge base.

4.3 Device specific relationship

This kind of knowledge is specific to a particular device. The particular device in these esamples is the Nixdorf 8832 computer system. This may be regarded as typical for the class of electromechanical devices.

The first predicate defines the position of a specific object. Its first parameter is the name of the specific object. The fourth parameter names a more global object, generally the container of the current object, which is used as a positional frame of reference to describe the position. This frame of reference is regarded as generally being three dimensional, and cubelike, with six sides (top, bottom, left, right, front, rear). The side permitting access to the specific object is named as the third parameter. This side in turn is regarded as being a twodimensional plane which is subdivided into nine regions like a tic-tac-toe board.

	left	middle	right
upper	ul	um	ur
centre	cl	c	cr
lower	ll	lm	lr

The particular region of these nine in which the specific object is positioned is described in the second parameter. The example below states that the repeater cable is positioned in the upper left corner of the left side of the peripherals chassis.

Example:

```
posn(rpc-cable, upper-left, left, peripherals-chassis).
```

The concept of position of an object does not bear up for connections such as electrical cables which however can be positionally defined by the positions of their ends. The predicate "cable" is used here. The first parameter is the unique name of the specific cable. The second parameter is the name of the FRU to which the cable is attached. The third parameter is the name of an object at one end of the cable, and the fourth parameter is the name of the object at the other end.

Example:

```
cable (rpc-cable, smc-drive, smc-rpc-panel, smc-rpc-slot).
```

If the cable is not merely attached at its ends, but is also clamped along the cable-run, then this is declared as follows:

Example:

```
clamped (rpc-cable).
```

Any particular FRU is usually also attached mechanically to its container. This case is covered by the opening- and closing-tool predicates. In the case where there are multiple movable attachements (e.g. telescoped mounts) each part holding the FRU and preventing its release must be declared. In the case of telescoped mounts the FRU also holds itself as shown in the example below. The first parameter is the name of the retention mechanism, and the second is the name of the retained FRU.

Similarly if access to a FRU is obstructed then this is declared as shown below, where the first parameter is the name of the obstructed FRU, the third parameter names the obstructins object, and the second parameter states which side of the obstructing object is relevant.

Example:

obstructs (smc-drive, rear, rear-door)

The penultimate set of predicates are related to safety aspects which are relevant during repairs. If an object has to be made safe in order that work may proceed beyond accessing it, then the necessary declaration is as shown below. The first parameter is the name of the mechanism which removes the danger. The second parameter states on which side of its container it may be found. The third parameter is the name of the dangerous object. If an object is intrinsically safe, but is not free-standing, then this is declared in the "is-safe" predicate.

Examples:

is-safe (screwed-cable)
makes-safe (mains-switch, front, mains-switch)
makes-safe (mains-switch, rear, mains-cable)

Finally, a bilingual phrase dictionary and language dependant grammar generators enable the fully automatic translation of repair plans from english (as used above) to other languages (e.g. german). This paper shows both, enabling one to judge the quality of the syntagen translator (correct and adequate translations, but in a rather boring style).

5. Automatic documentation of the knowledge base

All knowledge bases can now generate their own narrative documentation tracing all paths through the knowledge. Thus you do not ever need to document a knowledge base by hand any more. To generate the documentation, after a consultation you just type in:-

:-document.

Note that each rule (fault) in the knowledge base now should contain an "author" statement. This lets you and the automatic documentation, keep track of who wrote each rule and when, so that if there is later a problem in the KB then you know which expert to ask about it. The format is demonstrated as the examples later in this paper.

It is also possible to get a narrative documentation of a fault and its causes when online, by typing in as shown in this example:-

:-doc (<fault-abbreviation>)

You can also look at the repair plan generated for a FRU object thus:-

:-repair (<object name>).

Automatically generated narrative KB documentation

This knowledge base documents how to find faults in the system 8832. Its texts are in english. The knowledge base is organised into a tree of faults. The top fault of the tree is stated to be:- the 8832 has a defect.

The problem, the 8832 has a defect, is a logical one, which is abbreviated internally as :- sysdef. The knowledge about it was entered by :- Savory e05 tel 109 830911 1041. The corresponding symptom is determined by asking the question:- Are all of the 8832 currently working properly? If this is the first time the question is asked, then the user is told the following thing:-
Hallo, I am a symbiotic expert system whose knowledge base can assist you to track down faults in the Nixdorf 8832.

However, I can only trace the logic of the system, and so I need you to help me by answering things which I cannot determine alone, performing tests for me, and doing any simple repairs.
I will be able to help you by explaining exactly which repairs are needed, and telling you how they should be done.

Let us begin now :-

If the answer to the question is "n" then the problem is present.

The possible causes of the problem are as follows:-
    the peripherals chassis contents are suspect
    the electronics chassis contents are suspect.

The problem, the peripherals chassis contents are suspect, is a (multiple choice) testable one, which is abbreviated internally as :- p-ch. The knowledge about it was entered by :- Savory e05 tel 109 830911 1041.

If the answer to the question is "y" then the problem is present. The instructions given to the user are as follows :-

The diagnostic file contains records in this format :-

```
+---------------------------------+
| L |   |   | E | D | S | A | A |
| E | D | T | R | E | O | D | D |
| N | A | I | R | V | U | D | D |
| G | T | M | N | I | R | R | R |
| T | E | E | U | C | C | O | O |
| H |   |   | M | E | E | 1 | 2 |
+---------------------------------+
```

Look at the Device Field of the most recent record therein. If the problem is in the peripherals chassis then this field contains one of :- mp1, mp2,smc, sdr, dap, mkd.

The multiple choice question for the test is : - What value is it? The possible answers to the question are : - mp1 mp2 smc sdr dap mkd

If the answer to the question is mp1, then the possible causes are :-
disc 1 is suspect.

An automatically generated Repair-Plan

The following extract from a consultation session shows a typical repair plan which has been generated automatically.

Is the streamer mode cassette ok?

Using a key, unlock the front door at the centre right of the front side of the peripherals chassis. Now switch off the mains switch at the lower right of the front side of the smc drive. Using a key, unlock the rear door at the centre left of the rear side of the peripherals chassis. Now unplug the mains cable at the centre of the rear side of the smc drive. The smc drive is electrically safe now.

Using a screwdriver, unscrew the flat cable at the lower centre of the rear side of the smc drive. Now unclip the repeater cable at the top right of the rear side of the front door. Now unclamp the repeater cable at the upper left of the left side of the peripherals chassis. The smc drive is now free of cables.

Now release the safety latch at the lower left of the front side of the smc drive. Using both hands, pull out carefully the smc drive at the top of the front side of the peripherals chassis. Now press in the safety detents at the left and right of the both side of the smc drive. Be extra careful, because the smc drive is mechanically free now!

Using both hands, pull out carefully the smc drive at the top of the front side of the peripherals chassis.

Return the old smc drive to the Nixdorf Repair Centre, and replace it by a new smc drive.

Now I must ask you again : - Is the streamer mode cassette ok?
yes

The fault streamer mode cassette is defective which can cause the fault currently being investigated namely : -
the peripherals chassis contents are suspect, has been corrected.

The automatic translation of the repair plan into german delivers the following text: -

Die Streamer-mode Kassette ist defekt, dies muss repariert werden. Ein Austausch des SMC Laufwerkes ist erforderlich. Sie finden diesen Teil oben an der vorderen Seite des Peripherie-Chassis.

Nehmen Sie einen Schlüssel. Bitte die vordere Tuer aufschliessen. Bitte den SMC Hauptschalter unten rechts an der vorderen Seite des SMC Laufwerkes ausschalten. Nehmen Sie einen Schlüssel. Bitte die hintere Tuer aufschliessen. Bitte das SMC Netzkabel mitte an der hinteren Seite des SMC Laufwerkes herausziehen. Die Stromversorgung des SMC Laufwerkes ist damit abgeschaltet.

Bitte das SMC Repeater-Kabel oben rechts an der hinteren Seite der vorderen Tuer lösen. Bitte das SMC Repeater-Kabel oben links an der linken Seite des Peripherie-Chassis entklammern. Alle Kabel des SMC Laufwerkes sind jetzt entfernt.

Bitte den SMC Sicherheitsriegel unten links an der vorderen Seite des SMC Laufwerkes freimachen. Nehmen Sie beide Haende. Bitte das SMC Laufwerk vorsichtig herausziehen. Bitte die SMC Sicherheitsarretierung an den Schienen an der linken und rechten Seite des SMC Laufwerkes drücken.

Seien Sie besonders vorsichtig, weil das SMC Laufwerk sehr schwer ist. Nehmen Sie beide Hände. Bitte das SMC Laufwerk vorsichtig weiter herausziehen.

Befestigen Sie einen Begleitschein an dem alten Austauschteil. Darauf schreiben Sie den diagnostizierten Fehler : - Die Streamer-mode Kassette ist defekt. Schicken Sie die alte Einheit zurück an das Nixdorf Reparaturzentrum und ersetzen Sie diese Einheit durch eine neue.

Die Anweisungen zum Wiederzusammenbau sind: -

Nehmen Sie beide Hände. Bitte das SMC Laufwerk vorsichtig hineinschieben. Bitte die SMC Sicherheitsarretierung an den Schienen an der linken und rechten Seite des SMC Laufwerkes drücken. Nehmen Sie beide Hände. Bitte das SMC Laufwerk vorsichtig weiter hineinschieben. Bitte den SMC Sicherheitsriegel unten links an der vorderen Seite des SMC Laufwerkes befestigen. Bitte das SMC Repeater-Kabel oben rechts an der hinteren Seite der vorderen Tuer wiederanklemmen. Bitte das SMC Repeater-Kabel oben rechts an der hinteren Seite der vorderen Tür wieder befestigen. Bitte das SMC Netzkabel mitte an der hinteren Seite des SMC Laufwerkes hineinstecken. Nehmen Sie einen Schlüssel. Bitte die hintere Tür schliessen. Bitte den SMC Hauptschalter unten rechts an der vorderen Seite des SMC Laufwerkes einschalten. Nehmen Sie einen Schlüssel. Bitte die vordere Tür schliessen.

Die Reparatur ist jetzt durchgeführt.

As can be readily seen, the translation is factually correct and complete, it does however retain the same boring style of the english repair plan.

REFERENCES

GAS 81 — Gaschnig, J.
PROSPECTOR
in Infotech state-of-the-art Report 9, No. 3

HAM 82 — Hammond, P.
Logic Programming for expert systems.
M.Sc. Thesis at Imperial College, London 1982.

NOE 84 — Noelke, U. and Savory S.E.
PROLOG Systeme in Vergleich
in Angewandte Informatik 3/1984

SAV 83-1 — Savory S.E.
Das Prototyp Expertensystem von NIXDORF
Angewandte Informatik (Nov 1983)

SAV 83-2 — Savory S.E.
Expert Systems Research at NIXDORF
in Industrial Liasion Session
IJCAI-83

SAV 83-3 — Savory S.E.
A prototype Expert System
in Proceedings zum Industrieprogramm
13. Jahrestagung der Gesellschaft fuer Informatik (Oct 83)

ARTIFICIAL INTELLIGENCE: Towards Practical Application
T. Bernold and G. Albers (editors)
Elsevier Science Publishers B.V. (North-Holland)

A PROTOTYPE EXPERT SYSTEM IN P.W.R. POWER PLANT CONDUCTING

Jean-François Héry
Electricity of France
Clamart Cedex
France

WHY AN EXPERT SYSTEM IN POWER PLANT CONDUCTING?

1. Classical conduct

Today power plants are conducted according to written documents called procedures. These are series of orders to be carried out sequentially. The right procedure is chosen according to the present situation and objectives: in case of an accident, for instance, the procedure is identified through the diagnosis. Thus, procedures are an ordered representation of the knowledge about conducting.

2. Expert System knowledge base

On the contrary, we have described this same knowledge in a prototype base by the means of production rules.

Such a realization in afield that first did not seem propitious to this formalism, consisted in a double bet:

- we had to take into account some of the huge complexity of the system (a power plant);

- we had to "flatten" a most sequential and hierarchical form of knowledge into expert rules.

This bet led us to the realization of a 125 rules prototype, which describes in a satisfying way the starting sequence bringing the plant from a cold to a power state.

3. Advantages of an Expert System

An ES fits the description of the plant's states by the means of its main physical measures: this solves the problem of extra procedure situations (for instance, it may be impossible to apply the required procedure because some material is unavailable: in this case an ES can provide a solution, though the situation had not been previously planned).

An ES, thanks to its capacity of explaining the various steps of its reasonings, is well adapted to:

- computer-aided teaching in conduct. It could be used intensively as a training for the conducting staff;

- providing an aid in critical situations, for it can justify any advice it as given.

Finally, an ES, unlike a classical software, can cheaply be extended by adding new production rules. Thus, for instant, our present prototype is being extended in order to deal with accidents.

MODELIZATION

1. The plant

The representation chosen for the facts is the classical "Object-Attribute-Value" pattern. The plant is thus described in the present state of the work.

Objects	- Physical parameters (13) - Material and circuits (66).	
Attributes and values	- For parameters:	Value Final objective Current objective Various functions ....
	- For other objects:	State Position Availability .....

Let us show same examples:

OBJECT	ATTRIBUTE	VALUE
Primary pressure	Value	25
	Final objective	155
Steam Generator No.2	Availability	yes
Cooling circurit RRA	State	Isolated
RRA pump No. 1	Nature	RRA - pump

Here follow two plans among others, where are mentioned all relevant objects (i.e.; those who are described in the facts' base), as well as their lists of attributes.

2. The conduct

The behaviour of a nuclear power plant may be represented theoretically by a function

$$F\ (x_1, \ldots\ldots, x_n)$$

Where the variables x_i are the various positions of the various materials. In fact, the function F is unaccessible because of the large number of variables x_i- The only functions known are partial laws:

$$\frac{\partial F}{\partial X_i} \quad \text{or} \quad \frac{\partial^2 F}{\partial X_i \, \partial X_j}$$

We will simply call these laws. They describe the partial effects of the materials on the main physical parameters.

Let us emphasize that it was at first quite uncertain that a knowledge base limited to these partial laws would give an account of the total behaviour of the plant. We have proved this to the possible.

In order to clarify the mocel of the conduct we will divide the problem of the rules into two stages

- The "laws"
- The "restrictive rules".

a) Free conducting

If there were no limitations to the conducting of the plant, we would summarize the mental process of the conductor as the following pattern:

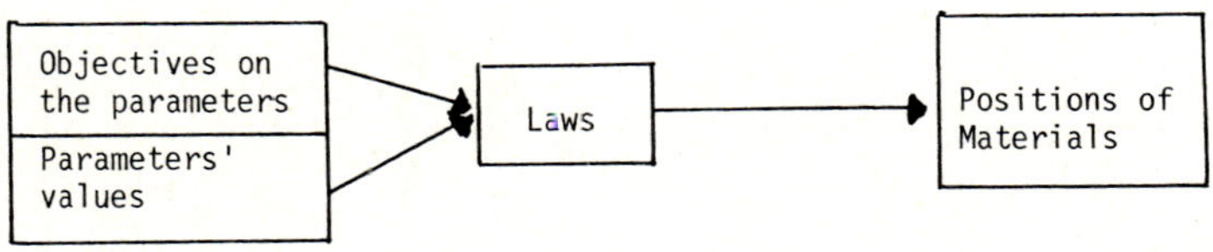

A simple comparison between the objectives and the values of parameters shows the desired tendency (plus, minus or stable). One or more laws then transform those tendencies into actions on the materials (e.g.: starting a pump, isolating a heat-exchanger, etc.). In terms of an expert system, these laws are rules, whereas objectives, values and positions of materials are facts.

Example of a law:

If Tendency (Pressurizer level) = Negative

Then State (Aspersion) --- off

b) Conducting under constraints

In practice numerous obstacles disturb the above pattern: those are technological limitations, exploiting directives, etc. We will take these obstacles into account as rules: we will call them restrictive rules.

Example of a restrictive rule:

<u>If</u> Value (Primary temperature) < 120°C

<u>Then</u> State (cooling circuit RRA) ← On
Current objective (Primary pressure) ← 25

The new rules are integrated in the pattern which becomes as follows:

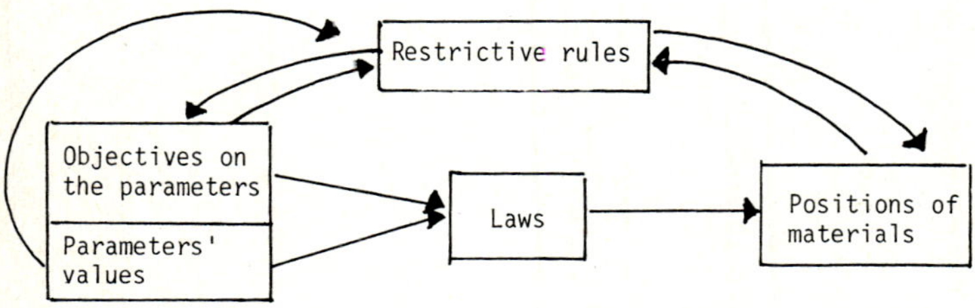

3. Inference and conduct

a) The ALOUETTE inference engine

The engine which we have used was designed in 1983 by D. Mulet-Marquis (EDF). It works in forward chaining until complete saturation of the facts' base. It handles rules in first-order logics (variables) thanks to a sophisticated combinatory management.

b) Procedure generation

In its final form, our Expert System should be coupled to a plant simulator. This coupling is due to take place in June 1984. A first operational outcome in computer-aided teaching is planned for middle-term future.

Both systems (the ES and the simulator) could then interfere to generate whole sequences of artificial piloting. The interference can be described by following diagram

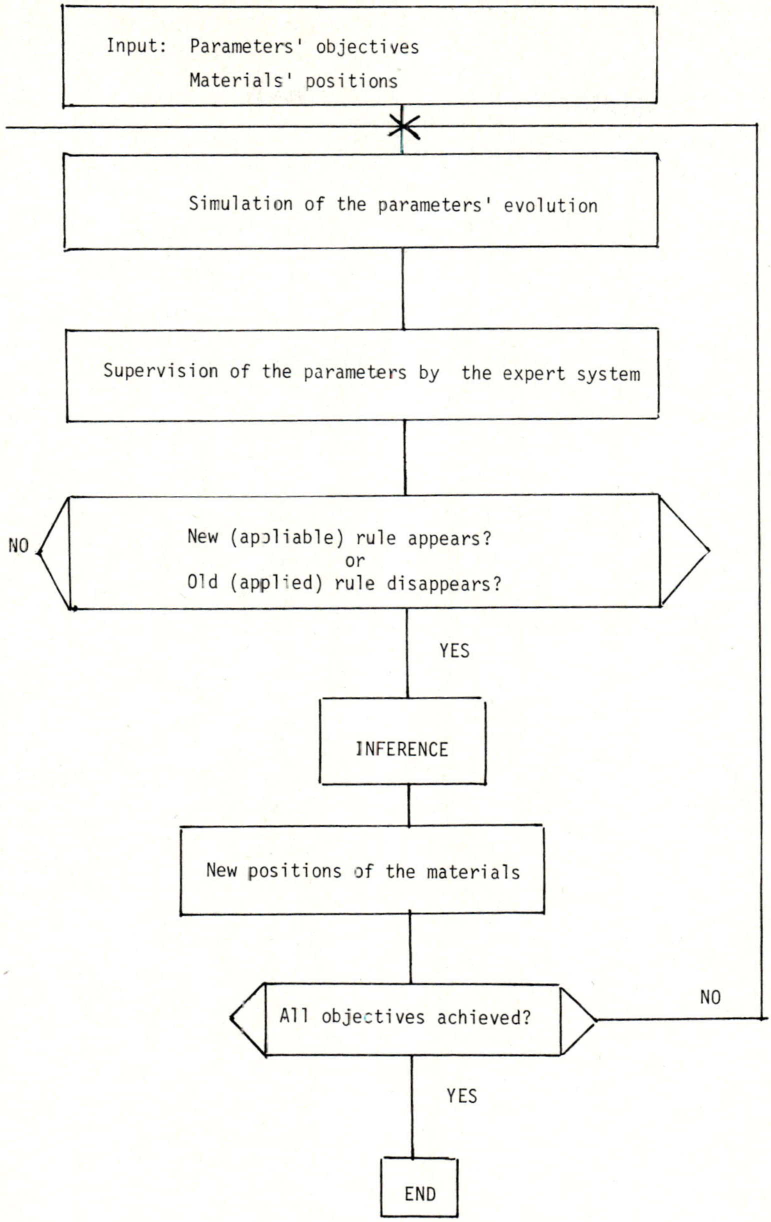

Input: Parameters' objectives
Materials' positions
Simulation of the parameters' evolution
Supervision of the parameters by the expert system
NO
New (appliable) rule appears?
or
Old (applied) rule disappears?
YES
INFERENCE
New positions of the materials
All objectives achieved?
NO
YES
END

Comments

1. Initialization

2. This is done by a simulator, not by the expert system.

3 and 4. The point is to detect whether it is relevant to start an inference, i.e. whether certain critical values are attained by the parameters, allowing new rules to be applied.

5 and 6. The inference is stared as soon as a new rule becomes appliable, or a formally applied rule becomes irrelevant. It concludes with a new configuration of the materials: this is the conducting stage, which introduces this configuration into the simulator.

7. End of the process: in the case that the given problem could be solved by applying a standard procedure, then the set of successive configurations computed by the inferences must match the very sequence ordered by this procedure.

FURTHER PROSPECTS

1. Extension of the knowledge base

Presently the prototype deals only with normal conduct. The most evident extension, and also the most useful, consists is writing accidental rules. Furthermore, the representation of the plant can be much more detailed, as well as certain subsets of procedures, which until now have been considered as a whole: connecting circuits, evaluating the reactivity level of the reactor etc.

2. Meta-rules

The size of a knowledge base related to both normal and accidental conducting leads to the introduction of meta-rules. These would handle rules' sub-bases according to the situation, emergency priorities, etc. It really seems impossible to lack meta-rules when the size of the rules' base grows up.

3. Problems of coherence

Large knowledge bases imply a control of both contradictions and loops among the rules. We are presently designing a program of detection of such irregularities. But since this detection cannot be achieved easily in a first-order logics environment, we are at the same time writing an inference engine in propositional logics.

ARTIFICIAL INTELLIGENCE: Towards Practical Application
T. Bernold and G. Albers (editors)
Elsevier Science Publishers B.V. (North-Holland)

KNOWLEDGE ENGINEERING IN CAE - FIRST INDUSTRIAL EXPERIENCES

Hubert Marchand

Battelle-Institute
(Department of Informatics)
Frankfurt
Federal Republic of Germany

This paper describes a knowledge-based system that automatically generates process plans for the manufacturing of rubber membranes. This work has been done in cooperation with a West-German manufacturer of elastomer products and is one of the first expert systems developed for industrial purposes in West-Germany. It shows the capabilities of expert systems techniques and the huge potential for AI applications in the field of manufacturing.

INTRODUCTION

It has been extensively reported about the necessity of integration of CAD, CAM and MRP (Computer-Aided Design, Computer-Aided Manufacturing and Manufacturing Resources Planning) for the factory of the future. Computer Integrated Manufacturing (CIM) is the goal to be achieved in the next ten years. However, many of the necessary requirements both at hardware and software levels are missing. Our thesis is that expert systems provide the solution for the software missing link.

Let us consider the CAD/CAM relationship and especially the process planning tasks.

Figure 1 shows the engineering activities to be integrated for preparatory purposes: production of drawing and lists of parts, production of the process plans and, eventually, of the respective NC-programs.

If we consider commercially available computer-aided process-planning systems, we see that two kinds of packages exist:

- process plan management systems, where new process plans are produced as updated copies of existing ones. These systems are only well suited to manufacturing processes with very few changes.

- variant computer-aided process planning systems, which allow to produce new plans after computation of parametric inputs of the part to be manufactured. These systems require a systematic and complete specification of the part and therefore become very rapidly too large to include all aspects of the planning process. Most of them are therefore devoted only to the calculation of the standard times.

A third approach, namely knowledge-based process plan generation, allows both comprehensive but cost-effective process planning and easy link to CAD.

DESCRIPTION OF THE SPECIFIC PROBLEMS FOR ELASTOMER PRODUCTS

Rubber membranes are used in fluidic components for separating two different media. Common applications are: pumps, relays, actuators and instruments. Most of the orders

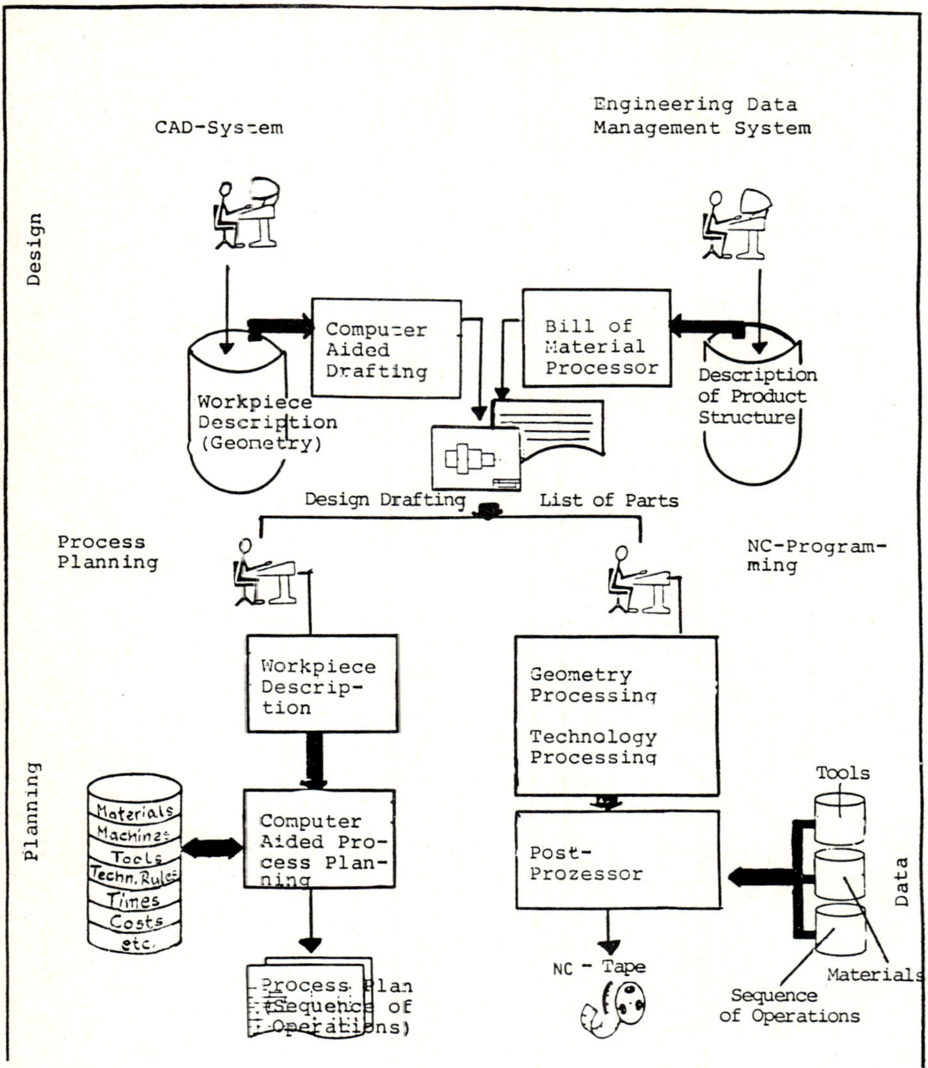

Figure 1 Computer-Aided Engineering

require a new design: starting with 4 basic forms (see figure 2), the combination of differing geometries, dimensions, materials, number of layers, types of textile layers, insertion of plastic or metal part lead to thousands of possible membranes and manufacturing processes. Besides rubber forming processes (injection, pressing, coining, stamping), different blank production processes are also to be determined according to the nature and the material of the blanks.

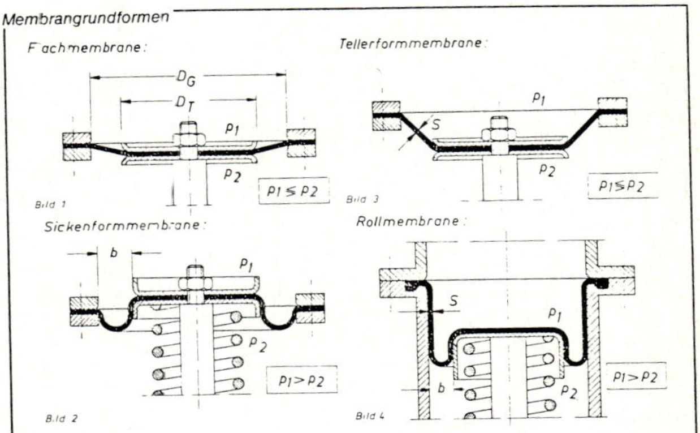

Membranform	Bild No.	Hub = $f(D_G, D_T, b)$	Druckbeaufschlagung einseitig	Druckbeaufschlagung beidseitig
Flachmembrane	1	$H = \pm 0{,}05\ D_G$		X
Sickenformmembrane	2	$H = 0{,}15\ D_G$	X	
Tellerformmembrane	3	$H = \pm 0{,}15\ D_G$		X
Rollmembrane	4	$H = \pm 0{,}85\ D_G$	X	

Figure 2: Basic forms of membranes

The work plans for the manufacturing of the membranes are normally written by technicians who receive as data a schematic representation indicating geometry, dimensions, tolerances and materials (Fig. 3).

The planner selects the appropriate rubber forming process and specifies the different blanks needed (rubber, textile, non-woven, metal, plastic, plastic sheet) and the fabrication of each blank. He then gives details of the rubber forming process (temperatures, times, pressures) and specifies any later manufacturing or inspection perations (drilling, stamping, visual inspection, etc.).

The process plan contains a sequence of manufacturing operations detailing work stations involved, dimensions, material and weight of blanks, tools and devices needed, data needed for the operation of the presses, etc.

Obviously the right choice of the process operations has a tremendous economic impact.

The main problems, the planning engineers had to face were the following:

- correctness of the process plans; in many cases this could not be achieved before tests were made at the production testing facilities and the plans reworked iteratively at the process planning department. Up to 20 iterations were sometimes required.

- quality of the process plans; as for all highly qualified tasks the quality depended a great deal from the experience of the engineer. A way to be found to make systematic use of this experience.

- improvability of the process plans: it proved necessary to develop a well-organized documentation of the reports established during the manufacturing processes and a continuous evaluation of these reports in order to integrate the observations made for better subsequent plans.

Attempts to systematize all aspects of the planning logic in form of algorithms proved not feasible: it would have led to large and complex programs, and to the well-known updating and maintenance problems. For this reason a new technique was chosen: expert systems.

THE EXPERT SYSTEM APPROACH

Let us precise the results we want to obtain: the resulting program must be able to

- determine the sequence of the manufacturing steps,
- define the blanks and their production and
- specify for each step the technical parameters (temperature, pressure, etc....).

The only input data must be

- the description of the part to be produced (geometry, tolerance etc.)
- the order quantity and the lot size.

The main difference between traditional software and expert systems is of architectural nature (fig. 4): an expert system has no fixed-coded logic, where all steps of the program are predetermined; instead it includes a knowledge base, which contains all rules necessary for the execution of the task and an inference system (in our case a deduction system) able to choose and combine the right rules until a solution to the task is produced.

Rule for deciding on the number of rubber blanks:

As a consequence the quality of the expert system depends both from the quality of the fules of the knowledge base and from the efficiency of the inference system to perform the right combination.

If both requirements are met, we achieve a program with many nice features:

- since the rules are expressed by the engineers and are used as such directly by the inference system we eliminate the "translation" problems between users and programmers

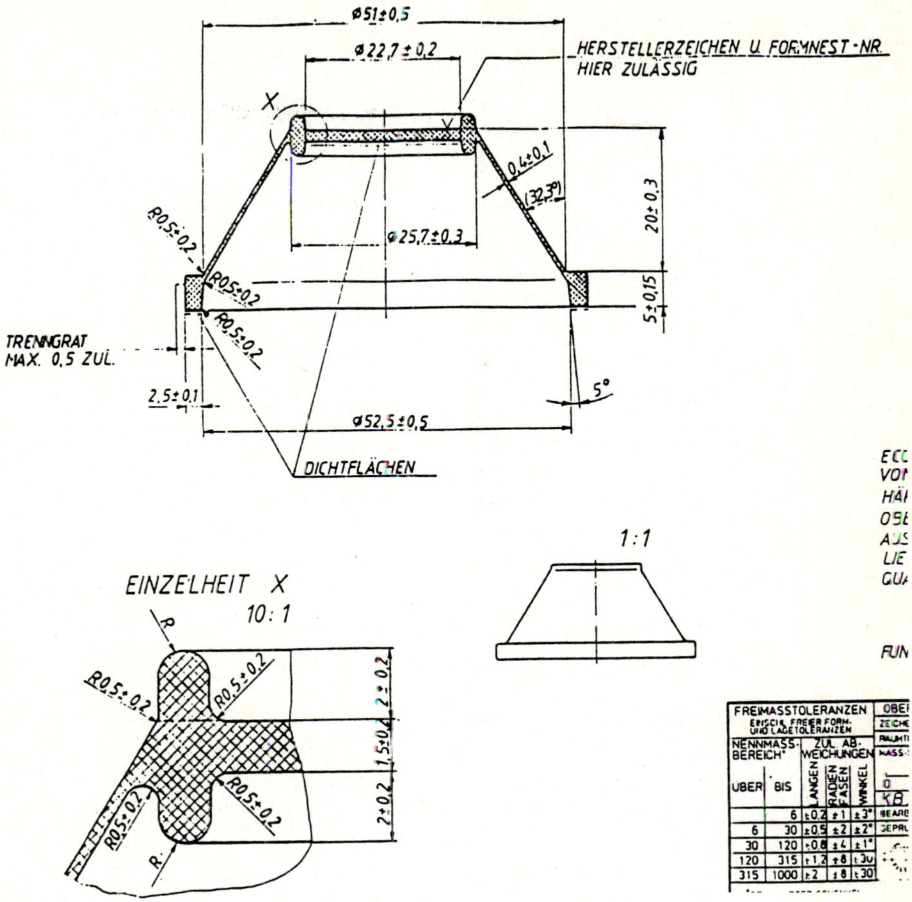

Figure 3: Geometrical input data for process planning

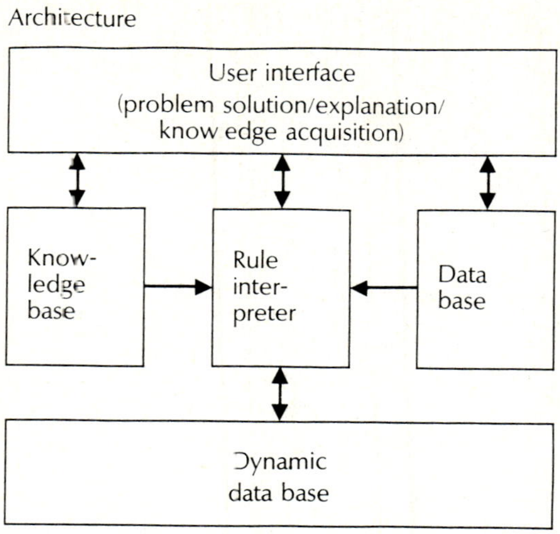

Figure 4: Architecture of expert systems

- we obtain prototypes in a short period of time, since the functions of the system can be shown independently from the amount rules. This is a good way to obtain confidence in the system from the user side

- the updating and the maintenance of the system is easy. In many cases, one needs only to add or update rules. Each rule is an independent unit without connections to others.

At present the program uses about 300 rules and produces plans for the basic membranes of the company.

Figure 5 shows two of the rules used in the system. They have in common following aspects:

- use uf concepts directly understandable by the engineer, who recognizes his knowledge in each rule and is able to correct possible errors

- IF (sequence of conditions) THEN (decision) format

- possibility to make basic arithmetics within the IF-part of a rule.

Rule for deciding on the number of rubber blanks:

IF (1) the main process is not stamping and
   (2) the main process is rot injection and
   (3) the number of layers is = 2 and
   (4) either the material of layer 2 is textile
       or the material of layer 2 is textile
THEN the number of rubber blanks is 1.

Rule for deciding on the main process:

IF (1) the thickness of the walls of the membrane is large and
   (2) the material mixture is of type M1 and
   (3) the membrane has only one layer
THEN decide as main process injection

As in R1/XCON, an expert system used by DEC for configuring computers, the rules are gathered into "contexts", which correspond to the subtasks performed by the engineer. After completion of one subtask, no revision of the decisions made within it is required. This means that, in this case we have a sequential planning system, the sequence of the contexts depending on the decisions taken within each context.

Of course this assumption may or may not apply to other manufacturing planning systems. However well-developed AI methods such as backtracking allow to cope with non-sequential processes as well.

LINKING THE CAD SYSTEM

As previously described in the rule example, expert systems use "symbolic" notation, i.e. the words used commonly by the persons involved in the task. Mathematical notation plays only a very small cole.

This leads to a problem encountered in many practical expert systems: how to let them communicate with traditional mathematically-oriented programs?

In a first version of our system no link was provided: the user had to describe the part to be produced in terms of menu-driven answers to questions asked by the program. Althrough membranes are geometrically simple parts, about 20 questions had to be answered.

Clearly this had to changed. The way choosed was to interpret the CAD files describing the part and to translate the sets of points and lines into characteristics like "the thickness of the walls of the membrane is uniform" or "the membrane is flat and circular".

All these facts are written in symbolicform into the knowledge base, so that in the present state the production of drawing and process plan is done in one step starting from the description of the part within the CAD-system and requiring no further inputs except lot size, order quently and material.

IMPLEMENTATION

Two implementations of the system have been done. The first one uses traditional hardware as existing at industrial sites: a VAX-11/780 computer running the FORTRAN CAD-program and the expert system written in PROLOG. The second implementation aimed at investigating the capabilities of special-purpose machines for expert systeme. We used a XEROX 1108 machine tailored to LISP programming. As a result we obtained a very impressive man-machine interaction at both input and output. The explanation capabilities, which are among the most useful features of expert systems, could be implemented in a straight-forward manner.

ARTIFICIAL INTELLIGENCE: Towards Practical Application
T. Bernold and G. Albers (editors)
Elsevier Science Publishers B.V. (North-Holland)

ADVANCED INFORMATION PROCESSING IN ROBOTICS

Jean-Claude Latombe

Laboratoire LIFIA
ENSIMAG
Saint-Martin d'Hères Cédex
France

Information processing is necessary to take full advantage of the flexibility provided by the actuators and the sensors of a robot. It is organized around the concept of robot programming, since its goal is both to provide a language in which the user can specify how the action and sensing functionalities of the robot are to be applied in order to execute a given task, and to interpret this language. This paper treats two aspects of information processing for robots. One concerns robot programming systems themselves: what are the different approaches? How a programming system should be architectured? The other aspect concerns the automatic generation of robot programs from CAD specifications. Although it is a long-term aspect in its whole, it helps understanding more about robot programming, and it is likely to provide new programming tools combining expressiveness and simplicity of use in the near future.

Key words: Robotics software, robot programming, automatic robot programming, Artificial Intelligence, geometrical reasoning, dealing with uncertainty.

INTRODUCTION

By definition a robot is a flexible machine:

- It is adaptable to perform a certain variety of tasks (not any) without major hardware modification. It draws this kind of flexibility mainly from the generality of both its mechanical structure and its actuators.

- It can adapt to variations of its environment with respect to a given input model. This second kind of flexibility derives from the sensory equipment of the robot which provides data on the actual environment.

Adaptability to the tasks makes it possible automating small and medium batch production. Adaptability to the environment reduces the burden put on the designer of the robot environment.

Information processing is necessary to take best advantage of these two kinds of flexibility. It is organized around the concept of robot programming, since its goal is both to provide a "language" in which the user can specify how the action and sensing functionalities of the robot are to be applied in order to execute a given task, and to interpret this language.

The definition of a robot programming system is a difficult problem for at least two reasons:

- First, it requires a deep understanding of what programming a robot is, and why a programming system is needed. Today many people still think that programming a a robot is easy, just because they make use of robots for automating simple tasks in well-engineered environments.

- Second, it requires specifying apparently contradicting requirements. On the one hand, we would like such a system being easy to use so that it can be accessible by the least sophisticated users. On the other hand, we would like it being expressive enough so that the users can describe the most complex tasks.

In this paper we focus on two aspects of information processing for robots. One concerns robot programming systems: what are the different approaches? How a programming system should be architectured? The other aspect concerns the automatic generation of robot programs from CAD specifications. Although it is a long-term aspect in its whole, it helps in understanding more about robot programming, and it is likely to provide new programming tools combining expressiveness and simplicity of use in the near future. Another important topic, which the paper does not address, is information processing for interpreting sensory data.

THE PROBLEM OF PROGRAMMING A ROBOT

Programming a robot requires to determine which actions of the robot are to be executed, which sensing is necessary, and how actions and sensing are to be embedded into an overall algorithm including conditional and loop statements, and possibly parallel processing.

This interweaves ramifications issued from two different types of problems:

1) Specifying safe positions:
A robot-manipulator is mainly a positionning device: it can move a part or a tool from one position to another. Therefore the core of robot programming is to define the sequence of positions through which the robot must pass during the execution of the task. This includes defining the positions at which parts are to be grasped and ungrasped, the position at which special-purpose end-effectors are to be operated, the trajectories to be followed by the robot, etc....

   A key difficulty in specifying positions is reachability: each position should be reachable without collision at the time it must be attained.

2) Dealing with uncertainty:
Both the environment in which the robot operates and the actions executed by the robot cannot be predicted exactly. Uncertainty is not a problem as long as it is lower than the precision requirements of the task, for instance the clearance between two parts to be assembled. However, this usually requires a carefully engineered environment.

   A general way, although not unique, to deal with uncertainty is sensory interaction. For instance, this includes inspecting and locating a part using vision, and locating two surfaces in contact using a force sensor.

Clearly these problems interact in many ways. For instance, computing safe trajectories requires to take into account uncertainty, especially in a congested environment; reciprocally choosing appropriate trajectories, for example the approach direction for mating two parts, may make the interpretation of sensory data easier if an unexpected situation occurs.

A robot program must be solution to both these problems. In addition this solution must be acceptable with respect to time and reliability considerations.

ROBOT PROGRAMMING SYSTEMS

1. Conciliating two approaches

Traditionally, one distinguishes between two different families of robot programming systems: one is based on the "teaching by showing" method, the other on textual programming.

- The "teaching by showing" method is the earliest one, and the most widespread today. Using an interactive pendant the programmer teleoperates the manipulator for performing a sample execution of the task. The motions of the joints are recorded so that they can automatically be played back later. This method is attractive both because of its immediacy and because it requires almost no specialized knowledge from the user. But it presents severe drawbacks that restrict its aplication to simple tasks: repetition of the same sequence of motions with minor changes at each iteration is fastidious to "program"; recorded "programs" are difficult to edit; sensory data cannot be used to face uncertainty of the environment; coordinating several robots is impossible.

  More recently the increasing interest in blending CAD and robot programming led to extend this method to simulated robots on a graphical display (Heginbotham, Dooner and Case 79) (Dooner, Taylor and Bonney 82) (Sata, Kimura and Amano 82) (Liegeois, Dombre and Borrel 82). Teaching by showing on graphical displays improves personnel safety. It also has the advantage over traditional teaching-by-showing systems to make it possible experimenting with different robots, different parts, and different world arrangements. However, it still suffers the limitations listed above.

- The limitations of the "teaching by showing" approach have led to the development of symbolic languages for programming robots, known as manipulator-level languages, for instance AL (Finkel et al. 74) LM (Latombe and Mazer 81) and AML (Taylor, Summers and Meyer 82). Most of them are extensions of traditional languages such as BASIC and PASCAL. They include both the main facilities of these languages and new constructs appropriate to robotics, for instance: world modelling, motion specification, and sensing. They give a large access to the basis primitives of the robot, so that they avoid most of the limitations of teaching by showing. But they are not directly usable by personnel with little programming experience. Indeed it requires clever programmers to take full advantage of all the functionalities of these languages.

For a long time these two approaches have been opposed. In fact, today they appear more and more complementary. Some commercial systems based on the teaching by showing method have been extended to incorporate some of the functionalities of textual language, for instance iterative control structure and guarded motions. On the other hand, it has been shown that implementing teaching-byshowing utilities is not only possible using textual languages, it is also very convenient (Grossman 77) (Bansard 83).

Today several robot programming systems are based on textual languages because of their expressiveness. In addition they include interactive programming environments with teaching by showing utilities and graphical facilities both for sophisticated and little experienced users (Taylor and Grossman 83) (Latombe, Laugier, Mazer and Miribel 84).

2. Functionalities of a textual programming language

Many textual languages have been developed for programming robots, including: WAVE (Paul 77), AL (Finkel et al. 74), PAL (Paul et al. 80), MAL (Gini, Gini, Gini and Giuse 79) VAL (Unimation 80), LM (Latombe and Mazer 81) (Miribel and Mazer 83), EMILY (Will and Grossman 75), AML (Taylor, Summers and Meyer 82), RAIL (Franklin and Vanderbrug 82). Some of them are commercially available today.

In addition to the traditional algorithmis facilities provided by programming languages (symbolic variables, conditional and iterative statements, input/output on files and terminals, subroutine), these languages include robot-specific constructs, which can be broadly decomposed into four classes: world modelling, specification of robot motions and operations, sensing and interaction with other devices, and flow of control. Some of these constructs are illustrated by the following program for inserting a pin into a hole:

```
function boolean INSERT (frame PIN, HOLE;
                         real FZMAX, EPS;
                         integer NMAX);
integer N; vector LATF;  frame HOLE 1;
begin
N:=0 ; HOLE1:=HOLE*translation (-vz, 10);
while N NMAX do
move PIN by transformation (PIN, HOLE1)
        until fz FZMAX;
if distance (PIN, HOLE) 1 then return (true) ;
        else
        LATF:= vector (fx, fy, 0);
        move PIN by translation (LATF, EPS):
        EPS:=EPS/2; N:=N+1;
        endif;
   enddo;
   write "INSERTION FAILED" on terminal;
   return (false);
   end;
```

A widely accepted method, although not unique, for modelling the robot environment consists in attaching cartesian frames to the object of the world and to the features of these objects. Several frames must a priori be known by the language interpreter. These frames include a fixed frame, which is to serve as the user's reference frame, and a moving frame attached to the extremity of the robot arm. In the program, the user can declare the frames he needs and define their positions by applying transforms, which may combine translations and rotations, to already known frames. A rotation and a translation can be defined using vectors.

Some languages, like AL and LM, permit the user to affix frames to other frames. Two affixed frames, remain in the same relative position in the interpreter's model of the world. If the position of one frame is known to be modified, let say by a motion statement, then the position of the other frame is automatically updated in the world model. Such a facility considerably simplifies programming when several frames are attached to an object and its features. For example, a frame F attached to an object may be convenient to define the position of the object, while other frames Fi are more suitable to model possible grasping positions of the object. If F and Fi are affixed together then they will "move together" in the world model. Affixments also allows the programmer to specify motions directly in term of the object frames (see the motions of frame PIN in the above example).

A more clever use of this facility deals with the automatic correction of the position of an object when contact information is obtained (Taylor 76).

The shape of the path for a motion can be described either in terms of joint coordinates or in terms of cartesian coordinate. The second possibility, which takes advantage of the existence of the world model, is usually the most convenient. If affixment among frames is an available facility, then each motion statement applies to the frame M which the user considers as the most appropriate to describe the motion. M must be affixed to the frame attached to the extremity of the robot arm. The final destination is defined by a frame D (for instance D may be a frame attached to an object of the world). M will coincide with D at the end of the motion. To attain this goal position, the origin of M may be translated along a straight path, and, if M and D do not have the same orientation, the axes of M may be rotated around a fixed direction. The interpreter does all the computations, involving trajectories planning and generation, and cartesian to joint coordinates transformations, and generates the servo set points (Paul 81). The user can control the speed of the motion. He also can describe non-linear trajectories by stipulating that M should traverse some intermediate positions before it reaches its final destination. More complex paths may be possible, but in general the planification of the acceleration profile of the motion requires off-line planning.

A motion may be guarded by a boolean condition involving sensory data such as exerted forces. This condition is periodically evaluated during the motion and the robot is stopped when the condition becomes true, for instance:

```
move PIN by TRANSLAT until fz FZMAX.
```

Languages like AL and PAL also include options to control both the position and the force exerted by the robot during motion, for instance:

```
move OBJECT to GOAL with force (vy)=FY.
```

Synchronization of several robots is offered in a few languages only. For instance AL includes a COBEGIN-COEND construct for specifying sections of programs to be executed in parallel. These sections may involve different robots operating asynchronously. Languages like LM and AML permits the user to get control back to its program as soon a motion is started; this makes it possible, for example, commanding another motion on another robot in parallel.

3. Facilities of a programming environment

The purpose of the environment of a robot programming language is to assist the programmer in implementing and debugging robot programs. The basic facilities to be offered include interactive interpretation, programming-by-showing utilities, graphical simulation, and interface with CAD data bases.

a) Interactive interpretation:

Programming languages can either be interpreted or compiled in a lower-level language. Compilers provide higher performance at execution time, but in robotics they lack the immediacy which is often required to implement a new program. On the other hand, the relative inneficiency of interpreters make the implementation of some programming functionalities such as parallel execution and sensory interaction difficult, or even impossible, with the current technology.

A good solution is to provide both a compiler and an interactive interpreter. The later is to be used for developing new programs (Finkel 76) (Gini and Gini 78).

It should include such facilities as specific text editing, hot debugging, breakpointing, etc. If a graphical simulator is available (see Section c), then execution of a piece of program by the interpreter may either occur on the actual robot or on the simulated robot.

b) Programming-by-showing utilities:
Consider the following robot program:

```
integer N,I; real D, A; frame POS;
file PROG-FILE;
begin
  read  N  on terminal;
  I:=Ø ; D:=1Ø; A:=1Ø;
  while I  =N do
    POS:=robot; teach;
    D:=distance (robot, POS);
    A:=angle (robot, POS);
    if (D Ø) or (A  Ø) then
       write  "move robot to", robot
                in PROG-FILE;
    else I:=N+1;
  enddo;
end;
```

This simple program can be used as a teaching-by-showing utility. It first asks the operator for the number of positions to be recorded (variable N). Then it iteratively gives the control to the operator on the teach pendant (statement "teach"). Each time the control is returned back to the program, the new position and orientation of the robot (frame "robot") are compared to the old ones (frame POS). If it is different, the new position is used to generate a move statement in a program file. The successive positions could also be recorded into a file to be used later by another program.

This illustrative example, although very simple, shows that textual languages are a powerful tool for developing teaching-by-showing utilities (Grossman 77) (Miribel 84) (Latombe, Laugier, Mazer and Miribel 84). These utilities can be easily adapted to various types of tasks, for instance: pick and place, palettizing, point-to-point welding, assembly,...

Such utilities can be used by operators with no programming experience. They also can be used by experienced programmers. Then it is useful that the utility does not generate only positions in a file, but textual code, as in the above example, to be inserted in the full program and edited.

c) Graphical simulation:
Graphical simulation is a tool both for debugging existing programs and for building new ones using teaching-byshowing utilities.

Debugging programs using graphical simulations has been studied in many places (Arai 83) (Heginbotham, Dooney and Case 79) (Laugier and Pertin-Troccaz 84) (Meyer 81) (Queromes 82) (Sata, Kimura and Amano 81) (Soroka 8Ø) (Tsujido, Kodaira and Oshina 83). The set points of the trajectories computed by the language interpreter are sent to a simulation program. This program runs on a world model which includes geometric models of the objects and the robot. The simulator uses the information sent by the language interpreter to update the world model, which is graphically displayed.

Graphical vizualisation requires that the user can include graphical commands in the robot program (Laugier and Pertin-Troccaz 84) to define how the scene is to be observed (view point, zoon,...).

The problem of simulating the execution of a robot is sensory interaction. Today this problem is not solved, but some sumulator includes interactive commands for emulating such data (Meyer 81))Laugier, Evieux and Pertin-Troccaz 84).

Teaching-by showing utilities implemented in a textual language can be used in the environment of a graphical simulator. The difficulty is that interactively guiding a simulated robot on a two-dimensional screen is not as easy as moving an actual robot using a teach pendant. An elegant solution is to replace the teach pendant in the simulator by a simple graphical language commands such as: move point P onto point P, move axis A onto axis A ,.... Such a language has been defined and implemented in the CATIA system (Liégeois, Dombre and Borrel 82) (Borrel et al. 83).

d) Interface with a CAD data-base:
Modelling the robot environment may be more convenient if explicit geometrical models of objects are available. Then the position of an object (the robot being a particular object) can be described by symbolic relations among this object and other objects. The positions of the frames attached to the objects in the CAD-base are automatically computed from these relations. The explicit geometric model are available only during the phase of developing a program. At execution time the robot system knows only about the necessary frames.

This kind of facility is provided by languages like RAPI (Ambler and Popplestone 75) (Popplestone, Ambler and Bellos 78) and LM-GEO (Mazer 83), which can be seen as input interface to more classical manipulator-level languages (for instance LM-GEO is a preprocessor of LM).

AUTOMATIC ROBOT PROGRAMMING

1. Overview

The goal of automatic robot programming is to automatically transform the description of a manufacturing task provided by a CAD system into a robot program, the execution of which will make the robot accomplish the task (Latombe 83). For instance, the CAD description of a mechanical assembly task includes both the models of the parts and the description of the assembly relations to be achieved among them.

There are several practical motivations for achieving the goal of automatic robot programming:

- The most obvious is to make robot programming easier. Automatic robot programming will make robots more flexible and programming more reliable.

- Another motivation is better CAD/CAM integration. An integrated system providing robot programs as a side-effect of the design process will put the designer in a better position for making design decisions resulting in easier manufacturing.

- Automatic robot programming facilicities the intelligent connection of sensing and action, because interpretation of sensory data, in particular digital images, often makes use of the same type of data as those which are included in CAD models.

Research on automatic robot programming has developedin the context of mechanical assembly. It involves action planning and environment plannings:

- Action planning includes process planning and phase detailing. Process planning basically consists in both ordering the assembly relations to be achieved and assigning the available robots to each relation. Phase detailing consists in planning the robot actions achieving a given relation.

- World planning includes the definition of the workarea layout and the selection of the part feeders, the fixtures and the robot end-effectors.

Until now, most of the research has focused on phase detailing. It has produced the notion of "task-level" programming of robots (Taylor 76). A task-level program consists of a sequence of goal assembly relations among parts together with models of the parts. Unlike a manipulator-level program, it does not specify the robot actions needed to achieve these relations.

During the early years of research on task-level programming, two systems, AUTOPASS (Lieberman and Wesley 77) and LAMA (Lozano-Perez 76) were defined, but they were incompletely implemented. The initial report on the AL language (Finkel 74) also included a task-level subset of instructions, which was never implemented. Languages such as RAPT (Popplestone, Ambler and Bellos 78) and LM-GEO (Mazer 83) provide constructs for explicitly describing spatial relations between parts, but the goal of these constructs is to facilitate the description of the robot position(see chapter Robot Programming Systems, Section 3. d.) These languages remain basically manipulator-level languages.

The first attempts to automate robot programming have shown that translating a task-level description into a manipulator-level program is a very difficult problem involving the kinds of ramifications introduced in the chapter on the problem of programming a robot. In fact, they helped very much discovering these ramifications and understanding why robot programming can be so difficult for humans.

The difficulties to be faced led most of the researchers to solve more deliminated subproblems of phase detailing, mainly grasp planning, transfer motion planning, and part mating planning (Latombe 82 & 83) (Lozano-Perez 82):

- Grasp planning consists in computing the grasping position of a gripper into a part together with the approach and deproach trajectories (Lozano-Perez 76) (Wingham 77) (Binford 79) (Lozano-Perez 81) (Laugier 81) (Laugier and Pertin 83).

- Transfer-motion planning consists in computing a collision-free trajectory for moving a part from its initial position to a goal position (Lewis 74) (Udupa 77) (Lozano-Perez 81) (Brooks 82a & 83).

- Part-mating planning consists in synthesizing a sensor-based program for controlling the motions of the robot when achieving a given relation between two parts (Taylor 76) (Dufay and Latombe 83) (Lozano-Perez, Mason and Taylor 83).

Confrontation with these subproblems has brought some light on two central issues of robot programming: computing safe positions and dealing with uncertainty (see Section 2 and 3 below).

There also exist some systems automating process planning using Artificial Intelligence methods (Descotte and Latombe 84) (Matshushima, Okada and Sata 82) (Tengvald 84). But these systems only consider the problem of planning metal cutting, although the underlying methods are more general, and might be extended to assembly planning in robotics.

A recent paper has proposed on overall architecture for an automatic robot programming system (Lozano-Perez and Brooks 84).

2. Computing reachable positions

2.1. The find-path problem

The basic problem in computing reachable position is the find-path problem, which can be stated as follows: given a part with an initial position, a goal position, and a set of obstacles located in space, find a continuous path for the part from the initial position to the goal position, which satisfies some collision and contact conditions.

Until recently most of the research on this problem derived from the CAD field and focused on algorithms for computing interferences among solids (Boyse 79) (Ahuja, Chien and Bridwell 80) (Powell 82). Various techniques have been devised: 2D projections, decomposition of volumes into cells, parallelpipedic and spherical approximations. These algorithms do not directly solve the find-path problem, and they must be embedded into an "hypothesize-and-test" algorithm (Lewis 74). Such an algorithm iterates the following three steps (Lozano-Perez 83): first hypothesize a candidate path; second check this path for possible collisions; third, if collision is possible, modify the path. This method works fairly well in rather uncluttered environments where crude heuristics can be used to generate candidate paths.

A more recent and general approach consists of explicitely representing the set of those robot configurations which are collision-free. Finding a path then consists in constructing a connected sequence of robot configurations in this set, starting from the initial configuration and terminating at the goal one.

A method based on this approach is the configuration space method, which has been introduced in (Udupa 77) and developed in (Lozano-Perez and Wesley 79), (Lozano-Perez 81) and (Brooks and Lozano-Perez 83). Basically it consists in shrinking the moving object -- let call it A -- to a point while expanding the obstacles -- let call them Bi (i=1,2,...) -- inversely to the shape of A. This principle can easily be explained in a two-dimensional world with a fixed orientation of A. Then the position of some reference point P (a vector with two components) of A is sufficient to specify the position of A. Each obstacle Bi restrain P to be outside some region Bi(see figure 1). Bi can easily be computed if both A and the Bis are convex polygons. Then finding a path for A is equivalent to finding a path for P among the Bi's. This new problem can be solved by partitionning the free space (i.e. the space outside the Bi's) into convex polygons (Chatila 81). A path is defined as a sequence of adjacent polygons, i.e. polygons sharing a common edge.

The configuration space method can rather easily be extended to non-convex three-dimensional objects. Extension to rotating objects is more complicate (Brooks and Lozano-Perez 83) (Chien, Ling Zhang and Bo Zhang 84).

Another method based on the explicit representation of free space has been proposed in (Brooks 82 a & 83). In the two dimensional world, this method makes use of pairs of edges of the obstacles to compute the spines of generalized cones, called freeways, representing the free space (see figure 2). The possible motions of the moving object are along the constructed freeways; at each point of the spine of a freeway only a subset of orientations is allowed. Motion segments consist of translations, with possible re-orientation, along segments of spines. A complete path is built by transfering from one spine to another where they intersect. At such points the moving object must have an orientation legal for both freeways. The method has been extended (Brooks 83) to find collision-free path for a manipulator with 5 or 6 revolute joints. Free space is represented as freeways for the hand and as freeways for the upperarm. Such a method works fast in relatively uncluttered worlds.

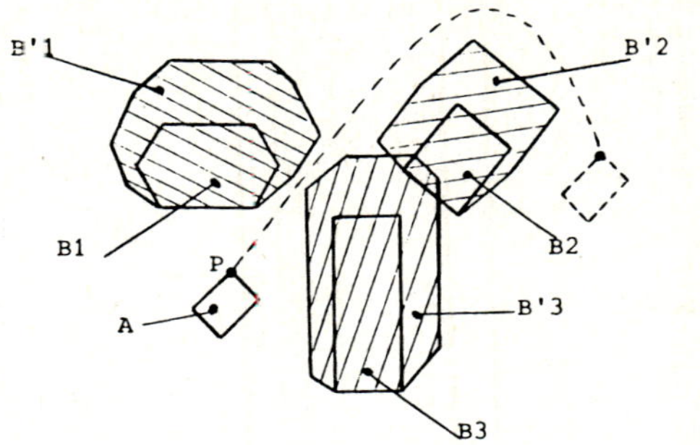

Figure 1 : Expanding obstacles

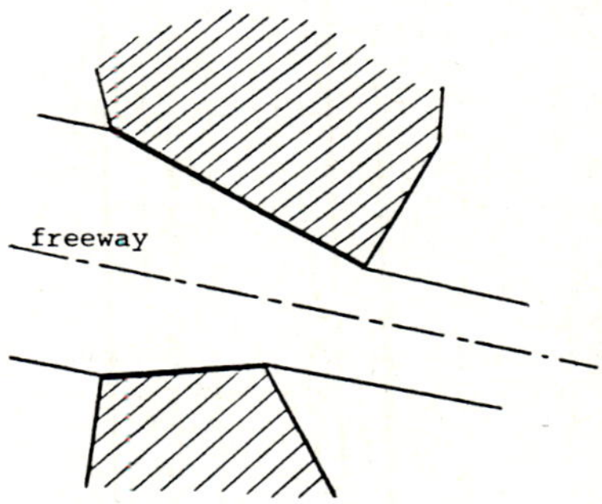

Figure 2 : Representing free space by generalized cones

2.2 Application to phase detailing

At first approximation, grasp planning, transfer-motion planning and part-mating planning can be regarded as instances of the find-path problem. However, at some deeper level of detail they differ considerably:

a) Grasp planning includes the additional difficulty of choosing the grasp position of the jaws on the part. The approach and deproach trajectories to be computed are short trajectories. The gripper and the part move close to obstacles.

Most implemented programs are based on the same general approach made of two steps:

- First, determine a set of candidate grasp positions on the object by considering local morphological properties of the object. For instance (Lozano-Perez 76) considers a small number of grasping position classes on simple volumes like rectangular parallepipeds and cylinders; (Winghan 77) searches for parallel faces on a polyhedron; (Laugier 81) makes use of a large collection of simple morphological properties including local convexity, parallelism, mutual visibility, matter distribution.

- Second prune the set of candidate grasp positions by analyzing reachability constraints both when the part is to be grasped and when it is to be ungrasped. (Lozano-Perez 81) and (Laugier and Pertin 83) analyzes reachability using the configuration space method, or an adaption of this method. The approach and deproach directions are computed during this second step.

b) Transfer-motion planning requires to compute long path sufficiently far from all obstacles because transfer motions are usually executed at high speed and thus may be inaccurate. In general these motions are performed in relatively uncluttered environments.

Methods developed for solving the find-path problem are almost directly applicable to transfer-motion planning. The fact that the environments are not very cluttered can be used to approximate objects in order to simplify computations.

c) Part-nating planning involves short trajectories executed in highly constrained environments (locally to the end-effector). The issue of dealing with geometric uncertainty becomes a crucial one.

The generation of nominal trajectories for mating two parts can be done using a method like the configuration space one. But it requires additional processing to include the sensory interaction which is required to deal with uncertainty.

3. Dealing with uncertainty

Until now, the problem of dealing with uncertainty has only studied in order to plan part mating operations. This is reasonable becuase it is the place where uncertainty plays its major role. However, it is not the only place where it can be taken into account.

If there was no uncertainty, a program for mating two parts would merely consists of a sequence of goal-oriented motions (possibly a single one). Each of them would achieve a desired geometric relation between the parts.

However, because of uncertainty, each motion may not achieve the relation it was intended for, so that it becomes necessary to check sensory data (typically force and position data) for determining whether the expected relation has been attained, or not. Unwanted relations require corrective motions.

Therefore, a program for mating two parts may be regarded as the implementation of a strategy to reduce uncertainty until the goal relation between the two objects is achieved. Such a program typically includes:

- goal-oriented motions to achieve wanted relations,
- corrective motions to improve position accuracy from unwanted relations,
- information-gathering motions to reduce position uncertainty,
- conditional statements, which implicity interpret sensory data in terms of spatial relations requiring different courses of actions,
- loops to repeat goal-oriented motions that were previously unsuccessful,
- variables representing uncertainty, and assignments to update them after both corrective and information-gathering motions.

A first approach to synthesize part-mating programs has been presented in both (Taylor 76) and (Lozano-Perez 76). It consists in filling in given procedure skeletons. A skeleton contains most of the ingredients for performing a task, but many parameters remain to be defined. Taylor (Taylor 76) developed a numerical method for propagating errors and tolerances through relations among part features in a world-model data base. Computed error estimates were used for deciding how to complete the concerned strategy skeleton; for instance, in the task of inserting a pin into a chamfered hole, the error estimate on the distance between the pin and the hole axes could be used for deciding whether to include a piece of code for searching the hole, or not. Later Brooks (Brooks 82b) improved the method for propagating errors by introducing symbolic computation techniques. The new method can be applied not only in the forward direction for estimating errors after a planned operation, but also in the backward direction for computing the ranges of initial values of some parameters which enable a program to succeed. Lozano-Perez (Lozano-Perez 76) developed mothods for computing the expected length of guarded motions and their termination conditions taking uncertainty into account.

The approach suffers from some drawbacks. First, many errors are difficult to estimate and error propagation techniques based on the "worst-case uncertainty" hypothesis may generate unrealistic over-estimates because error compensation phenomena are not taken into account. Second, the techniques developed so far for propagating errors are only applicable to linear programs; their extension to iterative ones would require to solve fix point computation problems.

These drawbacks have motivated investigating a second approach to synthesizing part-mating programs based on inductive learning from experiments (Dufay 83) (Dufay and Latombe 83). The method consists of assembling input partial local strategies described as "expert rules" into a complete manipulator-level program by processing the execution traces of several attempts to carry out the task. The execution traces are generated during the "training phase". Then the input rules are used to build plans in the form of sequences of situation and motions. Given a task, a first plan, called the ground plan, is built; for instance, if the task is to insert a pin into a hole, the ground plan may contain a single motion: starting from the situation where the pin and the hole are aligned (with some uncertainty) translate the pin along its axis until its extremity hits the bottom of the hole. After each motion of the plan is executed by the robot, the system checks position and force sensory data for determining whether the planned situation has been achieved. If this is the case, then the next motion of the plan is executed. Otherwise, rules are invoked for proposing a corrective plan starting from the current situation and having the expected (but not achieved) situation as its goal situation; for instance if the pin hit the chamfer instead of hitting the bottom of the hole, then the corrective plan may consist of first moving the pin along the force vector perpendicular to the pin's axis, and then moving the pin along its axis. The corrective plan is patched into the ground plan, and execution is resumed by the robot.

Due to geometric uncertainty, several executions of the same task usually produce different execution traces. Traces are represented by linear graphs, the nodes are the executed notions and the arcs are the encountered situations.

The assembly of the part-mating program happens during the second phase of the approach, called the "induction phase". It proceeds through iterative transformations of the execution traces by merging modes and arcs labelled by "equivalent" motions and situations. The result is a graph including branching points and cycles, which represents the flowchart of the part-mating program.

A third approach to plan part-mating operations derives from the configuration space method (Lozano-Perez, Mason and Taylor 83). Using this approach, the pin-into-hole task is first transformed from the original formulation shown by Figure 3.a into the problem of moving point p to the goal surface G shown by Figure 3.b (the pin has been shrinked to point p and the hole has been expanded accordingly). Then the "preimage" of G for a direction vi is computed. It is the range of all the position of p such that a single motion along vi would make p reach G (see Figure 4). If no prei age of G contains the current position of p, then the same prei age computation is recursively applied using each of the existing preimages as a possible goal. Therefore, the basic idea of the method is to chain backward from the goal towards the current position of p, characterizing at each step the preimage of the current goal. This idea has been extended for taking into account the effects of both uncertainty -- by introducing the notion of "stron" preimage (range of positions for which all motions within the range of velocity direction uncertainty will reach the goal) -- and friction.

CONCLUSION

During the last ten years, robots have considerably envolved under both the socio-economic pressure and rapid progress of basic technology. They have become truly flexible machines. Information processing, organized around the concept of robot programming, is essential to take full advantage of this flexibility.

It is more and more obvious that the cost of robot programming becomes an important economic issue in robot-based manufacturing. This issue has motivated the development of the general-purpose manipulator-level robot programming languages and their interactive environment.

Since the mid seventies and mostly during the last five years, part of the research has focused on automatic robot programming systems, which provide high expressiveness without requiring programming expertise. After the early ambitious attempts illustrated by AUTOPASS and LAMA, the trend has been to solve more delimitated subproblems: grasp planning, transfer-motion planning, and part-mating planning. Important progress has been made, and today there exist method for solving the three subproblems. Current work deals with improving these methods and integrating then into a single system.

Progress in automatic robot programming is likely to enter industry sson in the form of aids to programming. For instance, one may envision an interactive programming system including separate modules for proposing robots paths, grasping positions, and part-mating strategies to the user. Partial automatic robot programming should also be possible soon in some limited well-defined task domains, for example electronic components insertion on boards.

Robot applications other than manufacturing, including work in hazardous environment and service robotics, will also push for more information processing in robotics.

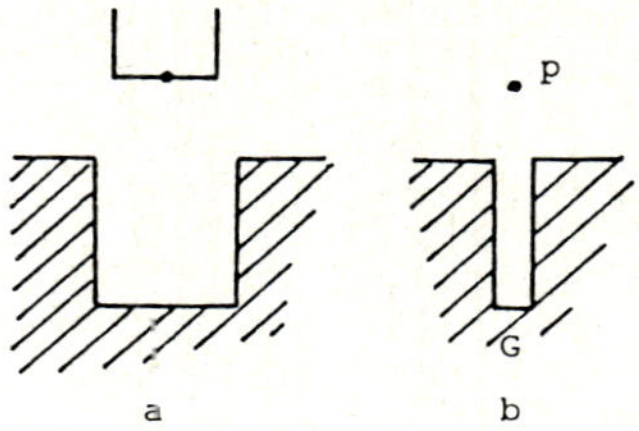

Figure 3 : Tranforming a part mating task

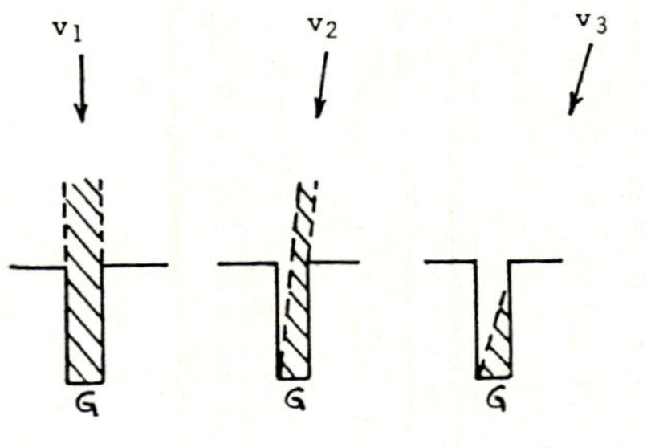

Figure 4 : Preimage of a goal G

REFERENCES

- H. Ahuja, R.I. Chien, N.Bridwell 1980: "Interference detection and collision avoidance among three dimensional objects", 1st American Association for Artificial Intelligence Conference, Stanford, August 1980.
- A.P. Ambler, R.J. Popplestone 1975: "Inferring the positions of bodies from specified spatial relationships", Artificial Intelligence 6, 2, 1975.
- I. Arai 1983: "A robot language system with colour graphic simulator", International Meeting on Advanced Software in Robotics, Liège, May 1983.
- J.P. Bansard 1983: "Le système LM-EX" (in French), IMAG, Grenoble, June 1983.
- T.O. Binford: "Computer integrated assembly system", Artificial Intelligence Laboratory, Stanford, 1979.
- P. Borrel et al. 1983: "The robotics facilities in the CAD-CAM CATIA system", edited by B. Rooks, IFS Publication, 1983.
- J.U. Boyse 1979: "Interference detection among solids and surfaces", Communications of ACM, January 1979.
- R.A. Brooks 1982a: "Solving the find-path problem by good representation of free space", 2nd American Association for Artificial Intelligence Conference, Carnegie-Mellon, August 1982.
- R.A. Brooks 1982b: "Symbolic error analysis and robot planning", International Journal of Robotics Research 1, 4, December 1982.
- R.A. Brooks, T.Lozano-Perez 1983: "A subdivision algorithm in Configuration Space for findpath with rotation", International Joint Conference on Artificial Intelligence, Karlsruhe, August 1983.
- R.A. Brooks 1983: "Planning collision-free motions for pick and place operations", 1st International Symposium on Robotics Research, Bretton Woods, August 1983.
- R. Chatila 1981: "Système de navigation pour un robot mobile autonome: modélisation et processus décisionnels" (in French), thèse de Docteur-Ingénieur, Toulouse, July 1981.
- R.T. Chien, Ling Zhang and Bo Zhang 1984: "Planning collision-free paths for robotic arm among obstacles", IEEE Transactions on Pattern Analysis and Machine Intelligence, Vol. PAMI-6, no. 1, January 1984.
- Y. Descotte, J.C. Latombe 1984: "GARI: an expert system for process planning", in Solid modeling by computers: from theory to applications", edited by J.W. Boyse and M.S. Pickett, Plenum Press, New York, 1984.
- M. Donner, N.K. Taylor, M.C. Bonney 1982: "Planning robot installations by CAD", Computer-Aided Design Conference, Brighton, March 1982.
- B. Dufay 1983: "Apprentissage par induction en robotique -- Application à la synthèse de programmes de montage" (in French), Thèse de 3ème Cycle, INPG, Grenoble, June 1983.
- B. Dufay, J.C. Latombe 1983: "An approach to automatic robot programming based on inductive learning", 1st International Symposium on Robotics Research, Bretton Woods, August 1983.
- R.A. Finkel et al. 1974: "AL, a programming system for automation", Memo AIM 243, Artificial Intelligence Laboratory, Stanford, November 1974.
- R.A. Finkel 1976: "Constructing and debugging manipulator programs", AIM 284, Artificial Intelligence Laboratory, Stanford University, August 1976.
- J.W. Franklin, G.J. Vanderbrug 1982: "Programming vision and robotics systems with RAIL", SME Robots VI, March 1982.
- G. Gini, M. Gini 1978: "Object representation with a manipulator", The Industrial Robot, March 1978.
- G. Gini, M. Gini, R. Gini, B. Giuse 1979: "MAL: a multi-task system for mechanical assembly", International Seminar on Programming Methods and Languages for Industrial Robots, INRIA, June 1979.
- D.D. Grossman 1977: "Programming a computer controlled manipulator by guiding through the motions", IBM T.J. Watson Research Center, Research Report RC6393, 1977.

- W.B. Heginbothan, M. Docner, K. Case 1979: "Rapid assessment of robot performance by interactive computer graphics", 9th International Symposium on Industrial Robots, Washington, D.C., 1979.
- J.C. Latombe, E. Mazer 1981: "LM 1981: a high-level programming language for controlling assembly robots", 11th International Symposium on Industrial Robots, Tokyo, October 1981.
- J.C. Latombe 1982: "Survey of advanced general-purpose software for robot manipulators", RR no 330, IMAG, Grenoble, November 1982.
- J.C. Latombe 1983: "Automatic synthesis of robot programs from CAD specifications", NATO Advanced Study Institute on Robotics and Artificial Intelligence, El Coccio, Italy, June 1983.
- J.C. Latombe, C. Laugier, E. Mazer, J.F. Miribel 1984: "Design and implementation of a robot programming system combining textual and graphical facilities", 2nd International Symposium on Robotics Research, Kyoto, August 1984.
- C. Laugier 1981: "A program for automatic grasping of objectswith a robot arm", 11th International Symposium on Industrial Robots, Tokyo, October 1981.
- C. Laugier, J. Pertin 1983: "Automatic grasping: a case study in accessibility analysis", International Meeting on Advanced Software in Robotics, Liège, May 1983.
- C. Laugier, C. Evieux, J. Pertin-Troccaz 1984: "Un système de simulation graphique de robots incluant une gestion élémentaire des incidents et des capteurs" (in French), RR no. 421, IMAG, Grenoble, March 1984.
- C. Laugier, J. Pertin-Troccaz 1984: "Graphic simulation as a tool for debugging robot control programs", International Symposium on Design and Synthesis, Tokyo, July 1984.
- R.A. Lewis 1974: "Autonomous manipulation on a robot: summary of manipulator software functions", Jet Propulsion Laboratory, California Institute of Technology, TM 33-679, March 1974.
- L.I. Liebermann, M.A. Wesley 1977: "AUTOPASS: an automatic programming system for computer controlled mechanical assembly", IBM Journal of Research and Development, July 1977.
- A Liégeois, E. Dombre, P. Borrel 1982: "Développement d'un système de CAD et de simulation de robots manipulateurs" (in French), Premières Journées ARA,Poitiers, France, September 1982.
- T. Lozano-Perez 1976: "The design of a mechanical assembly system", AI TR 397, Artificial Intelligence Laboratory, MII, 1976.
- T. Lozano-Perez, M.A. Wesley 1979: "An algorithm for planning collision-free paths among polyhedral obstacles", Communications of the ACM 22, 10, October 1979.
- T. Lozano-Perez 1981: "Automatic planning of manipulator transfer movements". IEEE Transactions on Systems. Man and Cybernetics, SMC-11, 10, 1981.
- T. Lozano-Perez 1982: "Robot programming", Memo no. 698, Artificial Intelligence Laboratory, MII, December 1982.
- T. Lozano-Perez 1983: "Task planning", in M. Brady et al. (eds.), "Robot motion", MII Press, 1983.
- T. Lozano-Perez, M.T. Mason, R.H. Taylor 1983: "Automatic synthesis of fine-motion strategies for robots", 1st International Symposium on Robotics Research, Bretton Woods, August 1983.
- T. Lozano-Perez, R.A. Brooks 1984: "An approach to automatic robot programming", in "Solid modeling by computers: from theory to applications", edited by J.W. Boyse and M.S. Pickett, Plenum Press, New York, 1984.
- K. Matsushima, N. Okada, T. Sata 1982: "The integration of CAD and CAM by application of Artificial Intelligence techniques", Annals of the CISP, Vol. 31, no. 1, 1982.
- E. Mazer 1983: "Geometric programming of assembly robots (LM-GEO)", International Meeting on Advanced Software in Robotics, Liège, May 1983.
- J.Meyer 1981: "An emulation system for programmable sensory robots", IBM Journal of Research and Development, Vol 25, no. 6, November 1981.

- J.F. Miribel, E. Mazer 1983: "The LM Reference Manual VI.7", ITMI, Meylan, France, October 1983.
- J.F. Miribel 1984: "Conception et implantation d'un systême de programmation de robots" (in French), Thèse de 3ème Cycle, INPG, Grenoble, September 1984.
- R.P. Paul 1977: "WAVE: a model-based language for manipulator control", The Industrial Robot, March 1977.
- R.P. Paul et al 1980: "Advanced industrial robot control system", School of Electrical Engineering, Purdue University, TR-EE 80-29, July 1980.
- R.P. Paul 1981: "Robot manipulators: mathematics, programming and control", The MIT Press, 1981.
- R.J. Popplestone, A.P. Ambler, I. Bellos 1978: "RAPT: a language for describing assemblies", The Industrial Robot, September 1978.
- E.G. Powell 1982: "An efficient collision warning algorithm for robot arms", 2nd American Association for Artificial Intelligence Conference, Carnegie-Mellon, August 1982.
- J.G. Queromes 1982: "Computer-Aided Design and Robotics: a full promise of cooperation", 12th International Symposium on Industrial Robots. Paris, June 1982.
- T. Sata, F. Kimura, A. Amano 1981: "Robot simulation system as a task programming tool", 11th International Symposium on Industrial Robots, Tokyo, October 1981.
- B.J. Soroka 1980: "Debugging robot program with a simulator", CADCAM 8 Conference, Anaheim, California, November 1980.
- R.H. Taylor 1976: "Synthesis of manipulator control programs from task-level specifications", AIM 228, Artificial Intelligence Laboratory, Stanford University, July 1976.
- R.H. Taylor, P.D. Summers, J.M. Meyer 1982: "AML: a manufacturing language", The International Journal of Robotics Research, Vol. 1, no. 3, 1982.
- R.H. Taylor and D.D. Grossman 1983: "The architecture of an integrated robot system", International Conference on Advanced Robotics, Tokyo, September 1983.
- E. Tengvald 1984: "The design of expert planning systems: an experimental operations planning system for turning", Thesis Dissertation, University of Linkoping, Sweden, May 1984.
- Y. Tsujido, N. Kodaira, M. Oshina 1983: "Realtime motion simulatior of robots", International Conference on Advanced Robotics, Tokyo, September 1983.
- S. Udupa 1977: "Collision detection and avoidance in computer controlled manipulators", International Oint Conference on Artificial Intelligence, MIT, Cambridge, August 1977.
- Unimation 1980: "User's guide to VAL: a robot programming and control system", Unimation Inc., Danbury, Connecticut, Version 12, June 1980.
- P.M. Will, D.D. Grossman 1975: "An experimental system for computer controlled mechanical assembly", IEEE Transactions on Computers, September 1975.
- P.M. Will 1978: "Computer controlled mechanical assembly", The Industrial Robot, March 1978.
- M. Wingham 1977: "Planning how to grasp objects in a cluttered environment", M. Phil. Thesis, University of Edinburgh, 1977.

ARTIFICIAL INTELLIGENCE: Towards Practical Application
T. Bernold and G. Albers (editors)
Elsevier Science Publishers B.V. (North-Holland)

THE LISP MACHINE ARCHITECTURE

David C. Schwartz

Principal Marketing Consultant
Symbolic Inc.
Cambridge
U.S.A.

The Lisp Machine has been called the U.S. reaction to the Japanes 5th generation computer project. It is not. Lisp Machines are 4th generation computer systems; Systems' who's hardware has been designed to explicity support the Lisp language and Operating System. In fact, Lisp Machines are being used as a research tool to aid in investigating new computer organizations, to study the concept of "personal sequential inference machine", as well as for symbol processing and AI software development. Better put, the Lisp Machine is a stepping stone to the 5th generation. The purpose of this presentation is to explain the architecture of the Lisp Machine (LM). There are currently three U.S. manufacturers of LMs. There are many similarities among the LMs currently on the market but of course there are important differences as well. I will make my talk general and draw on examples from all three to capture the key issues. Many of the examples will be drawn from the Symbolics 3600 Architecture. Before launching into a detail discussion on HW and SW, a brief background on the underlying forces motivating the entry of the LM into the technical systems market is useful.

The Lisp Machine is an important entry into the field of computing. LMs support the "paradigm shift" in software that is underway in the 80's. In the 70's we saw a hardware "paradigm shift" as mainframe vendors offering their computing cycles in more price competitive supermini class packages and supermini vendors succeded in further reducing the size and cost of their conventional architectures by introducing personal version of their hardware that ran the same operating systems and applications. Micro vendors have started at the personal scale and have successfully increased the power of their systems while keeping prices competitive. The net effect of the "hardware paradigm shift" is that the personal system is here as a host for the applications once run on systems that were cost prohibitive for the individual user. This trend will continue.

The "software paradigm shift" has begun and can be explained as follows. The programming techniques that have resulted from research in building artificial intelligence systems have been codified and are being used by more and more systems programmers to build advanced applications for users. These techniques include new ways of representing data in the form of knowledge that can be reasoned about. Also techniques for manipulation the data symbolically, algorithmically, as well as logically. Programming styles known as object oriented programming, rule based programming, metaprogramming (embedding new languages and control structures in the host language), data driven programming and logic based programming are being widely used. These techniques make it possible to solve more complex problems and permit systems programmers to build more advanced man machine interfaces. These techniques have been used most frequently in what have been called Artificial Intelligence programs. AI applications have traditionally required large virtual memory to support their execution. In addition the programs have been data intensive, making use of various forms of data representation that have been manipulated dynamically to produce desired program behavior. Artificial intelligence apllications have demanded more from the environment of the computer being used to support their development. An environment for interactive symbolic software development and software-reengineering has evolved to support AI applications primarily as a result of the fact that final specifications for AI systems were not possible. The system environment had to provide facilities for software-reengineering, the ability to both rapidly prototype program modules as well as change small portions of very large systems quickly and efficiently. These same properties apply to the new, advanced systems programs being developed for industrial use.

The properties of the application and environment described present an "orthogonal set of demands" on conventional computer architectures. The Lisp Machine incorporates software and hardware features to support these new application and systems programming techniques for both initial development and program execution more cost effectively and more efficiently than has been here so far possible. In addition, the fact that Lisp is an exceptionally good language for implementing other languages, LMs incorporate conventional software languages and utilities as well. As the techniques of AI and conventional programming are viewed as essential for building the next generation of both conventional and AI styles they offer the user a significant advantage. Examples include the integration of number crunching signal processing with AI for signal interpretation, the integration of text processing and AI for advanced OA, and the integration of data processing and AI for "decision processing".

This is to pinpoint the reasons for the appearance of LM's on the commercial market. We are familiar with numeric processing and systems programming. These are the areas where commercial machines have been most effectively utilized. We now observe two new forms of advanced systems programs known as extensive sympolic systems and advanced symbolic AI systems. This is, in fact, where we see the "software paradigm shift" occurring. An Expert System when viewed as a system program is an example of an extensive symbolic system. Many already exist including Emycin, OPS5, KEE, DUCK, etc. You have heard and seen a great deal about the nature and working of this kind of program already. Now, advanced AI systems would incorporate more procedures to control the semantics of the reasoning module, as well as advanced functions for the user interface such as for image processing, speech processing, language processing, and robotic control. Lets look at this problem space in terms of the nature of the system programs required for support.

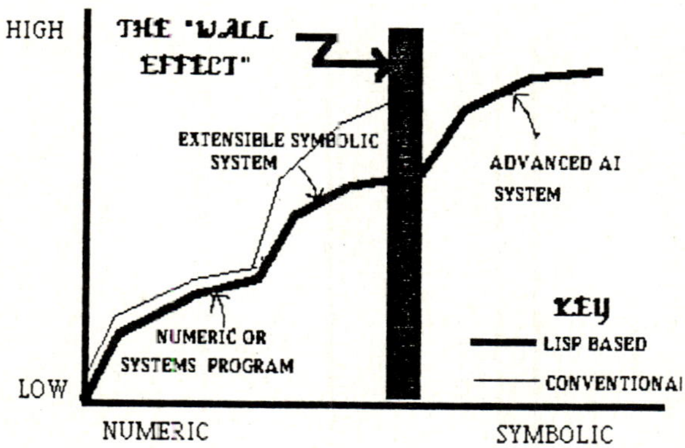

Depicted as a graph, if we move along the horizontal axis from numeric to symbolic and moving along the vertical axis from low systems programming effort to high systems programming effort the following observation may be made. For programming numeric or systems programs Lisp is about as easy to use as a conventional language. For programming an extensible symbolic systems such as en expert system, Lisp has a productivity advantage. For building an advanced AI system, if you choose a conventional language you encounter the "wall effect". The requirements of such an application make it nearly impossible to program it with a conventional language. For matter how much effort is invested. It is for this reason that Lisp machines were originally developed. It is for the same reason that the Lisp machine is becoming a popular industrial computer resource.

In summary, the advanced systems programs of the 80's are becoming more data intensive. This is forcing computer vendors to find ways to extend the acceptable performance range for their computer systems at a given price. These programs require fast pattern matching, flexibility for prototyping in various paradigms, efficient execution of diverse control structures language directed support for high resolution graphics, as well as systems level support for conventional computer features such as networking, file systems, and peripherals for various forms of I/O. Some vendors have discovered ways to push back the Von Neuman bottleneck to provide for efficient symbolic crunch as well as efficient overall system program operation.

The LM is emerging to meet the symbolic processing and Aritificial Intelligence programming needs in the 80's. New forms of software engineering are moving from the "work of glorified hackers" to the standard styles of the industrial system programmer. Lisp is able to be executed efficiently and has become more comprehensible due to the on going standardization efforts. Lisp is being used not only by researchers but by students learning programming for the first time. In fact, the availability of Lisp interpreters on conventional micros will aid in breaking the bottleneck of having a limited supply of good Lisp programmers. I have reviewed some of the driving forces that are bringing Lisp based systems into the lime light as well as the fresh attitude the market is taking toward new systems based on Lisp. Now let's turn to the architecture of the machine to see how it works and to further understand how it will be applied to complex problems.

The discussion on the architecture will be organized into 5 sections: the language, the hardware, the runtime facilities and software tools, networking and future directions. To begin, the Lisp language has evolved over a 25 year period to incorporate the best features of standard programming languages as well as to offer a set of unique features of its very own. Lisp is unique in it's uniform simple syntax and its common internal representation for programs and data. Many features such as list management, macros, type and boundary checking are implemented more powerfully than in conventional languages on conventional machines. Other features such as object oriented programming extensions have a unique and powerful embodyment in the Lisp Machine architecture. For example, list management with symbols and properties are implicit data structures in the language and are directly supported in the hardware as are the structures required for object oriented programming. Macros obey the simple Lisp syntax and hence can be compiled for more efficient executing. Complex data structures such as infinite precision numbers, arrays of mixed data types, arrays with infinite bounds (planes), and full user defined data typing make it possible to build sophisticated systems programs. The macro feature enables Lisp to be extended and you may already have heard of Planner, Conniver, and Amord as logic programming languages embedded in Lisp (before Prolog was a popular term). Macsyma, DPL, and ASAS are other modern examples of languages embedded in Lisp. As I mentioned, Lisp has conventional features such as structured programming, number crunching, I/O processing, bit manipulation, etc. It is important to remember that the Lisp machine not only provides efficient interpretation and compilation of Lisp but also support an environment comprised of over 10 thousand functions that aid the system programmer in his programming efforts including powerful text handling functions, searching and sorting routines, protocol management routines, etc. The 3600 offers a number of compilers for convertional languages since not only is Lisp good for embedding other languages but also is known as the machine language of high level languages. These compilers take full advantage of the LM environment such as debugging tools, window systems, etc. and are offered with their own language directed tools such as symbolic debuggers and editors. Offering conventional languages in the same address space as Lisp permits the melding of AI systems programming features with conventional application features. All of these software capabilities are provided in what is known as "a single level" memory environment. This enables the development and execution of programs in the full gigabyte of logical address space provided on the 3600 without concern for physical memory management.

The hardware of Lisp machines are a price performance breakthrough for Lisp. Lisp was invented in 1958 but was only available on expensive mainframe time sharing systems for a long time. Even then Lisp execution was computationaly intensive and consequently used for more resource that most time sharing users were willing to accept. The Lisp machine as we know it today is a personal system with dedicated symbolic processing power and provides the power of a full time sharing system at the finger tips of a single user. The block diagram of the system is conventional in its organization. In fact, all the modules of a regular Von Neuman machine are present including device controllers for low and high speed peripherals, memory subsystem, memory controller, microcode store and sequencer, and data path and arithmetic and logic control unit. The key difference is that all the data paths in each of these hardware modules have been organized to support Lisp directly. For example, the stack feature is implemented in the DP/ALU and has a buffer feature which takes advantage of virtual memory access. The microcode word of 112 bits was designed to support ZetaLisp (3600 Lisp dialect) directly. And the macrocode (the language codes into which Lisp is compiled) execution is tightly integrated with the microcode machine permitting the microcode to interrupt the macrocode execution. Combine this feature with the hardware type checking of data at runtime and it is possible to see how generic operations are implemented and supported in the machine. Of course the user interface is comprised of high resolution bit map graphics for both black and white and color. In each case, the architects of the Lisp machine have made every effort to provide fully integrated systems features. For example, directly manipulated screen objects are available through a mouse sensitive interface. In addition, the color system memory is viewed as part of the single level memory system and many of the commonly accessed color hardware features are supported directly in firmware such as pan and zoom. The large memory system supports the mapping of 3 different pixel data formats for fast color editing and redisplay.

The symbol processor is designed to support Lisp directly. This direct support can be identified in 6 specific areas including hardware support for data types (memory tagging), hardware support for memory collection (garbage collection), hardware implemented generic operations, Lisp primitives implemented directly in hardware, demand paged multi-level virtual memory with 28 bit addressing, and stack architecture with virtual buffer capability.

At the surface, the Lisp Machine looks like a conventional personal computer, a full array of optional devices is available including add on memory, a variety of fixed and removable disks, cartridge tape, modems, and a laser graphics printer.

The software facilities available at runtime include among other capabilities multiprocessing, dynamic error handling, hash tables, sorting, etc. and a robust local and remote file system capability. There are a number of powerful utilities for program development and program execution management.

These include a powerful and user accessable window management system, a language directed text editor (ZMACS), a full function mail system (ZMAIL), PEEK system resource monitor, an interactive display oriented symbolic debugger, and a Font editor. In terms of networking, both Lisp machines and other mainframe and supermini computers are supported. The support includes file system access, electronic mail, remote tape and printer service, name space service among others. The network link is a 10mbit per second Ethernet. Symbolics 3600 provides the service facilities through a high level protocol known as Chaosnet. The firm is moving toward support of TCP/IP.

In summary, the Lisp Machine is a powerful high performance single user computer with dedicated symbolic crunch. The computer is an excellent tool for embedding or writing other languages with runtime facilities and software tools in a totally integrated system. As we approach the issues of managing knowledge in the 80's, the diverse representations, diverse control strategies, special algorithms, symbol processing, and special purpose hardware required will best be served on Lisp Machines. In the 60's, the break through was the symbolic assembler. In the 70's the breakthrough was high level language on economical timesharing systems. In the 80's the breakthrough is symbolic programming on high powered personal computers. It is this new style of problem solving and computing that is helping us break through the complexity barrier in traditional application areas such as CAD/CAM, Training and Simulation, Medical Diagnosis, etc. And, as we move from basic research to application development for in-house use, the cost of Lisp Machines are coming down in price. The lower cost machines will enable the wide spread commercial distribution of this new and important form of problem solving computer.

ECONOMIC IMPACTS

ARTIFICIAL INTELLIGENCE: Towards Practical Application
T. Bernold and G. Albers (editors)
Elsevier Science Publishers B.V. (North-Holland)

MARKET TRENDS IN ARTIFICIAL INTELLIGENCE IN THE UNITED STATES AND JAPAN

Karl Wiig

Director Artificial Intelligence Program
Arthur D. Little Inc.
Cambridge
U.S.A.

Before I start this talk, I should tell you that my perspective on the AI market and its trends is that of a practitioner as well as an observer. In our organization we are biased as practitioners since we are making a business from applying artificial intelligence technology and since we perceive that artificial intelligence will develop significantly with time. Therefore, we are espousing a particular perspective that builds upon assumptions that reflect our particular background. In other words, there is a partisan world view behind the market perspective that I will present to you. As a matter of fact, I will make an experiment with you, a simulation experiment, trying to take you through what might happen in artificial intelligence. To put it differently, what I have been asked to do is to observe a dynamic system that can be characterized as a large billiard ball sitting on a table. On top of the billiard ball there is a small marble. And you have asked me to predict: in which direction will the marble roll off?

First, I would like to talk briefly about different transition forces and then take you along on a thought experiment which involves projecting into the future what is happening in the world today. Let us look at the driving forces (Fig. 1) that currently appear to be present in the market.

Driving Forces

- **Applications of AI are becoming practical and of commercial value.**
- **Decision support systems will increasingly incorporate AI knowledge-based technology, and will for the first time spread into broad use.**
- **Computer hardware costs are decreasing to where it is economically sensible to provide AI-based technology into broad real life applications.**
- **Gradual realization that complete, highly integrated workstation environments are needed to support knowledge workers — anything else is just "stopgap."**

Figure 1

We see that applications of artificial intelligence are becoming practical and of commercial value. We see also -- and this is where our bias comes in --- that decision support systems will increasingly incorporate AI modules. The cost of computer hardware has been brought down to where it now becomes economically realizable to consider AI tools and artificial intelligence approaches. We find that it is possible to supply highly complex workstations to provide extensive support to knowledge workers, when that is desired. These are some of the driving forces at this time. But there are a number of barriers against adopting AI technology (Fig. 2): it is the friction that prevents the marble from rolling off the billiard ball one way or the other. We have heard over the last two days that there are only a few people who know how to practice artificial intelligence.

Barriers to Broad Adoption of AI

- **AI technology is very complex and only mastered by few.**
- **AI-based systems take much longer to build and finalize.**
- **Management's philosophy does not yet support capital investments of $10,000-$20,000 for each knowledge worker under *any* promises!**

Figure 2

A question is: how fast we can make the field advance because there are so few people? It is also inordinately difficult to build AI-based systems. They take much longer to build than the traditional decision support system with mathematical models that incorporate, for example, linear program solution. Building AI systems involves digging much deeper into the subject matter than building conventional systems. We are perhaps not prepared as professionals, and, we are certainly not adequately prepared as managers and businessmen to go that deeply into creating a system when we don't yet know its economic advantages. Also, I think a major obstacle is that business managers are not yet accustomed to the thought of investing $10,000 to $30,000 or more in a knowledge worker's support system. Business managers are used to high investments per worker in factories, because of the large machines, but it is now people's brains that are in need of support with capital equipment. And, we see this is now becoming a new competitive requirement.

We have a number of trends (Fig. 3)--some extablished, some that are emerging.

Established Trends

Trends

- **Suppliers provide powerful AI development computers**
- **Suppliers are building AI development tools**
- **Applictions development teams are built by retraining non-AI'ers**

Emerging Trends

- **AI workstations technology suitable as delivery vehicles for 'bank tellers' and 'assembly line supervisors.'**
- **Software delivery environments suitable for use by 'ordinary people.'**
- **A realization among corporate leaders and other managers that AI has real — perhaps very large — business potential. But that it must be deployed both carefully and differently from traditionally DP.**
- **Inhouse AI development programs are emerging with development systems and staffs.**

Figure 3

Very powerful computers and super workstations are being provided for artificial intelligence to be part of the established trends. New development systems and suitable workstations are emerging to be used for delivery vehicles. We see that suppliers are building development tools and we see that application development teams are being built by quite a number of individual firms. Many of these development teams consist of non-AI'ers. This indicates that it is indeed possible to train individuals who do not have formal AI training to perform tasks in support of building AI-based systems. Some of the emerging trends include: A number of manufacturers are making highly powerful workstations with bit-mapped displays and quite large computer power. These systems might be suitable to place in front of a bank teller, for example, or you in front of a knowledge worker in a factory or a firm. I don't know that those of who have looked at the Xerox machines, Symbolics machines and the large DEC workstations in the exhibition hall feel that they are yet ready to go into those positions. I have some questions about that myself. But, I think the suitable workstations for final delivery to the user are coming very soon.

We see the emergence of delivery environments of software environments which can be used by ordinary people: people who did not grow up with computers; people who might be able to operate a keyboard; and, people who would never know how to get out of a broken Lisp expression as presented by some systems today. We see a real belief by many corporate leaders and other managers that AI has really potential. And, we see in some instances, for people who had a chance to observe it, that artificial intelligence has real business potential and that very high profits can be obtained from using them. We also see a number of industrial in-house programs emerging: in oil companies, in metals companies, chemical companies, etc.

Financial institutions are developing their own groups with AI development systems and staffs. So, things are happening at a rapid pace.

Based upon this set of initial conditions I have made some projections that I would like to share with you to look at where the marble might roll down from the billiard ball. Based upon the initial conditions, we can create a number of hypotheses and make a dynamic system model that evolves from these hypotheses (Fig. 4).

Market Forecast Hypotheses

1. **AI-based applications will spread throughout society to eventually support every knowledged worker.**
2. **The dynamics of adoption of AI technology will follow traditional patterns:**
   - **a. Automobile**
   - **b. Electric light**
   - **c. Television**

   (50% penetration reached in 14 years)
3. **Year of commercial introduction in the United States: 1983**

Figure 4

Hypothesis number one deals with the fact that AI-based systems will spread throughout society, (not necessarily like wild fire) in a very controlled and traditional way. We will adopt as a hypothesis that artificial intelligence will spread as fast as previous technologies. Perhaps as fast as the automobile spread through society or the electric light or television or the telephone, or a number of other technologies, which showed the interesting characteristic that they reached about 50 percent market penetration after a period of roughly 14 years. Given that hypothesis, we postulate that in the United States the year of first commercial introduction of AI was in 1983. That means we have the capability of projecting into the future what may happen in artificial intelligence for the next several decades. In our projections, we have focused on knowledge-based systems and their use (Fig. 5), their development, and tools for applications development and hardware (both for applications development and for workstations as knowledge-based delivery vehicles).

Emphasis of Forecast

- **Knowledge-based systems**
  - **— their use**
  - **— their development**
- **Tools for AI applications development**
- **Hardware for**
  - **— AI applications development**
  - **— AI workstations as KBS delivery vehicles**
- **Deemphasized:**
  - **— Military systems**
  - **— Robotics**
  - **— Imbedded systems**

Figure 5

I have not looked specifically at military systems or robotics and embedded systems. Perhaps more importantly, I have not looked extensively on the whole set of associated activities, dealing with trading of knowledge bases and how firms deals with knowledge within their own organizations. The latter point is very much part of artificial intelligence but it is not necessarily part of the section of artificial intelligence that we computernics think of first, which is mostly hardware and system software and things of this nature.

We have looked briefly at what is being traded (Fig. 6), various computers for AI development and application systems.

What Will Be Traded

1. **Computers**
   a. **Large development systems**
   b. **Small development systems**
   c. **Workstations**
   d. **Large central AI processors**
   e. **Imbedded and portable systems**
2. **AI developments — tools and building blocks**
   a. **AI languages (LISP, PROLOG, etc.)**
   b. **Specialized building blocks — graphics systems, inference engines, DBMS, etc.**
   c. **Knowledge-based systems development environments**
   d. **Knowledge bases (Lexica, Tax Laws, etc.)**
3. **Application Systems**
   a. **Knowledge-based systems**
   b. **Natural language systems**
   c. **Computer-aided instructions**
   d. **Vision systems**
   e. **Robotics**
   f. **Software development environments**

Figure 6

The different items that are being traded are essentially the traditional ones.

Now, let us look at the total artificial intelligence market in the United States as it might evolve (Fig. 7).

How Large Proportion Will AI Be of Total Computer Industry?

Year	AI Revenues ($ Billion)	AI% of Total	Total Computer Industry Revenues ($ Billion)
1984	0.15	0.1	148
1985	0.25	0.16	158
1990	11.8	4	267
1995	67	20	348
2000	113	26	422

Figure 7

It is enormous. In 1985, we expect that the total artificial intelligence market will be worth about $250,000,000. It breaks down, as you see in this particular table. (Since the tables are quite complex, I will just highlight a couple of interesting aspects here.) The way that these figures are shown and the way that we have perceived the evolution of the market, we see that there may be a significant activity in artificial intelligence workstations for the individual knowledge worker. This figure becomes large in the future since it must be expected that a larke number of knowledge-based systems that we today consider being software, will be incorporated in the workstations as firm ware. As we project into the future, there will be significant value pricing involved, and the workstations will incorporate functions such as natural language understanding and speech recognition. As we approach the year 2000/2005, workstations might even incorporate such functions as emerging common sense, although, those of you who have worked in that area will wonder if that ever is going to be possible. The workstation price in the year 2000 is high because it will incorporate more than a dozen complex AI functions. The total revenues six years hence may be $11,000,000,000 for artificial intelligence based products and services. When that is related to the total computer industry, it is not very large. In 1984, the artificial intelligence market in the United States is one-tenth of one percent of the total computer industry revenues. We project that by 1990, the AI market might increase to be just above four percent, which is not very large, except that it is a fifty-fold increase of what it is today. Now you start seeing why I have problems projecting in which direction the marble is going to roll off the billiard ball.

Number of People in AI Industry

Year	AI Workers	In Total Computer Industry
1985	2.6 thousand	1.8 million
1990	100 thousand	2.3 million
1995	486 thousand	2.5 million
2000	650 thousand	2.5 million

Figure 8

The number of people in the industry (Fig. 8) might change from about 2,500 people today to about 650,000 people in the year 2000. I think these estimates in one sense are conservative because many more people might potentially be concerned with the dissemination of knowledge, the organization of knowledge, the building of knowledge bases in an organized way, in ways that we never really have properly considered.

In the charts that accompany this talk (Figures 9-14), there is a discussion of the number of systems that will be traded in different categories: development systems, large and small, and workstations.

Total AI Market in the United States
($ Billion)

	1985	1990	1995	2000	2005
All AI Software	.089	3.3	28.6	46.0	46.0
AI R&D	.021	.17	.88	1.4	1.6
AI Workstations*	.048	7.2	32.0	56.6	70.0
AI Development Systems	.096	1.2	6.1	8.9	9.1
Total AI	.254	11.8	67.6	113.0	126.7

*As time passes, considerable applications firmware will be imbedded in workstations.

Figure 9

Near Term Market Changes
($ million)

	1985	1986	1987	1988	1989	1990
Applications	35	125	390	1,130	1,826	2,500
Tools	55	90	160	320	510	750
R&D (Software)	21	27	40	70	120	170
Workstations	48	260	980	2,500	4,500	7,200
Development Systems	96	155	250	490	725	1,150
Total	254	655	1,829	4,106	7,700	11,777

Figure 10

Sales of AI Application Systems
($ million)

	1985	1990	1995	2000
Commodity Systems	—	63	1,300	2,600
Generic Systems	23	817	6,500	11,700
Corporate Systems	7	900	7,900	12,300
Individualized Systems	5	750	8,000	12,000
Total	35	2,530	23,700	38,600

Figure 11

AI Personal Workstation Market
(Number of Systems)

	1985	1990	1995	2000	2005
New	2,700	500,000	3,500,000	3,000,000	1,500,000
Replacement	—	150,000	1,800,000	8,000,000	12,000,000
Total Sold per Year	2,700	650,000	5,000,000	11,000,000	14,000,000
Workstations in Service	3,000	1,000,000	11,000,000	30,000,000	40,000,000
Fractions of AI Users Served by AI Work Stations	1%	5%	40%	90%	99%

Figure 12

AI Development System Market
(Number of Computers)

	1985	1990	1995	2000
Small Systems	800	11,000	70,000	120,000
Large Systems	700	9,000	45,000	60,000
Total Systems for AI Development	1,500	20,000	115,000	182,000
Total AI Development Systems in Service	3,100	50,000	400,000	1,000,000+

Present Status

	1983	1984
All Types of AI Systems in Service	600	1,600

Figure 13

Sales of AI Tools

	1985	1990	1995	2000
Total Sales ($ million)	54	751	4,729	7,228
Tools per Development System (Averages)				
Small	1	2	2.25	2.25
Large	2	4	4.5	4.5
Applications per Workstation				
	2	4	7	8

Figure 14

One aspect is the number of AI system development tools that will be installed on the different development systems. These tools include Xeros's Loops or IntelliCorp's KEE or other knowledge-based engineering environments. Development systems will, in the future, have quite a number of such tools. Similarly, the number of applications on individual workstations might increase to about eight of nine by the year 2000 (Fig.15).

Sales of AI Tools

	1985	1990	1995	2000
Total Sales ($ million)	54	751	4,729	7,228
Tools per Development System (Averages)				
Small	1	2	2.25	2.25
Large	2	4	4.5	4.5
Applications per Workstation				
	2	4	7	8

Figure 15

In other words, each individual will have eight or nine different knowledge-based systems, either specifically designed for a particular work function, or generic systems for common use. The workstation hardware will in the short term consist of such systems as the SUN workstations and Apollos DN350s, and other specifically configured systems.

JAPAN

Japan is in a similar situation to the United States, except it is not as far along. As a matter of fact, I don't know if the marble has been placed on top of the billiard ball yet. Whereas in the United States you might say that we have 2000 AI development systems in place today, including the specifically designed VAX's and DEC 10 and 20 systems as well as the Symbolics, Xerox and LMI computers which are specifically designed as AI development workstations.

Assumptions

- **Japan's AI activities are now about two years delayed compared to the United States.**
- **Japan's rate of adoption will be slightly faster than in the United States — 50% penetration in 11 years.**
- **Japan will tend to create imbedded systems for the world market in addition to domestic uses.**
- **Japan's domestic market potential about 50% of U.S. market.**

Figure 16

In Japan, you might have 100, perhaps 150 systems in existence. On the other hand, Japan is abreast with the United States when it comes to development of the Fifth Generation computers as we all know (Fig. 16). We can see that Japan might lag the United States in applications, however, by a couple of years. We also might hypothesize that Japan will ramp up much faster than the United States whereas in the United States we expect that the 50 percent market penetration point will occur after some 14 years, in Japan it might occur only after 11 years. If you look at that, you will have a projection for the Japanese market which roughly goes like this: In 1995, the Japanese AI market will achieve revenues of about one-half of what it is in the United States in that year (Fig. 17).

Total Japanese Market
($ billion)

	1985	1990	1995	2000	2005
All AI Software	0.02	1.4	13.2	16.9	19.6
AI R&D	0.03	0.1	0.6	0.7	0.8
AI Workstations	0.01	3.1	30.0	32.7	38.8
AI Development Systems	0.05	0.5	3.4	3.8	4,2
Total AI	0.1	5.1	47.3	54.2	63.3

Figure 17

A major area of uncertainty with the Japanese market is associated with the extent Japan will be successful in selling AI-based systems to the developing world. This includes their ability to provide embedded systems for people who do not have any capabilities to run large-scale special software systems, but who want to buy AI systems in small hand-held packages by the year 1995 for medical and technical diagnoses and advice among other applications. If this AI market segment develops strongly, AI revenues in Japan may be much higher than those projected.

By taking you on this little tour I am trying to tell you that the artificial intelligence market in economic terms may be rather significant from what we can see. It is promising to be a very important industry which means that, technologically and economically there will be quite a number of opportunities. But I think the real impact is that we only can guess at, at this stage. Nobody thought that society was going to be changed extensively by the emergence of the automobile or the horseless carriage. Nobody thought that the telephone was going to change the world significantly. I think that people knew that television was going to change the world somewhat, but not to the extent that it has. I think it is up to you, as AI practitioners, to assist in changing the world with artificial intelligence.

ARTIFICIAL INTELLIGENCE: Towards Practical Application
T. Bernold and G. Albers (editors)
Elsevier Science Publishers B.V. (North-Holland)

SPECULATIONS ON THE FUTURE OF KNOWLEDGE ENGINEERING IN EUROPE I

Antony G. Baker

Manager Operational Technique Section
Unilever Research Laboratory
Mersey Side
Great Britain

I run an Operational Techniques Section at Unilever Research, Port Sunlight Laboratory. The Section provides support to the laboratory in Mathematics, Statistics and Knowledge Engineering. Later, I will define the term Knowledge Engineering, since people use the term differently.

In Unilever, we use four different methodologies:-

1. Inductive systems

About 12 years ago we started on this subject with regard to classification and hypothesis generation application.

2. Expert systems

About 5 years ago we started studying the subject and we have now generated 5 demonstrable systems. We use LISP and PROLOG.

3. Knowledge systems

These are 'working' text books or reports that deal with specific problems. We use our version of SYNICS, a dialogue processing system, in FORTRAN, which was developed by Professor E. Edmonds of Leicester Polytechnic. We have been working in this area about 4 years.

4. Working data bases

These are data bases that not only provide the information that is required, but also provide all the algorithms, data manipulation and graphics that are required to effectively use the information.

These four areas show why I use the term Knowledge Engineering rather than Artificial Intelligence, for many people would consider that only 1 and 2 are parts of Artificial Intelligence.

I would now like to discuss some of the terms used in these subjects.

Hamlyn's Theseausarus gives: -

Synonyms for INFORMATION are evidence, notes, details, results, figures.
Synonyms for KNOWLEDGE are cognition, learning, erudition, expertise.

These synonyms show that Knowledge is a better word than Information for describing our work.

I define Knowledge Engineering as the methodologies that enable knowledge to be put into a convenient usable form. Thus if you write a report that gives knowledge in a convenient usable form, then you are functioning as a knowledge engineer. Some people immediately react by pointing out that the definition makes everyone a knowledge engineer. I reply by agreeing for I see Knowledge Engineering as the natural development from pen, pencil, paper, printing etc. In the main, Knowledge Engineering can be used by most people and my definition reflects that viewpoint.

One plea that I have, because of what has already been said at this conference, is that we must not waste effort on questions like: "Is traditional computing at odds with artificial intelligence". There is too much to do and there is no need to waste time on such questions.

We can demonstrate

(a) 3 Expert Systems that are based on our own LISP empty shell, 2 in analyticial chemistry, 1 in packaging.

(b) 2 Expert Systems that are based on our own PROLOG empty shell, 2 in analyticial chemistry.

(c) 3 Knowledge Systems all of which are in the field of process engineering. One of the systems is particularly important since it was developed by a chemical engineer with only our background support. Before we had completed our first application of SYNICS, the chemical engineers said that they wanted to develop such systems themselves. A 2 day course was arranged and now several chemical engineers are developing Knowledge Systems themselves.

Our approach to applications is based on the following basis:_

The problem is the key issue	- Knowledge Engineering methodology exists or can be developed at least to a helpful stage.
Applications must be needs led	- Trying to find problems to fit methodologies is not as successful.
Systems must be transportable	- Otherwise sizeable problems.
Methodology must be teachable	- Knowledge Systems, 2 days Rules into Expert Systems, 2 days.
Use of systems must encourage expertise development	- black boxes weaken the expertise base.

The lastpoint is very important. We try and develop systems, the use of which increases the expertise of the user. We should not weaken our human skills by using only black boxes.

The pay-offs from such developments are: -

1. Ensure that an adequate base of expertise exists.

2. Transforms expertise into a capital asset.

3. Reduced experimental effort required.

4. Expertise is tidied-up. Application areas are dealt with and only need revision when new insights and/or materials become available.

5. Company is able to exploit opportunities provided by emerging technologies.

Today I will speculate where Europe is going in Knowledge Engineering. Any speculation has to depend upon our views of the present. If you agree with me that Knowledge Engineering should be built into every vocational course, then the subject can and will be the pencil and paper of 10- years hence. Such a view is very different to that held by those who consider the subject to be very complex and difficult.

We have to consider how society can be enriched by enabling people to think about and use several disciplines. If we can double or treble the scope of the human mind by the use of such systems, human life can be considerably enriched. If we take the other view, then the development of such systems will have uneven effects on society.

If we consider the hardware, software and communication developments that will be coming out of Europe, Japan and the United States, there is no doubt that the scope of Knowledge Engineering will expand considerably. How such developments are used depends on our viewpoints. We have time to evolve with these developments. We have demonstrated within Unilever, that the tools of knowledge engineering can be used by non-computing disciplines. Should we continue to produce graduates from our universities who have no experience with these methodologies?

We now have some very useful tools that can be taught to all undergraduates so that the tools can be used within their professional courses. I believe that the educational process will be improved by using such tools. The assembly of academic knowledge so that real problems can be solved is rarely a trivial exercise. On the contrary, such applications will generally be mind-stretching.

Summing-up: -

If we have the WILL, then

> Knowledge Engineering can be an everyday approach that is widely used throughout Europe within 10 years.

The potential, consequential enrichment of human minds opens up wide horizons. The developments that are now coming from Artificial Intelligence fit in well with the changing culture.

The Esprit, Alvey developments along with those from Japan and USA will ensure that a wide range of very useful hardware and software will be available. Society, via Knowledge Engineering can start tapping these developments and thereby prepare for the future. Europe needs to accelerate the application of these subjects so that it can adapt.

$$\text{ADAPT} \geq \text{RATE OF DEVELOPMENT} \rightarrow \text{SUCCESS}$$

$$\text{ADAPT} < \text{RATE OF DEVELOPMENT} \rightarrow \text{PROBLEMS}$$

ARTIFICIAL INTELLIGENCE: Towards Practical Application
T. Bernold and G. Albers (editors)
Elsevier Science Publishers B.V. (North-Holland)

SPECULATIONS ON THE FUTURE OF KNOWLEDGE ENGINEERING IN EUROPE II

A.W. Pearson

Director R + D Research Unit
Manchester Business School
Manchester
Great Britain

As a participant at the conference as well as a speaker I have been very conscious of the different interpretations that have been given to three groups of words: Artificial Intelligence, Knowledge Engineering, and Expert Systems. My colleague and co-presenter in this session, Tony Baker, has stated that he is actively involved in knowledge engineering and has provided us with his definition of this area. However, no-one has specifically raised the question what makes an expert? Who is an expert? What knowledge is implied in any definition and how is this knowledge used in practice?

Managers are experts, accountants are experts, teacher are experts, doctors are experts, craftsmen are experts, anyone who has some knowledge or some skill that we personally do not have can be thought of as an expert. Where do these skills come from - some of them may be thought of as given - the artist, the painter, perhaps - but many of them are actually learned either through formal or informal processes. The net result is that some people actually obtain power in systems because they have some knowledge for some skill that we have not acquired or could not acquire easily. For example, an accountant can remember which side of the balance sheet the debits and credits go on, and will know that it may be different in different countries. Those of us who cannot remember such things may find our access to the profession barried, and hence will not be able to develop other skills which will influence our future career paths and in some cases the quality of life. Professions set boundaries and establish norms which must be adhered to. The important message from this conference is that developments in 'expert systems' offer the opportunity to change many of the boundaries set by history and open up the possibility of a new professional and managerial revolution.

At the present time the technology is pushing. We are seeing developments in microelectronics which offer improved performance, improved quality, reduced costs, etc., and whether or not we choose to use such developments these trends will continue. On the market pull side there is an increasing demand for quality, for speed, for cost reduction from many sources. For example, in the health service worldwide we are conscious that we have not enough money to spend on the system that we are going to require to satisfy the future needs. Therefore, governments are demanding that we produce a more efficient and effective health service. And if there is a piece of technology that may help in this respect it must be given serious consideration. At the same time, as individuals we would like to think that the medical staff have available to them the most effective methods of treatment, and would expect that the medical staff - who are professionals by any definition - should want to be in the forefront, backed by technology and systems which enable them to make the best use of their skills.

A professional, whether a craftsman, an accountant, a teacher, should be aware of and seek out the tools that are going to enable the job to be done better. Tony Baker made the point in his illustration of the chemical engineer who takes the view "I have seen that, I like it, I want it, because it is going to help me professionally". We are looking now at those experts who are not told what to do, but who are saying "because I am an expert, because I am a professional, I want to use the best available tools". This is the way to create demand for a product, from the people who are going to use it, and this demand will be increased if those who use the system also gain from it.

What are the major considerations then in terms of making sure that those gains are achieved by all people? Clearly, there is going to be a learning time, there needs to be some software, there will inevitably be some standardization, and there may be significant development costs. Unfortunately, there seems to be a quite wide diversity of opinion as to the costs, with again the experience of Unilever suggesting that the costs need not be too high, and the potential benefits very considerable.

There is also an important need to consider the effect upon many groups of people This is probably going to raise some of the biggest issues, including the obvious one of unemployment. This is too large and difficult a subject to cover here, but it must be accepted that in some countries, and companies - and certainly in areas of business - there is a shortage of qualified labour. In such cases anything that can put more power to the elbow through technology is going to be used. Where we already have unemployment the situation is less easy to assess. The need for competitiveness will always encourage better approaches and as mentioned earlier the demand from professionals can be a driving force.

However, it must be recognised that there could be some very significant changes in the power structure. Going back to earlier remarks, we are going to have to redefine skills, and in so doing we are going to provide opportunity for a lot of people to enter the employment market in different ways. For example, a handicapped person can now use the word processor to good advantage; the person who could not hold a pencil straight and could not draw without shaking can now make use of developments in computer-aided design. The sort of people who could not add a hundred numbers up in a row and get the same answer every time can now do many things that were, for example, seen as accounting, or even management. You can change the whole skill base by the use of a computer-backed (if you like to call it that) information system. And now, we can all buy the software which will enable us to do our own tax returns without the need to resort to advice from an accountant.

If legislation is changed in such a way as to reduce the power of some professional bodies, we will in fact find that more people undertake work from which they were previously excluded. We may even have a revolution in the teaching profession. In this respect it is interesting that many comments have been made about how much easier it is to introduce new ideas and systems into a productive sector, because it is possible to measure the effects upon output more easily than in the service sectors.
In some cases this may be true, but there are standards in the service sectors, and if we look closely at those standards we might find that the present training programmes are not well designed to satisfy the demands which will be made upon the professions in the future.

A possible development is the extension of self-education to more people, many of whom are well able to handle computers and to benefit from 'expert systems' technology.
A distributed educational system could be a big issue, with the next or perhaps even the current generation of children buying software in the local micro shop and also developing their own expert systems from home. There are many who would not like such a development to take place, and if it did it is clear that there would need to be other changes, e.g. in social interaction patterns. But do we have a choice? Technology may be neutral, but in a competitive society unless we have an alternative technology that is going to provide the same and results, we do not have too many options.

We are now facing tremendous new challenges, new opportunities and new stimuli. The major stimulus may be competition but in addition there must be excitement, more control over the job, a widening of the job content, etc. So what will be the key determinants? User interest, user involvement, user demand, and perhaps an increasing reliance on people who are innovators. There are many people who really do want to see change, because they see benefits in it. There are many people who see the opposite. A need therefore is to get a variety of systems used by the people who really are the change agents in the organization. The positive benefits from them can then be seen by others, who will eventually follow. The initiatives must be from the grass-roots and not from outside.

In conclusion there are many, many opportunities. The technology is attractive, but may not be seen to be so by all people. There are obviously implications for education, and what may be most productive is to promote the exchange of information between the developers and the users with the possibility of adopting a Unilever-type model where the aim is to have 'user-developers' with consultants - internal or external - there to be called upon for advice and assistance as and when required.

ARTIFICIAL INTELLIGENCE: Towards Practical Application
T. Bernold and G. Albers (editors)
Elsevier Science Publishers B.V. (North-Holland)

THE INFLUENCE OF ARTIFICIAL INTELLIGENCE ON ORGANIZATIONAL STRUCTURE AND RATIONALIZATION

Hans-Willi Hüsch

Manager of the Institute for applied Innovation Studies
University of Duisburg
Duisburg
Federal Republic of Germany

Erich Staudt

Director of the Institute for Applied Innovation Studies
University of Duisburg
Duisburg
Federal Republic of Germany

RATIONALIZATION AND AUTOMATION [1] THROUGH TECHNOLOGY WITH INCREASED FLEXIBILITY

An analysis of business development processes reveals that in most businesses, full use has not been made of the available technical possibilities for rationalization, aimed at improved efficiency. Rationalization, in the sense of using technical advances, has supplanted out-of-date production procedures and structures, got rid of old-fashioned methods of manufacture, and free people from difficult - sometimes intolerable - tasks. However, a certain caution has always remained in regard to sources of technical rationalization. This is the result of the practical techno-economic constraints of the technologies available until now.

The root of the problem is that a workable rationalization policy based on automation (taken to be technology used for operating processes in production and administration) must endeavour to keep a certain degree of flexibility. This allows a business to survive in a changing environment by adapting to changing conditions. The theory that automation and business flexibility contradict one another is to be found in much that is written about and practised in business management. It satisfied, and even today in certain areas still completely satisfies, conventional ideas on the technical possibilities of automation. Everywhere examples can be found of extreme automation making only mass-production possible. When, however, in the course of further development, it is possible to make use of today's contrasting technology in artificial intelligence with higher flexibility, that is, with increased ability to change the kind and amount of goods and services, then the conditions in business and work organisation alter decisively.

An examination of industrial development up to the present reveals a trend towards three movements in rationalization. Two examples from production and management organisation will be outlined. (see chart 1)

1) see: Jörg Biethan/Erich Staudt (Hrsg.) (rest of footnote in German)

Starting with a craftsman-like production the result of the earliest rationalization movement was that manpower was partially replaced by a rigid, central technology which the works and organizational structure determined, and considerable falling off in flexibility had to be tolerated. Practical technical and economic consideration led to mass-production by assembly lines or a flood of information by databank systems.

In the second rationalization movement the further expansion of mass-production with manpower playing the controversial role of stop-gap, in a technology-dominated work process, resulted in greater efforts to optimize the technology by upgrading automation. This development led to transfer lines or databank systems with communications interfaces and program generators.

With the different third rationalization trend, entirely qualitative changes now appear possible. Flexibility has taken a remarkable leap forward and is hardly to be recognised from the automation technology available up till now. Robot production or expert systems are only two examples. The use of the new technologies with increased flexibility is resulting in a substantial increase of choices for work and organisation arrangement, and their potential can hardly be grasped.

ORGANIZATIONAL POTENTIAL OF "ARTIFICIAL INTELLIGENCE"

When one looks at today's widespread "production type" in industry, services and management it becomes clear that most business and works organizations spread out from central production and procedure technologies. The rest of the functions, carried out by the worker in such organisations, are to be found in the areas of control/direction and manipulation/operation of the technology installed in the course of development (see chart 2).

Because these technical appliances are often installed as an isolated solution in a partial zone of a business their rigid limits have a restrictive effect on the work procedures of those who are dependent on them. Whereever, this technology proves incompatible with the workers it is usually the workers themselves - being far more flexible - who are made to adapt to the unyielding interfaces of the technology. The enduring tasks of control, direction and operation devolve on the human being. He is thus tied, in place and time, to the technical equipment. His flexibility compensates for the inflexibility of the equipment and restricts the installation of further technology which appears technically impossible or economically pointless.

It is in recent years that a new direction of research, artificial intelligence (AI) has come to the fore. Aimed at reviewing applications, it takes upon itself to soften the "rigid interfaces" of earlier automation and to arrange them flexibly.

Depending on the observer's point of view the basic principle of this new technology can be described as:

- the processing of symbols instead of numbers
- the equal identity (isomorphism) of cognitive ability between men and machines.
- the development of methods and instruments which makes possible what was hitherto the reserve of men, that is to simulate ways of behaviour by means of the computer and to make accessible scientific considerations in particular concerning their technical consequences.

Five elements are usually to be distinguished, [1] although there is some overlapping:

- deduction systems
- expert systems
- natural language processing
- computer vision
- "intelligent" robot technology

Refined techniques and new developments in already well-known automation technologies are notable with AI. In particular:

- in micro-electronics and its related fields
- in information and communications systems, especially data processing, numerical controlled methods, telecommunications and telemation, connected with
- mechanical engineering.

Artificial intelligence differs from already known technologies in that:

- part of the work process, in particular controlling and operating, which was done by men because it was impossible to do it with technology, can now be turned over to it,
- at a price which makes use of men in these areas seem hardly cost-effective,
- and in many cases faster, more flexibly than men, whose capacities in these directions are sometimes overestimated.
- in addition there are further techno-economic advantages such as smaller energy requirements, longer exploitation, greater load capacitiy, miniaturization and integratibility.

The use of this new generation of automation technologies demands changes in the product spectrum and in the framework of manufacturing and management processes. It widens the variety of conventional goods and services and contains sources of considerable reationlization and innovation.

The organizational potential (see chart 3) of these substituting, rationalizing and innovating procedures is that what men at present regard as simple control functions, can be carried out by robots which in the future will do them more cheaply (chart 3). Hand-in-hand with the functional changes come economic effects resulting from the ever-lowering price of processors and memory elements, so that this "substitute for human flexibility" can be offered for sale at a price which not only places them in serious competition with human workers but also presents society with a chance to make a leap forward in the quality of working life through flexibility in business and works organisations. It is now much more possible to substitute functions of manipulation which still exist, with a cost-effective appliance of lower intelligence which will release men from the stultifying, monotonous tasks of assembly, mounting and information processing.

The robot is totally indifferent to adverse working conditions. It therefore economises on extra pay for difficult work and, for the first time, jobs can be done which would damage the health of worker. The advantages of intelligent operational technology are especially to be seen in the field of assembly work. Because of the high cost of assembly in proportion to the total cost of manufacture - up to 50% - this new robot technology takes on a decisive meaning, even with the installation of smaller and medium batch sizes of up to 500,000 units [1].

1) see: Bibel, W./Siekmann, J.H. (Hrsg.): Künstliche Intelligenz, Berlin 1982

A marked improvement in the economic working level of assembly of every kind is found, for example:

- in the field of precision assembly robots (Scora-concept of Prof. Makino Japan)
- in the field of plastics machines with robots operating the loading and unloading,
- in the field of NC-toolmachines with universal robots of higher intelligence and sensors to change tools and parts.

In West Germany today about 70% of industrial robots have been installed as tool guides and the remaining 30% supervise the manufacture of components.[2)]

In addition to the humanizing aspect of doing jobs like cast iron cleaning, paint spraying, welding etc. it is the increased quality and maintained standards of quality together with higher flexibility and often considerable production improvement that are inducing a greater readiness to install these robots. At the moment difficulty is being experienced in installing robots in assembly-line welding and coating.

With the advancing automation of operations which up to now were areas of human activity dependent on information- or materials-flow, the interdependence of machines and men serving them begins to decline.

Since, however, the operations technology requires, along with its self-regulating functions, a higher level of management and direction, there also appears in the operations area a vertical division of work through the separation of performance from direction and management. The improvement, for example, in robot-direction, and the simpler programming that goes with it (with joy-sticks in the teach-in-method for example as well as the reasonably-priced small robots for testing and training) offer an opportunity to put the new technology to use at a favourable cost. Integrated micro-computers equiped with textual and verbal communication initiate the new user automatically into their techniques.

With the growth of automation the dependence of personnel on the flow of materials and documents is undergoing a transition which is steadily becoming more noticeable. Staff is increasingly dependent on the flow of information at managerial level. This makes clearly meaningful the potential of the new information and communication techniques for the further development of the organisation.

The advances in the field of artificial intelligence, in specialised software and in technical help, are leading to automation of recording, processing, storing, transfer and issue of information. Information processes which men carry out with their own brainpower will increasingly be supported or even partly replaced by the use of:

- expert systems
- data, text, sound and image processing systems.

Expert systems are being developed, for example, for the medical diagnoses and treatment of bacteriological illnesses (Mycin) or for oil prospecting, to replace specialists or relieve them of routine tasks. A search is going on to move from mechanical responses to perception of form. The aim is to substitute the alternating relationship between eye and brain with an artificial image-comprehension technology and to link the environment with machines.

1) see Wirtschaftswoche Nr. 14 v. 30.03.84, S. 96 ff.
2) Ibid

In the realm of communications too, exchange of information is the result not merely of direct personal contacts but, to a growing extent, and with the assistance of technical systems, of the further development of data processing and information technology, as in:

- telecommunications or, in addition
- natural language access systems, etc.

Thus, for example, the EIES system (Electronic Information Exchange System of Professor Turoff, Institute of Technology, New Jersey, 1976) makes it possible to communicate round the clock, over any distance and at asynchronic times thanks to terminal connections and telecommunication equipment (appliances) to a communications computer network. The system allows the other person in the dialogue to have his own work pattern. No one is forced to confer at times when he is perhaps relaxing or tired. In addition the system offers (partially) automated support functions like project tracking, budgeting or making available works or conference reports, etc.

The goal of the endeavours in the field of artificial intelligence is to facilitate entry into and communication with the computer, for example by voice control, and in this way to raise the level of flexibility in computer technology.

The stiff, complicated man-and-machine dialogues common until now will increasingly be adjusted to the "normal" voice sensation of the user. Immediate applications are to be seen in the coupling of voice control systems with a databank, perhaps with an expert system or a robot.

In this way technology can now be used (see chart 4) at exactly those points where the limits of rationalization once stood. These limits were necessitated by the dependence of personnel on the supply of materials and documents, and by links combining the direction and management levels with the executive units (chart 4).

With the development of new technological units with artificial intelligence and with a higher potential for flexibility than previour automation, the rationalization frontiers are pushed back and lead to changes in the division of work. Above all, from the point of view of economic advantage, these have important consequences in allowing greater latitude for production organization.

Installing the new technology means that in production, the interfaces between men in machine-minding and skilled work move towards the periphery. The job of stop-gap which men did in the partially automated process can be taken over extensively by operational robots. The intervention of men in the flow of material is placed at the outside edge of such production zones. Instead of using direct intervention he has industrial robots and transport systems at his disposal and can program their operation and control the execution.

In the vertical division between men and machines, the possibilities for self-regulation by technical devices increase with the degree of automation.The phases available to men in the remaining control/management functions or in machine operation are increasing. This detaching can be carried so far with the help of the new technologies that only one regulation relating to despatch or withdrawal is required in one shift, so that, for example ghost shifts will be set up.

All the new possibilities for beaking linkages show that the processing of materials can be executed, to an ever-growing extent, independently of personnel.

But also in the field of purely human processes, the man-to-man relationships, the availability of information-processing installations and appropriate storage systems weaken the need to work together. Where formerly the written word was relied on there are now databank and retrieval systems at people's disposal. Such systems allow co-operation processes to be detached from time and so relegate the co-operation problem to a consecutive problem by the use of man-machine dialogues. A simple example of this is the cash dispenser at banks where the payment of money is separated in time from the control of the customer consultant or cashier, and the customer is independent of the bank's opening times.

As this simple example shows, technology is beginning to help in the purely human organization process, and is being used there, where formerly there was none. But new interface problems are arising, particularly in the service and management sectors, between men and machines, whose aspects the present-day (Bildschirm Diskussion) only partially touches upon.

With the installation of the new telecommunications systems, further solutions are offered to problems where only humans are concerned.

The opportunities for co-operation, even over long distances, where recourse to documents is necessary are now offered through central databanks and by telecommunication. The old problem of being present is reduced to the technical one of the availability of video terminals and telecommunications links. Again the question arises of the proper work-place and the need for change from the present-day centralized work-place to the concept of work that is removed in distance and time.

The last and most important growth-point resulting from the installation of AI-technology is the possibility of a new division of work between men and machines (see chart 5).

Formerly, conventional manufacture required the presence of the machinist who determined the running time of all the machinery, because production could only be thought of as being synchronized with human control, or because quality could only be ensured through the continual intervention of men regulating the machines. The outcome of this has been that today a single man involved with several complicated processes is often overtaxed. One has only to think of what is involved in spaceship coupling manoeuvres, reactor control or low-level flying.

The function of steering, as may be seen in the programming of industrial robots, can be entirely removed to the office and thereby separated from the manufacturing area in time and place.

The new generation of programming and storage systems for steering and control information allow the steering/control software to be created and made available at entirely different times. It need no longer be for the use of an individual machinist and one can steer and control without stress and with recourse to the experience of others. Associated with the integration of these new-won technical possibilities there are, however, far-reaching processes of qualification and disqualification.

THE INFLUENCE OF ARTIFICIAL INTELLIGENCE ON QUALIFICATION AND DECISION-MAKING STRUCTURES IN BUSINESS

Technological changes in the arrangement of work places and production methods require supporting sociological strategies which, with the modernization and adaption of business training and further education programs, make it possible for employees to master the new technologies without their working or social positions being downgraded. But people at management level too, must involve themselves in these new learning processes.

Upper management must learn to think innovatively about technical, economic and social correlations as well as about breaks with present trends. It must accept the fact that being open to innovation is to a certain extent "antagonistic" to organisation because "innovative management", in contrast to organisations which regulate routine tasks, may not look on any problem as being finally solved and, because of the complexity of the problems, cannot respect any departmental frontiers. [1)]

Middle management will have to exchange its control of material and documentation flow for co-ordination tasks in the areas of information and communication, not least because the limits of rationalization have moved back and automated production zones have pushed men out to peripheral areas. The growing possibilities for flexibility in work-organisation can only be put into practice through decentralized automated control mechanisms because linked, central, command structures which are not infallible lead back to practical technical and economic constraints. Rationally constructed artificial intelligence programs can be created with the help of computers of the fifth generation which imitate the subjective reasoning, the "psycho-logic" of the decision-making man.

But in addition to scepticism as to the technical feasibility, business undertakings see several other unanswered questions:

- who shall the risk, inevitable in all decisions, devolve on when artificial intelligence does the deciding, and what consequences will there be for the hierarchy and power divisions when artificial systems take over responsibility for decision-making?
- to what extent can rationally put-together artificial intelligence take over the "irrational" thinking and the contrasting creative thinking of human decision-makers?
- will it in fact be possible for "ideal" feasibility schemes in the problem-solving machine to give realistic help in resolving the uncertainties as to the overall trade area, required by special circumstances, and the substitution of rational thinking with personal opinions and far-reaching expectations?
- Can it be said with certainty that the human "box of tricks" for solving problems is capable of being described once and for all - a consideration which has special significance from the point of view of costs.
- Even if it were possible to refer back the problem-solving to a routine procedure model with a large enough range, would that not deprive the simulated individual of all creativity?

Qualities of active creation and unconscious resentments have no place in information processing. The unmistakable moment of relief for the brain-worker comes when in the process of solving problems artificial intelligence transfers in the shortest possible time an unimaginable amount of data of many different kinds into new classification and structuring models.

1) See Staudt, E. (rest of footnote in German)

The interdependence of reasoning and intuitive phases in the solution of problem still evade technical algorismic treatment. [1)]

TECHNICAL AND ORGANIZATIONAL POTENTIALS OF THE CHANGE IN INDUSTRIAL SOCIETIES

Present-day practices in business and industrial structures are the result of very long social development. Since the beginning of the industrial revolution, of the resulting incursion of mechanization, and of the progressive division of work in the achievement of industrialization, the absorbtion of men into the process of operations has been fraught with problems.

The arrangement of work is dominated by technical and economic considerations which restrict the latitude and potential in work organisation. These practical constraints have not only become more important in the theme of industrialization but also implicitly and explicitly accepted as the determining link in a great many deliberations about change in industrial society. The ideal of determining the functions, position and working-times of business and works structures on the basis of given technical and economic facts hides the growing freedom for manoeuvre in the progress of the latest technical development of artificial intelligence. [1)]

The neglect of this manoeuvrability through the micro-economic conversion of suitable technological developments leads to two false evaluations in explanations of the change. They are typified by two areas of uncertainty:

- the shortage of micro-economic analysis in highly aggregated macro-economic research in technology assessment and
- the domination of technical and economic consideration in studies of technology consequences towards personnel.

1. Scarcity of integrated explanatory evaluations of the change.

Many highly integrated explanatory evaluations of the change in industrial societies are based on a kind of short -circuit forecast in which politico-cultural, economic and social change is connected directly to technical developments. Very often all the adjustment at micro-economic levels is skipped. The entire complex of work division, specializing, organizing, substituting, etc. is dismissed as no problem although these elements carry great weight in the social structure . [1)] In other words the relationships between the introduction of technology and economic organizational objectives, as well as work divisions and rationalization strategies are neglected.

If on the other hand, it is considered that, in free-market systems for technical development , the bulk of the scientific technical research as well as the conversion of scientific-technical knowledge into production, products and services are carried out by enterprises, then it becomes obvious that innovations in market systems gain acceptance only if they seem to make "economic sense" and not because they are technically workable or socially desirable.

Decisions which will lead to changes in structure take place in small-scale areas at business level. On the one hand, the economic ability to convert to new techniques determines the success of a firm while, on the other, the analytical forecasting of these very processes of change allows for statement only on their consequences.

1) see Staudt, E. (rest of footnote in German)

Meanwhile, global studies of problems involving technical and economic development are a matter of everyday politics. A study is still far off of business convertion with its necessary supports and compensations and the micro-economic considerations that go with these. This deficiency makes it all the more difficult to consider practical business consequences and problems of installing new techniques without getting lost in speculations and vague suppositions. There is a gap in research which must be closed before generalized statements about the global consequences of technology are ventured upon.

In spite of, or because of this lack of research, attempts at explanation of the technical change in industrial society continue to be made. They are usually based on material techno-economic forces but these, on closer examination, prove to contain contradictions. Thus, for example, it is assumed on one side, that the problems of installing a new technique are easily overcome, and this is intended in a positive sense, because the question of how to convert the existing technology is simply not raised. But on another side, in order to reckon with levels of high integration, dynamic responses, such as solutions with creative variants, are not attempted for the businesses included in the analyses.

The projections of technological results usually relate to fictitious conditions in a static economy and if a static employer-employee attitude is supposed, that allows of as few variations as attempts at interpretation or forecasts are in a position to work on. But the scarcity of micro-economic analysis of the practical answers to organising technical introductions begin in fact one stage earlier. It is the linkage created by individuals that joins together technological, economic and social factors in change, and this linkage has not been sufficiently analysed. [1]. The tradition of man coupled in fuction, place and time to the work process is taken for granted. Moves to uncouple him remain unattempted.

2. Technical and economic necessities in attempt to consider the position of people in relation to change.

In the second line of approach of technology forecasting and assessment, based more on social sciences, conceptions of rigid, determining relationships between technology and its consequences on competence, employment and work organisation are still widely held.

At the centre of these considerations is man, and the effects of technology on man are eveluated, as if there was an unmistakable causal connection between special technical capacity and human circumstances in a relevant production or service.

This sort of consideration ignores the fact that technical results stem not directly from technology itself but from conditions in specific areas of use to which it is put.

Numerous controversies about the usefulness or otherwise of specific technologies ought to touch upon this misunderstanding. For if technical results are the results of specific uses of a piece of technology, then differences which emerge in estimating technical effects are often the result of surveys based on differing ways of using the same machine. If one simply regards modifying the area in which it is used as influenceing technology and technical development, one fails to recognise the latitude offered by the increasing flexibility of technology, for example, with decentralised, distributed artificial intelligence. Instead, the matter should be considered from the opposite direction.

1) see (rest of footnote in German)

Rather than starting with technical optima or the technical imperative in the search for solutions to work organisation, it is necessary to establish and make practicable the possibilities for business and work re-organisation using the growing flexibility of technology, if the great potential for innovation in the new generation of technology is to be inserted economically. The use of this kind of scope, however, seems limited in market economy systems.

Just where conditions for installing the technology are worth influencing, there is a second factor added to the technical imperative. It is the economic imperative.

The increasing work divisions and mechanization required, in the case of industrial development, a harmonization of function, place and time by large groups of workers, with each other and with the locations and working times of existing technical aggregates.

- From the co-ordination of a fairly large group of people fulfilling the same job together came the first linking force, namely the sharing of work and synthesis in a man-and-man operating process.
- The increasing partial replacement of man-power by machine-power produced a further linkage - the sharing of work and synthesis between employees and mechanical groupings in a man-and-machine coupling.

According to the character of the job to be done and the basic method in which the work is divided two further ways of coupling may be distinguished.

These are:

- co-operative coupling, where different functions in jobs are separated and executed jointly in the working process,
- consecutive coupling where jobs are cut up into piece work, each part being completed independtly from another. The allotment of this piece work can be done, for example, according to specialised skills.

Co-operative coupling suffers from the constraints of synchronism while consecutive coupling represents, in principle, independent operations. Here the tie with time schedules results from additional, economic considerations, such as:

- lowering the throughput time,
- minimizing the waiting and stopping times
- reducing the stock of the organisation
- and the carrying out of work in the information and materials flow connected with all this. 1) (p. 27)

These material considerations narrow down the scope for arrangement in business structuring and work organisation and are then the basis of economic assessments.

Proceeding from a quantitative frame-work, taken to be the determining factor, these traditional considerations fail to appreciate:

- that emphasis is placed on numerous rational-seeming economic decisions which in general have absolutely no rational foundation.[1) (p.28)]

1)(p.27) see (rest of footnote in German)

1)(P.28) see (German) Demonstrated with the example of experiments in work organization in industry. At the same time, a criticism of attempts at decision orientation in business studies.

- that conventional, widely practised, estimates of efficiency leave room for considerable latitude. 2) (p.28)

Simplified monetry portrayals of the quantitative frame-work abstracted from implied flexibility, and decisions based only on certain facets of reality, admit of a further conclusion - that still more manoeuvrability for the arrangement of business and works organisation is emerging micro-economically through the introduction of artificial intelligence and the flexibility it offers.

Conventional economic assessments thereby fails even more.

The want of clear outlines which is occuring results from the impossibility of determining technically the links in man-and-machine operations or of forming definite, formal economic opinions on them. Lack of consideration of uncoupling scope and of its economic shift, is the source of many false appraisals in correlations of actions.

The existence of such ill-defined areas tells against the technical and economic imperatives, which are not always made clear, and against the correlations of action in industrial society which are determined by such imperatives. At the same time such ill-defined areas imply considerable potential of flexibility and elasticity for the change in industrial society.

SUMMARY

On the basis of selected examples from areas of change, the possibilities of influence for the newly emerging generation of automation technology, "artificial intelligence", were outlined. Micro-economic analysis shows that the much-criticised inflexible confrontation between men and machines can be removed, since new techniques blur the borderlines and thus contain options for arranging a technique, which, from the point of view of those involved in using it, will be more "flexible" to organise.

The possibilities for uncoupling in the man-and-machine system invalidate the most important, classical, economic argument for strict on-the-spot control and for regulation of working times. The machine is no longer the restricting factor round which the organisation must adjust itself. Instead, it is a cost-effective source of flexibility which can operate far apart from human beings. Proceeding from staffing and social units it will permit cost-effective technical potentials to be co-ordinated with the easing of work loads. To a far greater extent than at present, social and technical organisations and related personal and social needs can be harmonised with each other. At the same time, an increase in flexibility of economic capacity may be used along with possibilities for product changes and, above all, the individualizing and further development of goods and services.

Whether these options can be used depends largely on how far it will be possible to alter built-in patterns of organisation, among legislator, trade-unions and employers, which have become established in response to earlier technical and economic conditions. Here, for the moment, lie the most important remaining limits to uncoupling, which still prevent the threshold of practical applications from being crossed on a wider front.

2) (p. 28) see (rest of footnote in German)

LITERATURHINWEISE

Bibel, W./Siekmann, J.H. (Hrsg.): Künstliche Intelligenz, Berlin 1982

Biethan, J./Staudt, E. (Hrsg.): Automation in Industrie und Verwaltung - Oekonomische Bedingungen und soziale Bewältigung, Berlin 1981.

Hinz, H.:Der Bankrott des Tylorismus. Qualität der Arbeit - Qualität des Arbeitsplatzes. In: Biethahn, J./Staudt, E. (Hrsg.): Der Betrieb im Qualitätswettbewerb - Von der Qualitätssicherung zur offensiven Qualitätspolitik, Berlin 1982, S. 65-77.

Staudt, E.:Wachsende Freiräume in der Gestaltung von Arbeitsorganisationen. In: Mitteilungen aus der Arbeitsmarkt- und Berufsforschung, MittAB, 17. Jg., 1984, Nr. 1, S. 94-104

Ibid: Bedürfniserfüllung - Anspruch und Wirklichkeit. Wege und Irrwege zur Technikbewertung aus einzelwirtschaftlicher Sicht. In: Rapp, F. (Hrsg.): Ideal und Wirklichkeit der Techniksteuerung. Sachzwänge - Werte - Bedürfnisse. Reihe: Der Ingenieur in Beruf und Gesellschaft. Hrsg. v. Verein Deutscher Ingenieure, Düsseldorf 1982, S. 147-179.

Ibid: Entkopplung im Mensch-Maschine-System durch neue Technologien als Grundlage einer Flexibilisierung von Arbeitsverhältnissen. In: Meyer-Abich, K.H. / Steger, U. u.a. (Hrsg.): Mikroelektronik und Dezentralisierung, Berlin 1982.

Ibid: Widerstände bei der Einführung neuer Technologien - 'Anwendung der Mikroelektronik' als Herausforderung an Technologiemanagement und -politik. In: VDI-Z 7/1982, S. 233-241.

Ibid: Betriebswirtschaftliche Beurteilung neuer Arbeitsstrukturen. In: Zeitschrift für Betriebswirtschaft, 51. Jg. (1981), H.9, S. 871-892.

Ibid: Die Bedeutung der mirkoökonomischen Analyse zur Beurteilung und Durchsetzung neuer Arbeitsstrukturen. In: Mitteilungen aus derArbeitsmarkt- und Berufsforschung, MittAB 3/1979, S. 328-339.

Ibid: Planung als "Stückwerktechnologie". Demonstriert am Beispiel arbeitsorganisatorischer Experimente im Industriebetrieb. Zugleich eine Kritik entscheidungsorientierter Ansätze in der Betriebswirtschaftslehre, Göttingen 1979.

ARTIFICIAL INTELLIGENCE: Towards Practical Application
T. Bernold and G. Albers (editors)
Elsevier Science Publishers B.V. (North-Holland)

EVALUATION OF ARTIFICIAL INTELLIGENCE WITH REGARD TO SIZE OF CAPITAL INVESTMENT AND RISK

Jörgen Biedermann

COMOR AG
Computer- und Organisationsberatung
Zurich
Switzerland

The subject which has been allotted to me calls, in this circle, for a contradictory and almost provocative point of view. While on the subject of investment volume and risk, one must reckon with a Controller of Finances, totally biased because of his very status. It would also therefore be completely natural if his first reaction upon hearing the term "Artificial Intelligence" would be, "who is trying to slip me another oil-tracking aeroplane?" If one comes along with abstract explanations of technology such as selflearning models, distribution and integration of mathematical processes and other such things, one automatically awakens memories of costly "l'art pour l'art" projects which were restricted to use in the Data Processing Department. With self-learning models, it is possible to be unlucky, as the memory of the 'sixties is not yet quite erased.
You certainly remember the stories of stock control where these pseudo-optimising calculations were put forward, whereby it was claimed how wonderfully, with the help of a computer, stocks would be reduced. Then came the era of playing around with equalising factors, such as alpha equals 0,8 - 1,1 - those were already religious wars. What was then the effect of these stock control systems, when one left them to their own devices? Left them to their forecast projections and to their formulae? Unfortunately, stocks increased rather than decreased as promised when one left automation have its own way and allowed no human being to influence decisions. We have, so far, mentioned two areas, which are basically to be viewed with scepticism when it comes to any project involving artificial intelligence:

1. The first large complex involves the very critical question of our own capabilities, our own capacity for following through the logical analysis of our thought and decision-making processes in a correct and complete manner; to glean the relevant influences and above all the interdependencies of these relevant influences. Exactly there, I believe, exists the greatest danger that one forgets these intermediate correlations, which lie in the background and are therefore not obvious.
I am also rather disappointed when I hear in this connection of successful "Expert Systems" which contain about 50-60 rules. Take one simple model out of the Operations Research era and you will remember that with 50 or 60 conditions only very simple, student-level models were able to be described - are the self-learning system elements really rationally covered in connection with these interdependencies? In short, are the model and the method at all related to reality?

2. Now for the second point - are the computer systems at all powerful enough to perform all processes quickly and accurately? Can the necessary input data be made available at all? Input data and the connections between these data, and their analysis have always been a big problem. We must therefore ask ourselves: are the fundamental assumptions for any model correct? This is the critical point: the model is correct for some special condition, but the fundamentals of these models change. Are the fundamentals actually mutable? How can one maintain them in the form of data?Does there exist - if one so wishes - some sort of master file maintenance?

And, last but not least, what is produced as output? What is the end result of the system? Is it digestible?
So, to summarise, there remain critical questions regarding the efficiency of the machinery and its establishment in the system environment.
To return to our sceptical Controller of Finances. When we explain to him that the so-called Artificial Intelligence is in fact only the application of a sophisticated advanced information system, he will growl at us and laugh at this new-fangled, pompous name in computer jargon, but he will at least listen to the project idea. The next hurdle is that one can credibly present benefits so that the project is not banished to the realms of fundamental research, possibly with State-financed universities. If one then presents the suitable analogy of the artificial intelligence projects, namely development of complex operating systems for computers, one has a good chance of finally being dismissed with the remark that already much bigger companies, even belonging to the computer branch, have gone bankrupt because of operating systems problems. And examples of these failures can be given with no difficulty, on both sides of the Atlantic. However, let the negative criticism suffice.
One key-word has been mentioned, which is the actual clue to it all, and that is the benefit. To present this in a credible and interesting way, one must depart from a concrete project application. Then the benefit can be presented, as one would optimally wish to see it from the view of the Company Management, and in a way which a Board of Directors can understand: that is, in terms of money, in terms of United States Dollars, German Marks or Swiss Francs. There are some benefits which are directly measurable, such as increase in productivity, headcount savings, reduction of investment of capital and so-called "intangibles" which are not easy to value through means of Cost Accounting by the Financial Administration. But also, for example, improvements in quality have a market relevance and therefore, even with a degree of uncertainty, are to be evaluated in monetary terms. From the measurable and estimable benefits is calculated the allowable investment. As we are still very much at the beginning of the technology of Artificial Intelligence, each individual project will, until further notice, be judged on costs and possible returns.
The technical risk involved, as shortly mentioned, makes costing estimates at least as unsure as any prognosis of benefit. One should therefore give priority to projects which, if successsful, promise a high multiplicatory effect through the number of applications. All unicates, meaning by this applications with a slim chance of being used again, must justify themselves by means of a comfortable distance between estimated cost and benefit. Because of the implied technical difficulties and because of negative experience collected with regard to the analogy of the development of systems software for computers, the estimated benefit should be at least three times as much as the estimated costs.

There is then the possibilitiy that one escapes with minor damage also if, as usual costs and time estimates were too optimistically judged, but still reasonable to a certain extent. With projects where there is the promise of great repetition, all development costs should, to be on the safe side, two to three years after the start of the multiplicity of applications, result in benefits out-distancing the cost volume threefold. I would also recommend to set more restrictive time limitations, and not to accept promises of results in 5 or 7 years from the gentlemen experts. The three-year period is drawn from the observation, as it is at the moment also valid for the development of Hardware-Technology, that one obtains within three years striking progress in the Price to Performance ratio.
As to the type of project application, an important distinction should be made. All projects which come under the heading of "Process Control" for example the control of complex and flexible manufacturing systems, which would include the disposition part, can still be logically and reasonably kept within bounds and could quite easily be reduced to the demanded functions if they came up against too great difficulties persuasively and relatively easily be justifiable as far as the technical mastery of the risk is concerned.

Added to this, comes the fact that such production units in which the Artificial Intelligence are to be used, quickly reach a value of 20 Million Dollars and more, whereby the cost of the artificial intelligence itself does not play a decisive role.

Much more critical are the possible application projects in the area of organisation. In already classic, commercial-administrative data processing there is a whole range of, in themselves, dissatisfying areas of application, which actually with the help of the technology of Artificial Intelligence, should be taken towards a solution. The Sloan School, as one knows, makes a distinction between three hierarchical levels of application, namely the operational, the tactical, above it, as well as the strategic application, at the top. Formulated differently, one calls them Decision Support System.
Here it would mean, on the basis of mass data processing, which we practise today on the operational level, condensing data on the next highest level, in order to offer so much through self-learning systems on the highest level that a man can limit himself to his own associative and creative capabilities on the most important issues. Here the criticism really starts. On what level is it actually already all over for the machine and where is mankind with its association capabilities still way ahead of these models? There are enormous doubts that it is at all possible to achieve the logical analysis of actual decision processes and above all to analyse realistically the interdependencies of influencing functions. Before judging the machinery, we should critically evaluate our own capabilities in the conception and development of models. When one recalls with what jubilation we lanced into the use of operations research and how progress-convinced Management set up special departments reporting to themselves - only, hardly ten years later, to allow the whole story to die the quiet gentle organisation death - one should not reproach a computer technique which is today relatively weak as the machinery of that time was capable of inverting matrices. The difficulties were much more in the building of models and in the supplying of these with input data.
The second problem is and remains the performance potential of the computer. Let us take again the analogy of the building of complex operating systems. We all know today that one can suffocate even the largest computers in pure Parkinsonian self-government, if one tries to use all the possibilities of the systems software at the same time or to use it otherwise in a not too refined or intelligent way. What shall we think of Artificial Intelligence under these auspices? The basis of strategic decision support systems, not to mention self-decision making systems will in the commercial-administrative area always be the processing of mass data. And exactly this means the necessity of setting up powerful number crunchers. We are not speaking any longer of the combination of excellent processor-performance alone, but also of the peripheral mass data storage channels and all the rest. The question of performance potential is therefore raised in projects of Artificial Intelligence in this area. Let us imagine that in a pilot project you receive a suitable model and get it to function with test data, then the critical question is the performance with real, i.e. a considerable greater volume of data. Let us further imagine that one of the companies involving itself with Artificial Intelligence guarantees the performance potential by reason of their pioneering trust in the pilot or test model. When it then does not function, the danger of this company's bankruptcy is very real and for the user the problem is not solved, and the money spent(which he has up) until now (invested) is lost. In this way, nobody has gained anything. For such projects, the background of very large, financially strong firms would be required. To come back yet again to our Controller of Finances, employed by such a financially strong company, he will certainly ask why the large computer manufacturers, which do most of their business in the region of commercial/administrative areas, have not fully embarked upon this technology of Artificial Intelligence.

He will imagine that they have not, or maybe only slightly, missed the boat in the new developments in computer science, and that they in the first place estimate the risks of a large scale application too high against the possible benefits. His conclusion is, therefore, technology is not yet so far advanced that it would be of interest to his Organisation.
This means that it is still much easier to invest in COBOL programmes.Even if this is old-fashioned, one can easily obtain a credit for a million, whereas one hundred thousand for a project in the field of artificial intelligence is almost impossible. We should not forget, in commercial data processing, that more money has been invested in COBOL programmes, quite normal primitive commercial programmes, than in hardware. These investments must be protected. Therefore, the apparatus and systems of Artificial Intelligence must base themselves thereon. They must be compatible. In this commercial-administrative region of application, the competition remains the conventional methods and all our experiences teaches us that here the human being is hardly to be replaced in the decision-making procedures. Artificial Intelligence would soon be very interesting in spite of this, if its technology can break through in such a way that it could also be accepted as conventional, that is, proven and verified. Until then, it seems that the use in relatively risk-free technical process control areas is more reasonable, due to the easier Cost/Benefit evaluation.

ARTIFICIAL INTELLIGENCE: Towards Practical Application
T. Bernold and G. Albers (editors)
Elsevier Science Publishers B.V. (North-Holland)

POSSIBILITIES AND LIMITATIONS OF ARTIFICIAL INTELLIGENCE

Panel discussion

Careful but optimistic pragmatism characterised the expectations of panel and audience about the future of Artificial Intelligence (AI). The discussion reflected the sincere interest in a realistic assessment of AI with a specific emphasis on Expert Systems and Knowledge Engineering. The shortage of manpover, economic considerations, limitations of the current technology and questions focussing on the social impact were identified as the critical issues for the further development of this field of Advanced Information Technology.

The shortage of manpower rather than economic considerations seems to emerge as the main obstacle for a rapid development of AI in the near future. The basis, particularly in Europe, has to be strengthened, stress the scientists. They fear a new wave of the braindrain to the United States which would deprive Europe of the most creative and gifted talents, jeopardizing severely Europe's chances in world-wide computer competition. The establishment of AI as a branch of computer science is urged as well as a better and up to date computer environment.

A solution to the current problems could be achieved by a better cooperation with industry as demonstrated in the USA. Such a model could provide an early exposure to practical problems of applications, complementing the theoretical training and education. Nevertheless, there is no generally accepted model available yet and one has to recognize the considerable regional differences in the size and effectiveness of the European scientific infrastructure.

Regarding the obvious lack of trained people differentiation nevertheless is necessary. A closer analysis of an Expert System Project reveals a structure of four basic levels of functions in development and use: writing the Expert System shell, interviewing the expert and designing the architecture, programming the system which means coding and modifying the rules and finally its actual use. Obviously the end user shouldn't need any training at all whereas the work on the shell requires a profound training and knowledge about the complex technologies of AI. In other words there are more people who can work in this field than those who have only had the formal education.

A third point of view regarding the problem of manpower derives from the well established fact of the multi- and interdisciplinarity of AI-research. There was the notion of unmined resources among people who so far were not believed to be able to contribute much to building AI-Systems. They are people having backgrounds in philosophy, psychology, liberal arts such as literature, linguistics, etc. Much to the surprise of the specialists they had often a better capability of formulating, synthesizing and conceptualizing systems than people with a computer science background. Sussex is one of the universities which recognized this fact early, institutionalizing an interdisciplinary undergraduate and graduate program with AI as the intellectual core but with philosophy, psychology and linguistics as equal cooperating partners.

AI is still a young and evolving subject of computer science with an obvious need for basic research. Despite the current spread of practical applications in Expert Systems and related fields it is difficult to conduct an economic evaluation. Not many systems can yet prove a return on the initial investment which is a difficulty in a business world where quick profit is a basic philosophy. Nevertheless, costs seem not to be a predominant problem. Thus it is rather the question of believing in the usefulness and future of the methodology and of being part of its development, that companies have to answer.

It is a common experience too that getting into AI and building internal capabilities is much harder than envisaged. It usually takes in the order of one to two years to train people to do relatively simple tasks, to work in teams and to design their own objectives. The example of Unilever showed however that it is possible to establish credibility in Knowledge Engineering on a comparably restricted budget. The project started on a small scale and expanded slowly, quietly in an evolutionary manner with the specific aim to be demonstrable and useful.

This example defines one end of the spectrum of current developments. These systems may be characterized as relatively simple, small and task specific. On the opposite side we find the work on the technological limits of today's state of this science. The problem of automatic knowledge acquisition were mentioned as one of them. Progress is not expected to be fast because it involves some of the most difficult questions about cognitive processes. Nevertheless, nobody felt that these obvious limitations would be of any relevance to today's applications.

Perhaps it is a lack of imagination that makes it so difficult to envisage and discuss the social implications of technology in general and Artificial Intelligence in particular. The need has been recognized and the panel voiced this concern in saying: "I think we have overlooked in our quest for technology, in our preoccupation with computers and computer software, the human side of things". Regarding the future development of AI this could mean assisting the human being to be more creative.

Thomas Bernold

INFRASTRUCTURE, RESEARCH AND TRAINING

ARTIFICIAL INTELLIGENCE: Towards Practical Application
T. Bernold and G. Albers (editors)
Elsevier Science Publishers B.V. (North-Holland)

PROBLEMS OF THE INFRASTRUCTURE: THE BOTTLENECKS IN RESEARCH AND TRAINING

Stefano A. Cerri

Department of Informatics
University of Pisa
Pisa
Italy

A frame for discussion means that what I will tell you is at a "high" mental level, i.e. it consists of words with which everyone can agree or disagree and on which many arguments can be made; the bottleneck metaphor, viewpoints on AI as a discipline, needs and compliants of industry and acadamia (by academia I mean the set of universities, public research centers and government institutions which are more or less concerned with supporting education and research without expecting necessarily any short term reward in financial terms); tentative interpretation of the problems in terms of a causal chain; and suggestions of solution by industry and academia.

Here is a set of statements which relativise what I will tell you in the following: meanings of words are often ambiguous, many issues may seem obvious and thus irrelevant. What is not irrelevant is actually the unsolved bottleneck problem of education and training in AI. Different decision makers may be sensitive to opposite arguments. Unfortunately, there is no recipe for solving the problem and, as in AI, solutions are best found by tentative strategies, multiple reasoning, cooperative distributed interacting architectures and so on, and finally, the motto of the first step for solving a problem is to be aware of its existence.

What is the bottleneck metaphor. The situation at the end of 70's could well be this one: at the top of the typical Tuscany wine bottle, above the bottleneck there is to some extent AI expertise and possibilities of growing the people in the green-houses into the universities and the research centers. And there is a very tiny need from industry - at the bottom of the bottle - for many reasons. The situation changed practically at the beginning of or mid 80's, due to the crisis which seems to be partially overcome by now. Pressures come at the top of the bottle, from governmental cuts in budgets and from the crisis in general, which has a delayed impact in the resources of the public sector. The bottleneck becomes even smaller and the bottomside of the bottle becomes bigger, due to success of applied AI system, cheaper hardware, limits of software engineering methodologies not in the general sense, but in solving particularly complex problems like VLSI-design problem. Another component is new needs arisen from new problems to be solved, namely more complex problems on the one side, which are illdefined as I said, and on the other side, needs for a more natural or friendly interface with a so-called casual user, the unskilled user. So, the present situation could be sketched in this picture, and the temptation of the companies is of course to turn the bottle, this is not only a temptation, it is a fact in many cases, certainly in the United States, and even in Europe. Turning the bottle means to exploit all of the resources but finish the wine.

I have a few sentences about AI as a discipline. These issues were addressed here in the first 1 1/2 days. AI, I believe, can briefly be defined as the formal study of knowledge, in particular, the way you can handle knowledge by representing it in a machine. Concerning the difference between AI and traditional computer science, the most important aspect is certainly the migration from an attitude considering computing systems as procedures operating on data, to an attitude of considering these systems as embodying descriptions of the word. This is a very basic attitude and I will say one more word which relates also to my own contribution from the audience this morning. The descriptive nature of knowledge in AI makes it very different to design an AI system with respect to a traditional system. You do not have an algorithm beforehand, you will have to try and describe situations instead of planning the exact sequence of steps executed by the machine. This makes it theoretically and practically different.

I find a difference between basic and applied research on AI, and within basic research, I distinguish between theoretical and experimental research, and a point I want to make is that too few efforts are spent in academia on experimental research on AI and in general on basic research in AI. The estimate of research efforts spent on AI in acadamia in Europe - referring only to my own intuitions as there are no studies on it - may be some 3% of the overall efforts on informatics. And within AI, 80% is theoretical, may be 15% is applied and the remaining 5% experimental, making advanced prototype systems, embodying new architectures, new structures, new ways of describing knowledge, etc.

I have a provocative slide for you, which starts with the motto: Education in AI is almost equal to training in AI research. This was stated also by - I think Prof. Raulefs. So, AI Education is not just to pour some knowledge into some pupils. It is both telling them something and letting them learn how to use this something, it is the training also.

If all the projects: ESPRIT (1500 million ECUs), ALVEY (1000 MECUs), the German project (2000 MECUs), the French, Italian, Dutch projects and so on (may be 1500 MECUs), will start in a year or two, we will have in Europe something like 6000 MECUs in 5 years for research on information technologies which comes to 1250 MECUs per year in the stable state when all these projects have started. If 50% is given to manpower, we have 600 MECUs per year in manpower. If the average costs of a man year in Europe is 60 KECUs, which is different from the estimate from Howard Austin in the States (Knowledge Analysis Inc. 1983) which was 125 K dollars per year (so Europe is cheap in this respect), we come to 10000 professionals per year within 2 or 3 years, and if 40% of the should be knowledgeable in AI - I do not want to argue about what knowledgeable means - we come to 4000 AI experts, and if the number of European universities capable of providing AI education and training in AI research is roughly about 20 (a very optimistic estimate), we come to about 200 AI experts per university. And if the expected trainer/trainee in AI is 1:5, which is a very optimistic evaluation, and the expected exposure time for an AI expert is from 2 to 4 years (where even the TEKNOWLEDGE representative agrees with), then we come to something which is - I believe - absolutely non-realistic.

I challenge the audience to contradict these figures.

What are the needs and complaints of industry? Academia should produce more graduates in the field of AI, it is too theoretical, it is not cooperative, it is selfish, it does not keep appointments, and many more.

What are the needs and complaints of academia, of - let's say - university people? Students and duties are increasing enormously, tremendously. Resources are proportionally decreasing. Our task is to provide education, not training. If we spent time on training people for research, we would want them to stay with us. Industry wants simply to exploit our ideas, industry does not invest on long term research; project management is not our task, for which we do not have any resources. If industry wants us to do research, they have to accept our proposed themes .... and compensations, and more.

I have a tentative interpretation of the situation in terms of a causal chain. The premise, I think, is the most important of all statements. This is stated as a fact, and you can argue about that. I just put it as an axiom. I do believe that the research-prototype-engineering-production cycle of advanced technologies, for instance information technology, and particularly AI, is not harmonious in Europe. And the well-known factors are the traditional role of the European economy, the traditional attitude of the European industry and the traditional behaviour of European governments. They have always brought Europe to a second role within the general distribution of concerns, particularly in the economic and industrial world.

The consequence, which is premise number 2, the lack of status for instance of AI, as a discipline within the whole academia, links to questions like: should AI be embedded within computer science of informatics, or be an interdisciplinary effort? I am very glad that this issue came up this morning. I strongly believe in what has been said by Prof.M. Boden, e.g. that contributions of linguistics and psychology and training people in these disciplines are relevant aspects. Even informatics needs a status within mathematics and engineering. In Italy, all the research is financed via the committees for mathematics or for engineering. There is no computer science committee.

Consequence number 2 is the lack of resources. The academic interest in AI is casual: the academic reward is low, (chairs in AI are almost absent); often work on AI is done with resistence within departments. Formal courses and seminars on AI issues are almost absent (due to lack of chairs); theoretical studies are preferred to experimental or applied ones (due to lack of financial resources for machines and manpower); AI laboratories seldom exist, traditional equipment is preferred. The consequence to the lack of resources is the lack of impact of AI, as cultivated within academia, on industry.

Most computer science graduates never had education in AI. The few who did never wrote any AI programs. Industry is forced to spend years on training people in AI. That environment is not optimal for such training, better send them to the U.S., but then, they do not come back because of the money and status.

I have a few suggestions in the last few minutes. All these should be taken as very tentative and I am glad if you react to it. What should be done by industry?

First of all, industry has to decide about the danger of playing a subordinate role in advanced technologies. It has to take a decision similar to the one taken at the European level at present (ESPRIT). If it is too risky to play a subordinate role, then invest in European know-how. In order to invest, do not be impatient, investing only on applications, identify basic experimental research (and education) in AI within Academiaas a primary need. Identify the few promising research groups and build on the existent. In order to build on the existent, make pressure on governments, support joint projects like ESPRIT or ALVEY. Obviously universities who would be involved in projects should be 100% financed.

You can argue on this, but it would remain a problem. Companies should invest directly on long term research in universities as is the case, for instance, in USA, and found joint research centers for AI (cfr. BEN, SRI, ... in USA), a phenomenon which seems to take place also in Europe now.

The suggestions for academia concerning the premises: Do worry about economic and social changes caused by information technology! Recognize chances for autonomous growth in Europe and recognize danger of the increasing gap to economic survival. Concerning the choice of the field, it is important that research and education within government and academia be no longer seen as something nice to be done, mainly as a social issue, but as something which is a prerequisite and a necessary condition for economic growth. At present, this means an exceptional effort. Concerning the method in supporting this exceptional growth: identify experimental AI within academia as a key point and provide resources for an exceptional growth. Outstanding groups should be financed independently on academic status (notice that most of the AI skilled people are very young!); cooperation between experimental and theoretical AI scientists should be facilitated, researchers should be protected from the industrial pressure (e.g. money), bureaucracy should be made smoother, leaderships of groups should emerge spontaneously, and not automatically related to age.

As to the tools, I suggest a group size of 5-10 (cfr. 1-2 for theoretical research). Secretarial/administrative supports would be needed: and equipment - 1 workstation each 2 workers; and fertilization: specific courses.

Regarding the interface with industry: make exchange easy because bureaucracy is now too complicated. Furthermore, part time appointments should be possible. Finally, academic credits should be given to successful industrial research within academia.

I have a final conclusive slide: it is a little story. Bobby is trying to catch the pan, many of you would know already the moral of the story. The pan was hot, he tried to catch the pan with his right hand and burned it, so he tried with his left hand. The story brings you to the moral of thinking about the beginning of the 70's, when computer science was coming up and European industry had to sell traditional computers. The backtracking in Bobby's behaviour should be done with memory and previous mistakes should be avoided.

ARTIFICIAL INTELLIGENCE: Towards Practical Application
T. Bernold and G. Albers (editors)
Elsevier Science Publishers B.V. (North-Holland)

RESEARCH POLICY OF ADMINISTRATIONS - GREAT BRITAIN (ALVEY)

Brian Oakley

The reasons for a program which we are discussing could be many and various, but at least one of the roots is the fact that the information technology (IT) market in the western world is going at a phantastic rate. It is estimated to grow by a factor of 3 in this decade. The factor 3 does not sound very much until you realize that it means that the whole industry is going to have to grow in the order of 10 % to 20 % per annum. In fact, there is no doubt that such growth rates are being achieved, and indeed, in parts of the U.K. industry, this rate is being even surpassed at the moment. The U.K. share is estimated to be approximately 5 % of the world market. But what is perhaps more significant - and I would emphasize this - is that the Japanese have now got something like 15 %, and they say that in the early 1990s they are going to have 40 %. It is this fact that really has accounted for the flurry of cooperative programs, which is spreading now like a rash around the western world, rather than the Japanese 5th Generation program itself. Within the U.K., the results of the 5th Generation announcement in Japan was to stimulate thinking in a big way. A twelve member committee was made up of representatives of the major British computer companies plus participants from the Ministry of Defense and SERC (Science and Engineering Research Council) which was appointed by the Department of Industry. Chaired by John Alvey who has since become Director of Research at British Telecom the committee was charged with undertaking this study which led finally to the Alvey program.

It is a national program. It is concerned with the underlying technologies of Information Technology, focussing on four key "enabling technologies":

1) Very Large Scale Integration (VLSI)
2) Software Engineering
3) Men-Machine Interfaces (MMI)
4) Intelligent Knowledge Based Systems (IKBS).

VLSI is supported for the obvious reason that it is vital to the development of advanced Information Technology products. Regarding Software Engineering I would like to add that we expect in the third wave of Software Engineering projects that we are handling to be bringing about a concurrence with Knowledge Engineering. In fact, we expect that the third wave of programming support environments will be based on Knowledge Engineering-type techniques. It is the sector Knowledge Based Engineering which I now will principally speak about, and the Men-Machine Interface area which also contains elements of Knowledge Engineering.

The program is cooperative throughout the nation's IT communities. Any part of the IT communities can take part. It is funded jointly by industry and by three government departments: the Department of Trade and Industry, the Ministry of Defense, and the SERC, which of course is not strictly speaking a ministry but which takes its funding from the Department of Education and Science and is the body in the U.K., or one of the bodies in the U.K., that tends to fund academic research in areas like computing science.

The program is cooperative in a sense that we only accept proposals which do contain elements of real cooperation, just what that means is slightly fuzzy but in fact, experience is showing that this is the least of our problems. We had not expected that we would get proposals from industry which virtually always include academic bodies but this is the pattern which is emerging, even in areas where we did not realize that the universities had got any real strength. I must admit that this is leading to a certain overload of the good academic teams.

The program is worth 350 million pound sterling to be spent over 5 years. £ 57 million of it are intended to support research and training in academic institutions on a 100 % basis. £ 30 million are expected to be spent on the subject of EIKBS over the period of five years.

The directorate is set up as a cooperative effort in itself. People are secunded from industry at industry's own expense to the directorate. I have in the directorate some 13 people from a variety of different firms, I have people from the Ministry of Defense Research Estahlishment, from the Science in Engineering Research Council itself, and from the academic world. We do try to lay down a policy, we try to lay down priorities and we try to have what is essentially a directive program. But you must remember that it is a 50/50 funded program, and it is slightly difficult with a 50/50 funded program to have true direction. The responsibilities of the Alvey Directorate include drawing up contract specifications and awarding contracts, arranging for the monitoring of the projects, dissemination of the results to promote commercial exploitation as quickly and competitively as possible.

IKBS is another good example of the British attempt to confuse the Japanese. We invented the acronym IKBS because we were not very happy with all the other expressions. I personally do not like the use of the term "AI". It is irrelevant whether the word really is derived from an understanding of how the human being behaves or not. It frightens the community at large and therefore, it is undesirable. As a software community, we put the word intelligence in front.

The present status of IKBS in the U.K. is so similar to the status of elsewhere that I do not really need to lay any great emphasis on it, except to say that, although the research community in the universities is undoubtedly small and to some extent dispersed, it is quite strong in certain senses, notably of course Edinburgh, Imperial College in London, and I must say Sussex. Particularly the interest in expert systems is spreading amazingly fast. The British computer societies' expert systems group is growing constantly. I think it has a membership of 600 now, when I suppose that it had about 50 two years ago. Large parts of industry and commerce are taking a serious interest. I find to get requests from the city, from finance houses, insurance companies and so on. I cannot make up my mind whether it is a good or a bad thing to encourage them into expert systems. Of course, there is a severe shortage of experts, but I believe that is no reason for not diving in, obviously attacking the experts whenever one can.

We established the strategy through a working party which was actually set up and funded by the Science in Engineering Research Council and the Department of what was the then Department of Industry. Typical of this project is that the joint study between those two bodies was actually chaired by somebody from the Ministry of Defense Research Establishment. That study is published and is to some extent the bible on which we work in this area. There were three main aims of the program: To increase collaborative research and development between the industrial world and the academic world in this area; to promote the markets for IKBS. I think, in a sense that this is really the advantage of the program, to make the country aware of potentialities and then to increase the expert manpower and build up an infrastructure.

We have a variety of attacks, first of all the 'show-me' projects. One of the ways in which we are trying to increase the manpower is through distance-learning techniques. We are creating a set of videos, some being not far of talking head recording of experts like Bob Kowalski and Margaret Boden talking about their subjects, some taking examples of expert systems that actually exist in the country, like those at Unilever for example, and recording those themselves. And then we make what we call a 'starter pack' available to the community which will help people to get going, that contains things like a documentation on one or two shells and leaders to where one can get advice himself.

We have also got demonstration projects throughout the program which are the nearest to applications that we have got, and they are particularly strong in the Expert System area, where it is necessary to make the techniques now. We are talking about six different communities and getting large cooperative projects going and we ask maybe 20 firms to get together to fund a particular project, where they take part in the specification, albeit they take part in the problems as they go along. They may not actually be involved in monitoring the work.

Then we have a set of research themes. We have leaders for each research team. Thoses leaders are always one person drawn from the academic world and one person drawn from industry. Amongst the research themes are parallel architectures that, I think, is a particularly important part of this whole program. I think the U.K. is relatively strong in what is perhaps the most important part of this field, that is the software part, the part of how to harness the raise of - let us say - transputers.

Other parts of the program consist of declarative languages. I do not think I have to go into that, a fair amount of work is directed here, but I think a program like this can perhaps be at its strength in trying to get the community at large to concentrate on a limited number of software attacks. Clearly, where one is in an area of immaturity, there is a lot to be said for letting a fair number of flowers bloom, but perhaps not too many. We do hope to be able to get a reasonably organized attack on that.

In the Men-Machine Interface part of the program, Speech Recognition and Image Analysis are both back to AI in various ways, so that there are parts of the program which are concerned with Artificial Intelligence.

We also have a limited set of what we call <u>large demonstrators</u>. These are major projects which are designed to pull a whole program together, to set the objectives. The demonstrators will be difficult projects, they will take five years of the program to pull through. At present we are going through study phases with the teams evaluating the proposals in detail.

Almost all of these have Expert Systems included in them, and at least three of them are sectionally based around Expert Systems. I think, that is really very interesting and very encouraging. One that I think that will be launched is concerned for example with trying to turn into a rule base the way in which social security people - the people who look after the poor and the needy - work with their whole set of regulations.

I will simply say that I feel that it is easy to be overruled by what is happening elsewhere and indeed, when one looks at the scale of funding that is going into Information Technology, particularly in Japan, but also in the United States, although it is there somewhat less coherent but still on a massive scale, it is easy to feel that we inevitably will get left behind. I must say that I do not share that feeling, I believe that we have in Europe qualities of excellence in our work, and if we can really get together and cooperate to bring through the best of it, I believe we should be able to maintain our position in this fast growing field.

ARTIFICIAL INTELLIGENCE: Towards Practical Application
T. Bernold and G. Albers (editors)
Elsevier Science Publishers B.V. (North-Holland)

COOPERATION BETWEEN UNIVERSITY, GOVERNMENT AND INDUSTRY

Excerpts of the Panel discussion

At the beginning of this decade, research and infrastructure of Artificial Intelligence in Europe had been underdeveloped compared to its state in the United States. This fact was recognized by industry and administrations at the announcement of the Japanese 5th Generation Computer Project, where techniques of knowledge based AI systems are planned to be used. It was realized then that only a close collaboration between the partners, mainly university and industry could improve the situation and become a factor of success. This philosophy is reflected in the structure of the programs of the administrations such as ALVEY or ESPRIT. State, Industry and Science should be interested to encourage a dialogue that reviews and analyses the scientific, organizational and political concepts as well as the decision making process. The following excerpts of the discussion is intends to illustrate aspects of the current developments.

G.A. / T.B.

Gallaire:
Just to be short, the center where I am coming from is called European Computer Industry Research Centre; it is an independent company located in Munich. It is a cooperative between three computer manufacturers, SIEMENS, ICL and BULL. The goal for creating this center was to share manpower in a common research center and to get results which would be fully shared and fully available to the three partners. The theme of research which has been selected is "computer assisted decision making", which is a way to say, AI plus Man Machine Interaction plus computer architecture. The kind of subjects that we are devoted to is mainly to work on tools and basic technology for these field's applications. It is pre-competitive research, so, for the three partners, it is a way to get common goals on future products. The personnel of this group is to be seconded partly from the three partners. Seconded means that they should be in the center about three years, and then go back to the three companies afterwards. The second part is made of people to be hired from the market, we talked about this already and everybody knows how difficult it is. The third point: People detached from research and academic centers can join this institute. The center was opened on January 1, 1984, and its objective is to have 50 researchers by the end of 1985.

Bibel:
Maybe first of all: I have been asked several times during this conference: What actually is ECCAI (European Coordinating Committee For Artificial Intelligence)? Let me briefly say, ECCAI is a supra-national organization with corporate members from most of the European countries. We have currently 13 members. The biggest one is the Society for Artificial Intelligence and Simulation of Behaviour, which was actually the first society for artificial intelligence being founded in Britain in 1964. I do not list all the other members. We have three more waiting to be accepted, so we will be 16 by the end of the year, 9 coming from the Community, me being the chairman of this organization.
We are supposed to talk about the relations between academia, government and business. This addresses actually three components: There are these relations, there are these individual bodies, so to call, and there is the environment. Let me start with the

environment.
In fact, I happen to have bought Newsweek this week, and maybe you have seen the front page, which says: "The decline of Europe". I think we tend to close our eyes that, from the outside, the state of the art in Europe is really not as it should be, although I agree with you that we should not be so pessimistic. But, nevertheless, there is a very bad doing in low-tech and no-tech industry. We have fallen behind in almost every major high-tech field. We have a lack - I would say - of leading goals for our old continent, and maybe this is the major reason behind all these problems.

The second point: What about the individual bodies? that is academia, business, government. I come from the university so I will address this part and do not say anything on the other parts, since I am not competent for them. There is a very bad general state of affairs in detail in the universities. I think, it has been addressed in particular in Prof. Cerri's talk before. Here is again a citation from this Newsweek article: "(Our) educational system... has gradually abandoned the notions of competition and quality (in Europe)". There are exceptions, but this is the general tendency. Let me even cite a Nobel prize winner of Germany who two weeks ago told me: "Well, even in the rank of professors, we have (let me say it in German) "überwiegend Flaschen". These were his words. A further point is: There are of course a lot of intelligent academic people, but they, because everything is equalized, lack the good infrastructure for doing their work. I could give you a lot of examples of that, but I think, the talk of Prof. Cerri has already indicated a lot of that.

Now about relations: between government universities and industry relations are bad as a consequence, as I see it, of this environmentally and individually bad situation. In particular I think, the relations are bad in all directions. University does not produce anymore that brilliant, creative people, that are needed in industry or government. Vice versa: The government - because it has a bad feeling about the university - is hesitating to give money back into universities. There is also hesitation from industry to transfer something into universities in contrast to the United States, for example, where there is a lot of equipment sometimes simply given as a present to the universities, because they know that they will get something back from them. The situation is really at the moment, I cite another Professor, who actually is in "exile", a German professor in "exile" in Switzerland. He has written a letter to a computer magazine saying that it was very attractive for him to leave this sad situation. It seems to be a little better at least in Switzerland. He also said that in particular one seems to forget that the transfer of hardware is very important to go from industry into universities and not vice versa. ....

Audience (Industry):
We are hearing many pessimistic statements and perhaps we are at a time where the interface is not ideal. I have not heard any suggestions from the people who are making all these pessimistic remarks as to how to improve it. I see here in Switzerland that there are very good signs of improvement. A good one is the program that has been started at the Swiss Federal Institute of Technology, where they have very much encouraging the students, encouraging on their demanding, that the students during the period while they are going to school, must spend what we call a "practicum" in industry. They must spend 3-4 months working with a company as part of their school program. This whole program is the beginning of a good interface I think between industry and the high-tech universities.

Bibel:
I see a hopeful sign. In speaking you always exaggerate, but if we continue the old style, I think, the situation may be very bad in the future, may be even worse in the future. We have a broad cultural background, a very good intellectual basis so to call, still a lot of tradition in education, so that, if we have a common goal, there will be a good success in the future, but not if we go on like we did in the last 20 years.

Gallaire:
Maybe one way to improve this relationship is to ask people in industry to become more competent on the new technology we all want to develop. Maybe the ESPRIT program, the ALVEY and the German programs or the French one are steps in that direction. If you look at the main difference between the United States and Europe, there is some kind of mutual respect between people in industry and the academic world in the U.S. because people move back and forth between the two worlds and I do think this respect does not exist much in Europe. With these kinds of programs which are collaborative, if somehow we increase competence of industry in these advanced technologies, then there is the chance that the two worlds talk together. Maybe that is one important point.

Audience (Industry):
In my country, which is Sweden, we are conducting now a lot of experiments based on the American science park models, where we have industry working very closely with highschools and universities. And I would like to make one comment to Prof. Bibel on the subject of U.S. companies donating computers to universities and highschools. It is not only because of the fact that they get an output of educated people, but is also tax-deductible. I think, that is a very important fact, because it really is an incentive for a company to donate computers.

Audience (Software-Industry):
My company is a small company and that is exactly why I want to raise this topic. We hear about industry all the time, but implicitely it is being talked about big industry, large companies and so on. It seems that there is a general agreement that currently most new jobs are created in the form of small companies. Those companies by definition have little or no capital which creates a very difficult position for them to participate in projects such as ESPRIT: There is really no way that a small company could provide 50 % of the finances out of their own pocket because it is empty.

Oakley:
I simply would like to add that it is true that the small firm is a crucial ingredient of spirit life in the Information Technology (IT) field. But I think one has got to notice the number of small firms that go bankrupt too. There does appear to be a new phenomenon in the U.K. and I believe in Germany too of the growth of small firms centered around the universities. It is not just science parks. In the case of Cambridge there are now something like 60 small high technology firms round the university, most of them not on the science park in fact, almost all of them in the IT field in one way or another, almost all of them got links to computing science department in the university. Just to pick out one: The Acorn Company is the company that makes the BBC micros, if you remember. There are a fair number of millionnairs in Acorn now. The board consists half of people within the university. If you go to Acorn in the evening and find them all at work, you cannot tell who are the members of the firm, who are members of the university, who are postgraduate student, you cannot even tell if they are undergraduates in the university. This seems to me to be entirely healthy, a phenomenon which I believe we must do everything we can to encourage. As far as the ALVEY program is concerned we have formed a panel of finance houses to try to ensure that when we do hit a small high technology firm that really should be in the program, to produce the funds, that there are at least the maximum chances of getting funds into that firm. But I think I have to add a word of precaution: I am not entirely certain that it is a good thing for a small firm, which after all means that it has probably got very really highly qualified people, to spend too much of their time on the enabling technologies when perhaps they ought to be concentrating on the products that they have to get out of the door next year so that they can live.

Zehnder:
I was asked from quite a number of people here in the floor: What is the situation in Switzerland actually? Don't you do anything in the direction of artificial intelligence here? And therefore, just a few comments. I think that people in Swiss universities hesitate to use the word 'artificial intelligence'. This is something dangerous, they like to prefer some basic mathematics and informatics subjects and therefore, you have to look carefully to find out where artificial intelligence and expert systems and things like that happen. At the Zurich universities - both of them - there are at least four groups around professors working in this field two of them especially in the boundary field between informatics and psychology, both with large research groups. I mean Ulich at ETH, Moser at the University, so we can already see that things happen but they are not identified with AI. But a second point should be made. I am glad that it has already been made clear that in this small country we have a chance that people know each other, so the contact between industry and universities works quite well. It is not organized as it is in other countries, but there is a situation where people know directly where things happen, and when somebody likes to do something, he can. I think, the most important point is that young people have a chance to do something in these fields so that they can see what should be done and they get a chance to do it.

ARTIFICIAL INTELLIGENCE: Towards Practical Application
T. Bernold and G. Albers (editors)
Elsevier Science Publishers B.V. (North-Holland)

ARTIFICIAL INTELLIGENCE AND "NATURAL MAN"

Margaret Boden

University of Sussex
Brighton
Great Britain

Dr. Bernold asked me to talk about how people will react to AI, when it finally does come into the market place and becomes visible - not just a terrifying name, which is what it is now for most people, if it is anything at all. Of course, it is a very large topic. What I am going to concentrate on is saying a little about how I think people will compare themselves with computers running reasonable intelligent programs, because I think this has some important social dimensions.

At the moment, and I think certainly within the next few years, it will be true to say, that if people compare themselves with computers and what computers can do, they will find - perhaps to their surprise, because it surprised the computer professionals in the field - that by and large what we can do well, computers can do badly, and vice versa.

In fact, many of the sorts of problems which we keep hearing about with respect to expert systems at this meeting are indeed problems for specialists, problems for human _experts_. They are things that the average human being cannot do, which many people _believe_ they could not do, even if they tried and which are done in many cases by pretty well-paid and high-status human beings. Now those tasks, which most of us think are difficult, are relatively easy to program in AI terms.

But there are tasks which all of us can do, and all of us do all the time, the tasks we can do so well all of us, never mind what our educational level is, that it does not even occur to us to think of them as intelligent. I mean things like speaking a natural language, understanding a natural language, seeing things which are half hidden with your eyes and realizing what they are, even though they are half hidden. These sorts of things are - as you know - extremely difficult to program.

To some extent, the fact that people do not realize this is, you might say, socially dangerous. Because it certainly means that they do not have a good sense of what problems it is reasonable to think a computer might be able to tackle, and what problems it is not reasonable to think they might be able to tackle. But I think that is perhaps less important than some other issues, because it is fairly easy to point this out to people.

You can _tell_ people that what we do well, computers do badly and vice versa. You can even _give_ them a few examples. They can take the point. Indeed, most people are very ready to take the point. Most people are very ready to believe that computers are not nearly as clever as they thought they were. I remember about 7 years ago, I went to the Science Museum in London. They had just installed a really very simple computer system for planning underground trips on the London Underground. What you did was: You keyed in the station you wanted to go to and you had a very, very simple verbal interaction with this machine, and it told you the way to go. Now, it was very interesting watching the way people were reacting to this. There were people in the Science Museum - adults, not just children - who were quite clearly (from their dress and manner of speaking and commenting) not par-

Let me give you just one more example: As many of you may know, there is a certain amount of research going on at the moment in AI on what they call "non-monotonic reasoning". Broadly speaking what that means is the sort of reasoning where, on Tuesday, you can prove or accept a statement to your satisfaction given the evidence that you have, but on Wednesday, you find out - perhaps to your surprise - that that was false. In other words: A proposition can change its truth value as your knowledge progresses.

Of course, this is happening to us all the time. In most interesting real life areas, it is quite normal to have this happen, because we are working in situations where we do not have complete knowledge. We are using our intelligence - if you like - to guess. So we are taking things to be true or false, which later on we find out to be false or true.

A certain amount of work is going on in this area to try and make AI systems to be able to do this too, but at the moment, they cannot. John McCarthy, the great granddaddy of AI, the inventor of Lisp, has shown the problem in a very nice way, the problem that I want to address here.

You all know the missionary/cannibal problem, which many, many AI systems have used as an example, as something to cut their teeth on. There are 3 missionaries and 3 cannibals on one side of the river, and one rowing boat which can hold 2 people; everybody can row; how do they get across the river, given that (for obvious reasons) there can at no time on either bank or in the boat be more cannibals than missionaries? Now, the normal way of doing this, as those of you who know the puzzle will know, is to sketch out a series of steps in which one man or two men cross the river in the boat. That is the normal way in which you do it.

McCarthy imagines giving this puzzle verbally to a friend, a human friend. He states the puzzle, just as I did. And the person says something like: "Well, they walk across the bridge". "There is no bridge", McCarthy says. So then the friend says: "A crocodile swims up to the river bank, and they all go and stand on the back of the crocodile. And when the crocodile has swum across the river as crocodiles are supposed to do, they all jump off." McCarthy gets slightly more irritated and says: "No crocodiles". The next suggestion is: "They go to the nearest phone booth and hire a helicopter".

Now, two things are quite clear: First of all, that could go on forever. If the friend wants to tease McCarthy in this way, he could go on forever. With his common sense, his ordinary world-knowledge - he is not an expert, he is not a specialist - he could go on forever. Anyone can play this game, and anyone could go on forever. That is the first thing. And the second thing is that that is actually a relatively important fact about it, because if this was not a puzzle (a puzzle by definition is where all the relevant information is assumed to have been given), then it might happen to be useful to know about crocodiles. And it might be very useful to have somebody there who is one of these rare people who have some hypnotic power over animals, and who could actually induce the crocodile to cooperate and come across. It could happen.

Similarly, and this relates back to the "possibly/probably" example, if you imagine these 6 people actually on the riverbank trying to work out how to get across the river, one of them might say: "Well, there are some logs lying around there, and there are some reeds. Let us try to tie those logs together with the reeds and make a raft, and go across that way". Now, if anybody said that, and certainly if they happened to be one of the cannibals that lived in that part of the forest, I think you would assume that there was no bridge. In other words, you would assume that if the person suggested building a raft, they believe that there was no bridge. Because nobody with any common sense would suggest building a raft in these extremely difficult circumstances, if there was a bridge you yould walk over. This is very like the "possibly/probably" example.

Now, imagine a system with which a naive user is interacting, which sometimes comes up with what you might call a crocodile suggestion (in other words, one

ticularly well educated people. And they were having a whale of a time playing with this system. What were they doing? They were joking with it. They were giving it a completely unrealistic question and then roaring with laughter when it gave a stupid answer or did not give an answer at all. They got a great deal of delight out of that. So, I do not think that - in the short term at least - there is going to be any great difficulty, although it is a job that has to be done, in persuading people that computers are not nearly as intelligent as most people think that they might be.

What I think is perhaps much more difficult to deal with and potentially much more socially dangerous is that, in the future, if we are going to develop the sorts of systems that people have been talking about in this meeting, if we are going to develop anything that could reasonably be counted as a 5th generation machine, we are going to have to develop at least two things. First of all, a really impressive natural language user, which we do not have today, and secondly, something approaching common sense reasoning, which all of us can do but which computers cannot do and at the moment cannot even approach.

Both of those topics are being mentioned in some of the meetings that I have been to in this Conference, so they are in the air. But I would like you to think for a moment about the dangers of providing these facilities.

We seem to have been assuming, certainly in the meetings that I went to, that obviously, it would be a good thing to have better natural language facilities. And obviously, it would be a good thing to be able to provide your programs with common sense reasoning. But I am not so sure. I am not so sure about this, until the point at which you can do the job absolutely perfectly (a point which, if it happens at all, will not happen for many, many years). I think this is questionable. Let me give you just a couple of examples to suggest why.

Suppose that you are a naive user. You know nothing about computers, nothing about AI, and you are having a conversation (perhaps over the teletype, perhaps through speech recognition, it does not matter) with this system which is using words in your natural language. Now, if it is doing this in a relatively unstilted way, if it appears to be using a reasonably rich vocabulary, I think the naive user is going to be very likely to interpret the language of the machine in the sort of way that they would interpret the language of one of their friends.

One thing we constantly do when we are using natural language is this: When somebody uses a word, we assume (we do not usually think about it consciously, but sometimes we do) not only that they have chosen to use that word, but that they have chosen to use it in preference to certain other semantically related words.

One very obvious example of this is: Suppose you ask me a question about whether I think something is going to happen, and I answer: "Possibly". That would normally be interpreted to mean: "Not probably". You would normally assume that if I had thought it was probable I would have said "probably". Since I only said "possibly", the implication is that I have decided not to use the word "probably". This is why you interpreted my answer accordingly.

Suppose that you had a computer system which could only answer "possibly", or "never". (Obviously this is a very simple example, and I think one would not have a system quite as simple as this; but it will do as an example). Then, the naive user I think could run into some potentially quite serious difficulties. For they would interpret that word "possibly" to mean "not probably", which is not what the computer is saying - and which in a specific case of the real problem might not in fact be so. Now, obviously, there are going to be difficulties if you scale that up to a large vocabulary, making rather more subtle distinctions, in areas which are not so easily understood. These words might be ones which cannot be translated straightforwardly into a numerical scale of probabilities, for instance (as "possibly" and "probably" arguably might be). And if a naive user is not aware that there are very grave restrictions on the vocabulary that this system could use, and on the criteria for choosing items within that vocabulary, there could be problems. So, that is one example.

which appears to have a certain degree of common sense). Again I think there is a great danger that the naive user may assume - not explicitly of course -: "Well, if this thing can think of crocodiles, it could have thought of rafts and bridges and helicopters and all the rest of it." The naive user may make the assumptions about (for instance) the non-availability of bridges, which anyone would make in the ordinary human situation.

So what I am saying is: A little common sense and (for essentially the same sorts of reasons) a little better natural language ability might be a very dangerous thing. Obviously, we are going on this way; we are not going to try not to improve the natural language facilities. And obviously, we are not going to have a perfect natural language facility or a perfect common sense reasoner in the near future. And therefore, I think we have to make very, very sure that the naive users are going to be aware of these problems. In other words, what we need is computer literacy in the users.

Somebody said earlier that they did not think that education of the user was going to be necessary, because the whole point of AI is that with these natural language interfaces, and reasoning power, and interactive facilities, the user is not going to have to know about computers. Certainly, they are not going to have to know about the way the thing is built, and they are not going to have to know about the details of the programming languages. But there are certain things which they _are_ going to have to know, and which I think are going to have to be taught. Specifically, they need to have some sense, not only of the general potential of AI systems (particularly those that might be used in the market place, in institutions, in commural organizations to support decisions which affect human individuals) but also about their limitations.

I think they need to be taught two things. First of all, that any particular program (unless we are thinking of an extremely narrow problem) is going to have some specific limitations. It might be as well for people who are actually writing and marketing these things to think of some way of flagging those limitations in the program, in such a way that they will become explicitly apparent to the user. That is one thing. But another much more basic and general issue which applies to all such programs is, I think, extremely important. Everybody in the community, whether they are actually using these things in their daily work or not, is within 10, certainly 15 years (it seems to me) going to have to recognize that you can always in principle question a computer program.

You can do this on three levels: You can question its data. That is to say you can ask: "Does it have all the necessary data, all the relevant data?" (because it may not). And you can ask: "Are all the data which it has actually true?" (which they may not be). In the same way, you can ask about a human being: "Do they know all the facts, and are all their beliefs which they take to be relevant, in fact true beliefs?" So, you can question a computer program in principle in that way just as you can a human person.

Similarly, you can always in principle question the rules of inference that the thing is using, just as you can in principle question the rules of inference that the human being is using. Just as you do not have to take somebody else's facts or beliefs as gospel, you do not have to take somebody else's inferential rules as gospel. In many cases, you had better look at them very carefully, and realize that they are unreliable. And thirdly, in principle, it is always possible to question the values, or decision criteria, which are built into the program - just as you can with human beings. What you think is "best" may not be what the programmer assumed was "best".

Now, I think we should add a general philosophical point, a general epistemological point about the sort of systems that AI programs are. They are basically knowledge systems. They comprise models of the world, and possible worlds, analogous in many ways to the models of the world which we all have inside our skulls. And those models are only models, and they must in principle be questionable in this way.

I think a lot of people today just do not realize that. They take computer programs to be objective systems. They take the answers, the judgments, the advice given by computer programs to be, if not absolutely objective, at least somehow more objective than the decisions of mere human beings.

In fact, I saw recently on British television an advertisment that very deeply disturbed me. I do not know whether it was meant as a joke. I suspect that it was not. But anyway, even if it was meant as a joke, I think it was a thoroughly pernicious one. The advertisment went like this: You saw six people sitting in front of six different "brands" of computers. The "voice-over" said something like: "We fed into each of these six computers, information about the price, the performance, and all the capabilities of all these six computers. And we asked them to choose the best. The X (I am certainly not going to advertise this firm any further because I think it was a pernicious advertisment) chose the X. So did all the others. It makes you think that a person ought to choose the X too." I wonder how many ordinary people sitting in British living rooms, even the sort of people who might have the money to think about choosing an X, would know that that is a completely illogical remark. Somebody had to write the choosing program. Somebody had to decide on what the criteria of the "best" computer were. And I would not offer any large prize for guessing which company employed that person, and which company in effect provided that program.

Now, that is a trivial matter. I mean, who cares (except the competitors of firm X) if anybody goes out and buys computer X? It does not matter. But there are many other decisions which social, political, and educational institutions will be making (within the next 15 years) with the aid of these sorts of systems, decisions which are by no means so trivial.

It is absolutely crucial that everybody realizes, even if they do not have the expertise to ask the questions themselves, that in principle questions of those 3 types can always be raised about a computer program. As long as people remember that, there is some chance of the human responsibility for decisions staying with us. If people do not recognize that, then it certainly won't. So, I think that is a sort of computer literacy which is very important for people to get.

I think there is no great problem, certainly within 5 or 10 years, about giving it to them. In fact, we at the University of Sussex have over the last 10 years developed a teaching system for AI (which is also a powerful research environment for AI) which is deliberately designed to do this. These issues can often be introduced to students on their very first day of programming experience. And these are students in the arts and social sciences, they are not particularly numerate students. Our system enables us to introduce to those students these two ideas: First of all, that an apparently intelligent program (an ELIZA-program which has a little conversation with you, or a program that talks about three - dimensional objects and shows them on a screen), although it may initially appear to be intelligent, is not infallible. That is the first idea. Secondly, they get the idea that that program can be changed. In fact, it can be changed in many cases (because we made it that way) by that student himself or herself, within the first few days or couple of weeks of their programming experience. They themselves can change it for the better. Obviously, that is not going to put them in a situation of being able to write fancy programs: that will need much longer. But these two points can be got over (with the right sort of programming environment) very early and very easily. I think this is absolutely crucial.

But you may stand back from that, and just say: "Well, wait a minute. You said something about why it is important to think about how people compare themselves with AI systems, when there are <u>specific</u> AI systems being used in the public domain. But you have not said anything about the more general question of how people may react to the mere fact that people are constantly making comparisons between the human mind and computer systems. Is that not", you may say - and certainly many people believe - "in itself dehumanizing? Is that not in itself likely to undermine people's sense of responsibility, their sense of purpose, and their sense of values, so as to undermine the social fabric in certain ways?"

Many people have argued that this is the case with respect to behaviourist psychology for instance (and for that matter, certain aspects of Freudian psychology). In fact, what psychologists tell us about the mind has an influence on the theories that ordinary people take into their heads, and use to think about their own mind in the future. Certainly, what you think the mind is can affect the use of your own mind. That is true.

Many people are worried because they say: "An AI program is a mechanistic system. It is not a system which has the sort of human psychological qualities that we value." And they believe that to the extent that these things become widespread, to the extent that these things become compared in people's minds to people's minds, they will have a dehumanizing effect.

I think that is wrong for two reasons. The first is less basic. It is that I think as a matter of fact the programs which will be available in the public domain will have very little (if anything) like emotionality. I do not think it is in principle impossible. But I think it won't happen, because it won't be profitable for people to build programs that do show emotions, by and large. So I think it is entirely possible that people may come to value the emotional dimension of human life more than they do today. Personally, I think that would be a good thing. It would be a good thing particularly for men as opposed to women because in our society the masculine role inhibits the expression, the recognition, and the development of emotionality in a way which I think oppresses most men. The more successful they are in our male-dominated terms, the more this tends to be so. And this is a bad thing, so I think it would be a good result if the change I have imagined were to happen.

The second thing is a much more basic philosophical point, but it is crucial. It is related to what I said before about the fact that you can always question a program at three levels: Fact, inferences, and values. And that is that the main thing about the human mind which all humanists have always valued, have always praised, and have always said (quite rightly) is completely left out of account by the natural sciences, is subjectivity.

Now that is a very airy-fairy word. But it is a perfectly familiar phenomenon. What it boils down to, is: Each of us has a mind which is different from other minds, in the sense that is has different beliefs, different experiences, different political values, and so on. This is something important about human beings. If you do not understand something about a particular person's value system and beliefs and cultural background, you will not be able to communicate with them very well. In fact, it is something which (particularly in our culture) is regarded as very valuable. The natural scientists cannot cope with subjectivity, they cannot recognize it as a fact, because sciences like physics and chemistry have no room for the concept of representation. And it is the concept of representation which is at the core of the phenomenon of subjectivity. It is true that the more theoretical psychologies have tried to be scientific, at least in the past, the more they have left out subjectivity. They had to. They had no way of talking about representation. (That applies for instance to behaviourism).

I think the philosophically most interesting and in some ways the humanly most valuable point about AI is, that the central concept of AI is representation, modelling, a symbolism. So it gives us a scientifically grounded, intellectually respectable way of acknowledging the existence of subjectivity. It enables us to accept it as a natural phenomenon which is of particular importance and value in human minds, and gives us a way of talking about it at the psychological level. It enables us to say that our minds are very complex models (dynamic, self-generating, and self-updating models) of the external world and of imaginary and indeed utopian worlds. These are the features of the mind which humanists have always stressed, and which up until now have been left out by scientists. The sciences have until now I think been insidiously dehumanizing. That need no longer be so, if you look at the mind with some of the concepts taken from artificial intelligence (which of course were originally taken themselves from talk about the psychology of human beings). These concepts were borrowed by the computer scientists from talk about human mind.

If you look at the human mind in that way, you at last have a scientifically grounded way of acknowledging subjectivity and perhaps talking about it in theoretically fruitful terms. So I do not think artificial intelligence is dehumanizing, in fact, I think it is re-humanizing.

General Reading:

Boden, M.A., Artificial Intelligence and Natural Man (Harvester, 1977).

Feigenbaum, E.A., and McCorduck, P., The Fifth Generation: Japan's Computer Challenge to the World (Michael Joseph, 1983).

Forester, T. (ed.), The Microelectronics Revolution (Blackwell: 1st edn. 1980, 2nd edn. -- very fully revised -- due end 1984).

APPENDIX

LIST OF SPEAKERS

Baker Anthony G., Manager, Operational Technique Section, Unilever Research, Port Sunlight Laboratory, Quarry Road East, Bibington Wirral, GB-Merseyside L63 3JW

Basu Rhada, European Product Manager, Hewlett-Packard GmbH, Medical Products Group, Herrenbergerstrasse 110, D-7030 Böblingen

Bibel Wolfgang, Dr.,Chairman ECCAI, Technische Universität, Institut für Informatik, Postfach 202420, D-8000 München 2

Biedermann Jörgen, Dr., Comor AG, Computer- und Organisationsberatung, Seefeldstrasse 63, CH-8008 Zürich

Boden Margaret, Prof.Dr., University of Sussex, School of Social Sciences, Arts Building, Falmer, GB-Brighton BN1 9QN

Burckhardt C.W., Prof.Dr., Ecole Polytechnique Fédérale de Lausanne, Département de Mécanique, Institut de microtechnique, DME (Ecublens), CH-1015 Lausanne

Cadiou Jean-Marie, Dr., Chairman of the conference, Director - Taskforce Information Technologies - ESPRIT, Commission of the European Communities, 200 rue de la Loi, B-1049 Brussels

Cerri Stefano A., Prof.Dr., Secretary ECCAI, Università di Pisa, Dipartimento di Informatica, Corso Italia, 40, I-56100 Pisa

Eibl Georg, Dipl.-Math., Dipl.-Wirtsch.-Ing., Laborgruppenleiter, Siemens AG, Zentrale Aufgaben Informationstechnik, Otto-Hahn-Ring 6, D-8000 München 83

Gallaire Hervé, Dr., Managing Director, European Computer-Industry Research Centre GmbH, Forschungszentrum, Arabellastrasse 17, D-8000 München 81

Héry Jean-François, Ingénieur, Electricité de France, Direction des Etudes et Recherches, 1, avenue du Général de Gaulle, F-92141 Clamart

Hüsch Hans Willi, Dipl.oec., Institut für angewandte Innovationsforschung e.V., Bürgerstrasse 15, D-4100 Duisburg 1

Jenny Christian, Dr., Leiter Anwendungsentwicklung - Koordination, Zürich Versicherungs-Gesellschaft, Mythenquai 15, CH-8002 Zürich

Kempf Karl G., Dr.,Manager Artificial Intelligence Group, McDonnell Douglas Company, St. Louis, Missouri 63166 / USA

Latombe Jean-Claude, Prof.Dr., Institut National Polytechnique de Grenoble (INPG), B.P.68, F-38402 St. Martin d'Heres

Langley Robert, Development Engineer, Schlumberger, 12, Place des Etats-Uris, F-92541 Montrouge Cédex

Marchand Hubert, Dr., Programmdirektor Expertensysteme, Battelle-Institut e.V. Am Römerhof 35, D-6000 Frankfurt/M

Neumann Bernd, Prof.Dr., Universität Hamburg, FB Informatik, Arbeitsbereich Kognitive Systeme, Schlüterstrasse 70, D-2000 Hamburg 13

Oakley Brian, Director, The ALVEY Programme, Department of Trade and Industry Millbank Tower, GB-London SW1 4QU

Pearson A.W., Director R + D Research Unit, Manchester Business School, Boothstreet West, GB-Manchester M15 6PB

Raulefs Peter, Prof.Dr., Universität Kaiserslautern, Fachbereich Informatik, Postfach 3049, D-6750 Kaiserslautern

Rees Brian, Artificial Intelligence Marketing Manager - Europe, Digitial Equipment Corporation International (Europe), 12, avenue des Morgines, CH-1213 Petit-Lancy 1/GE

Sagalowicz Daniel, Technical Advisor, Framentec/Teknowledge, 74, Bd. d'Italie, Monte-Carlo, MC-98000 Monaco

Savory Stuart, Projektleiter Künstliche Intelligenz, Nixdorf Computer AG, Pontanusstrasse 55, D-4790 Paderborn

Schwartz David, Principal Marketing Consultant, Symbolics Inc., 4 Cambridge Center, 12th Floor, Cambridge, Mass. 02142 / USA

Sieber Willi, Dr., Project CASP, Sandoz AG 503/506, CH-4002 Basel

Thompson Henry, Dr., University of Edinburgh/Artificial Intelligence Ltd., Hope Park Square, Mendow Lane, GB-Edinburgh EH8 9NW

Wahlster Wolfgang, Prof.Dr., Sprecher FA KI GI, Universität des Saarlandes, FB 10 - Informatik IV, D-6600 Saarbrücken

Wiig Karl, Director of the Artificial Intelligence Program, Arthur D. Little Inc., Aconpark, Cambridge, Mass. 02140 / USA

Wild Hanspeter, Masch.-Ing.HTL/ Oek KSZ, Abteilungsleiter Roboter, ASEA AG, Badenerstrasse 587, CH-8048 Zürich

Zehnder Carl August, Prof.Dr., Eidg. Technische Hochschule, Institut für Informatik, ETH-Zentrum, CH-8092 Zürich

Idea Exchange

At the conference in Zurich for AI Technology Assessment and Transfer the ECCAI organised a first "Idea Exchange" for Artificial Intelligence in Europe. The intention to sponsor an "Idea Exchange" has been based on the need to improve the liaison between industry and science. As the main conference was aimed to provide information to industry we wanted to open the possibility that all scientists and institutes working in the Artificial Intelligence area could present their work in an exhibition and in a short presentation. We thought, that such a central event could serve to improve the relationship. As some of the submission dates of new national and supranational research programmes supporting AI research, were short after the conference, the idea to establish that Idea Exchange proved especially successfull for research teams which could submit to this programmes.

PARTICIPANTS OF THE IDEA EXCHANGE FROM SCIENCE:

Bibel Wolfgang
Dr., Chairman, ECCAI, Institut für Informatik Universität München,
P.O. Box 20 24 20, D-8000 Munich 2, Tel. 0049 89 21052031
Research topic: Deduction-Systems, Expert Systems

Latombe Jean-Claude
Prof. Dr. of Computer Science, INTG (Institut National Polytechnique de Grenoble),
P.O. Box 68, F-38402 St. Martin d'Heres, Tel. 0033 76 514609
Research topic: AI Application in Production, Robotics

Mars Nicolas J.I.
Dr. Ir., Medical Informatics, School of Medicine, University of Leiden,
P.O. Box 9604, 2300 RC Leiden, Netherlands, Tel. 0031 71 148333 4559
Research topic: Coupling of large hospital information systems, data banks with medical expert systems.

Raulefs Peter
Prof. Dr., Sonderforschungsbereich Künstliche Intelligenz, Universität Kaiserslautern,
P.O. Box 3049, D-6750 Kaiserslautern
GMD-Gesellschaft für Mathematik und Datenverarbeitung, Bonn,
FB-Institut für angewandte Informationstechnik, Forschungsgruppe XPS,
Research topic: Knowledge-based Systems.

Stoyan Herbert, Mueller H.
Dr., Institut für Mathematische Maschinen und Datenverarbeitung (Informatik),
IMMD 6, Martenstr. 3, D-8520 Erlangen, Tel. 0049 9131 857885
Research topic: Data-bases, AI Languages, Parts-lists, Application of expert systems.

Trost Harald
Dipl. Ing. Dr., Austrian Society for AI, c/o Institut für medizinische Kybernetik,
Universität Wien, Freyung 6, A-1010 Wien, Austria, Tel. 0043 222 663281-0
Research topic: VIE-LANG, a German Language Dialogue System, MOSES, a System for Schema-based Modeling and Simulation, Decision Support for Primary Medical Care (ESDAT)

Wahlster Wolfgang, Neumann Bernd
Prof. Dr./Dr., INCA - Intelligent Computer e.V., Hamburg
Research topics: Natural Language-and Picture processing